1348468

Co
5/9/07

D1562832

Texts and Contexts

REFLECTIONS IN PACIFIC ISLANDS HISTORIOGRAPHY

EDITED BY

Doug Munro AND *Brij V. Lal*

UNIVERSITY OF HAWAI'I PRESS
HONOLULU

11 10 09 08 07 06   6 5 4 3 2 1

LIBRARY OF CONGRESS CATALOGING-IN-PUBLICATION DATA

Texts and contexts : reflections in Pacific Islands historiography /
    edited by Doug Munro and Brij V. Lal.
        p. cm.
    Includes index.
    ISBN-13: 978-0-8248-2942-1 (hardcover : alk. paper)
    ISBN-10: 0-8248-2942-5 (hardcover : alk. paper)
    1. Islands of the Pacific—Historiography. I. Munro, Doug.
II. Lal, Brij V.
    DU28.11.T49 2005
    996—dc22
                                        2005021026

University of Hawai'i Press books are printed on acid-free paper
and meet the guidelines for permanence and durability of the
Council on Library Resources.

Designed by Liz Demeter

Printed by Integrated Book Technology, Inc.

CONTENTS

ACKNOWLEDGMENTS

It is a pleasant final duty to thank the various people who helped in the making of this book. Oahn Collins in Canberra and Katharine Meacham in Wellington gave needed practical assistance; Justin Cargill of Victoria University Library provided bibliographic help; and the Stout Research Centre, Victoria University of Wellington, awarded Doug Munro a two-month Residency to work on this book.

We are especially grateful to Masako Ikeda, our sponsoring editor, for support and encouragement at every stage; and to the copy editor, Maria DenBoer, for her exemplary work on the manuscript.

The Text in Its Context:
An Introduction

I suppose that every one of us hopes secretly for immortality; to leave, I mean a name behind him which will live forever in this world, whatever he may be doing, himself, in the next.
A. A. Milne, quoted in Ann Thwaite, *A. A. Milne*, 486

AN ACADEMIC discipline always has a life of its own in which the defining moments are not always obvious at the time. A particular conference may have especial salience. An individual may be strategically placed and possess sufficient force of character to assume the mantle of impresario. Typically, however, the signposts of an academic discipline—at any rate, in the humanities and social sciences—are the more important monographs and journal articles. These are the markers that indicate what has happened and what might be the future directions. We hear that a book is a classic or that a text is seminal. But the word *classic* has been so overused that it is almost meaningless. The same might be said for *seminal*. Do these words connote that the text in question is still read, or that it sold many copies, or that it was one of a kind, or of admitted excellence, or any combination of these things? It is all too indeterminate. Perhaps the term *foundational* carries more meaning. Foundational texts are those that made an impact at the time of publication, or soon afterward, in contrast to the so-called classic, which attains that status in the fullness of time. Foundational texts may not have been best-sellers—not many academic books are. They often now have a dated air about them and are, we suspect, often dismissed as having passed their "use by" date. Yet they had a pivotal role in the development of the subdiscipline. They were the building blocks and stepping stones to greater things. The texts we have included in this volume fit that definition.

Pacific Islands historiography has its origins in the early twentieth century, if not before, with studies of a geopolitical nature that often incorporated the Pacific Rim and Australasia.[1] There was also, for example, Hohman's *The American Whaler* (1928), Kuykendall's first volume of *The Hawaiian Kingdom* (1938), Bradley's *The American Frontier in Hawaii* (1942), Furnas's general history, *Anatomy of Paradise* (1948), and Derrick's *History of Fiji* (1950). As well, there were the stout volumes on nineteenth-century imperial history that dominated the scholarly historiography.[2] So it cannot be said that Pacific Islands historiography was a clean slate when J. W. (Jim) Davidson went to Canberra in 1950 as foundation professor of Pacific history at the Australian National University (ANU). What Davidson did was to inspire a new approach to the history of the region and, in the process, to develop Pacific history into a recognized specialization in its own right. He played a seminal role in the evolution of the new subdiscipline. Paralleling concurrent developments in African and Southeast Asian historiography, the new Pacific historiography displaced imperial history as the dominant paradigm and focused instead on "culture contacts," "multicultural situations," and "indigenous initiatives."[3] A whole generation of doctoral dissertations emerged and several of these, in their published form, are considered in the present volume.

The Canberra department was the intellectual Mecca for prospective Pacific historians who journeyed forth to ANU and, three years later, armed with a doctorate and an island-oriented theology, branched out to preach their new gospel in different parts of the world. They were the new missionaries, confident about themselves and convinced of their doctrine. They were in the vanguard of a different order of things, building alternative interpretative structures on the ruins of the discredited Fatal Impact view of cultural encounters in the Pacific. The new theology was reinforced by the *Journal of Pacific History*, founded in 1966 under the joint-editorship of Davidson and H. E. (Harry) Maude. This flagship served multiple purposes, as these things always do, in providing a publication outlet, a symbol of identity, a badge of respectability, and, most important of all, a vehicle with which to influence the research agenda.

In the fifty years since Davidson delivered his inaugural lecture, proclaiming the new orthodoxy,[4] the field has grown in expected and unexpected ways. The founding generation has either passed away or retired. As Kerry Howe remarked in 1992, those "days of cosy homogeneity, indeed hegemony, of the ANU school of island-centred culture contact studies are long gone."[5] To switch the metaphor, there are other ships of state, under different navigators, following different stars, flying their distinctive flags, and each plying its own trade. A new generation of able seamen are at the helm. Many were not born when the field was founded but they are, or will be, at the various helms, manning the rigging, charting divergent routes, and negotiating reefs and inlets that were overlooked or discarded by Canberra. There are now several epicenters; there is no one dominant approach and rival journals, such as *The Contemporary Pacific,* have contributed to this diversity. In place of a unified approach, there were other "lines of descent" and each with their own "reproductive programmes."[6] The ways in which historical scholarship relating to the Pacific are framed, and the tone and terms of historical debate and enterprise, have also been fundamentally altered by new cultural and intellectual developments. Much new research is seen through the prisms of postmodernism, Cultural Studies, literary criticism, and history of consciousness. Historical experience, moreover, is presented in a variety of ways, through film, drama, museum displays, and music. This is particularly noticeable in the work of Islander scholars who have sought to combine indigenous ways of recalling the past—through chants, genealogy, and oral traditions—with the practices of Western scholarship. Archives-based research is seen simply as one among a number of ways of knowing the past. Canberra is still important as a center of postgraduate research but, ironically, the teaching of Pacific Islands history to undergraduates is now a practically abandoned field in Australia. A new Zeitgeist is abroad, and the center has been truly decentered.

Amid all the change, there have been obvious gains but at the cost of a diminishing sense of an intellectual past and the contribution of forbearers. There is but a hazy notion of how the specialization developed—what it developed out of and what it progressively transformed into—and the historians who made it happen. This loss of corporate memory is partly a consequence of the present-mindedness that has been encouraged by more recent developments. As Kerry Howe has pointed out, Pacific Islands history during the Davidson era was "not really informed by the Pacific Islands present,"[7] despite Davidson's own interest and involvement in contemporary island affairs. The Fiji coups of

1987 sharply and suddenly shifted the center of gravity from the nineteenth into the twentieth century as more and more practitioners took a serious interest in contemporary events and issues. The establishment of the influential journal *The Contemporary Pacific* was a direct response to this impulse, and its second issue was devoted to the coups. Worthy and welcome in some respects, such developments meant that scholarly inquiry was sometimes insufficiently informed by the Pacific Islands *past*. While the study of Pacific history was no longer hemmed in by a narrow disciplinary focus, the countervailing and broadening tendencies led not only to diffuseness but, in the case of the more postmodern analyses, to an emphasis on an authorial presence,[8] and this "focus on a personalised present, especially for the growing numbers of Pacific Islands researchers, leads inevitably to a reaching back into a recent rather than a remote past."[9]

A concurrent development during the 1980s was the unified approach of the Canberra department being displaced by a number of "self-reproducing clans, each with its own training grounds and theoretical interests. No longer is there a single line of descent . . . Nor is it easy any more to define 'mainstream' concerns. The notion of history has broadened: we face what one literary theorist has called a 'meltdown' of disciplinary approaches."[10] Confirmation of these developments, if not already evident, was unambiguously on display at the 1995 Pacific History Association (PHA) at Hilo, notably in its being split down the middle between an old guard of traditionalists and a new wave of postmodernists and/or Islanders. It was really two conferences with a fairly pronounced ethnic/generational divide. More so than previous PHA gatherings, the Hilo conference was strongly present-centered and multidisciplinary to the extent that the actual discipline of history was sometimes hard to find.[11] The event confirmed what Peter Hempenstall had said a few years earlier about the "series of conversations . . . going on, but not always meeting, in the crowded room of Pacific history."[12] There is nothing out of the ordinary in this state of affairs: the fractured academy of Pacific historiography simply reflects what is going on worldwide. The universal scenario is that growth leads to specialization, specialization to fragmentation, and fragmentation to the clannishness, separatism, and autarky that have become part and parcel of the historical profession and of academic life itself. In 1988, it was noted that the American historical profession had lost its cohesion: "as a broad community of discourse, as a community of scholars united by common aims, common standards and common purposes, the discipline of history has ceased to exist."[13]

There has been another development relevant to the changing nature of Pacific historiography. As well as the subdiscipline becoming increasingly diversified, fragmented, and present-minded, its literature has grown to unmanageable proportions. As elsewhere, such has been the exponential growth of the written output that keeping up with one's reading has become well nigh impossible. In these circumstances, the older texts tend to fall by the wayside, being seen as out of date, outmoded, and out of touch with the reigning concerns of our branch of the historical discipline. Of course, historical research involves the revision of received opinion, the overturning of orthodoxy, and a questioning of cozy past assumptions. Older texts are there to be displaced and their authors forgotten. For all these reasons, Pacific historians are beginning to lose sight of, or even to deny, the history of the development of their own specialization. It is made more acute when there are no *aides memoire* comparable to, say, Rob Pascoe's guided tour through Australian historiography or Peter Parish's small treatise on the historians of North American slavery and the histories they write, much less Meier and Rudwick's larger exercise on the same topic, or John Kenyon's study of the English historical profession since the Renaissance.[14] There are no volumes of essays on individual Pacific historians as one routinely finds in other branches of the historical profession.[15] There is a small and interesting corpus of autobiographical writings by Pacific historians.[16] This contributes to, but is by no means a substitute for, a systematic knowledge of the origins and development of the subdiscipline and its practitioners.

It is well to put these comments into perspective, because the disregard for intellectual ancestors and their works is widespread throughout the historical profession. When writing his biography of G. M. Trevelyan in the 1980s, David Cannadine gave a seminar at Cambridge University based on an earlier version of his second chapter to the eventual book. The majority of graduate students present had never read any of Trevelyan's books, and yet "Trevelyan was the most famous, the most honoured and the most influential and widely read historian during the second half of the twentieth century."[17] Such is the extent and depth of "posterity's disdain."[18]

Paradoxically, at the very time Pacific historians are likewise losing sight of their own past, they have become more willing to reflect on the nature of their discipline and their individual positions within it. More so than the earlier generations, they have become conscious—perhaps self-conscious—of the problematic nature and purpose of the construction of knowledge, the cultural and political contexts in which that knowledge is produced, and the uses to which it is put. And they have become much more alert to their own roles as researchers, their obligations and responsibilities. New lines of inquiry have been developed, theoretical debates chewed over, and fresh directions of research charted. It is part and parcel of the current state of present-mindedness. It is high time to take a backward glance that will, incidentally, make the current preoccupations of practitioners more intelligible.

The primary concern of *Texts and Contexts* is not with the authors, but with the texts and the various contexts that surround them. To concentrate on the text rather than the author is not unusual, whether within or beyond the discipline of history.[19] In any case, it is impossible to separate the author from the text itself. Each contributor was asked to examine a particular text—in some cases, complementary texts—in the context of its/their inception, production, and intellectual influence on a particular field of research. The contributors were not asked to write to a set formula but to work within certain broad parameters. They were asked to assess the significance of a particular text and explain why it was important or influential. Beyond that, they were free to shape their contribution as they saw fit. Was the text under scrutiny an expression of its time and historiographic fashion or did it break new conceptual ground? To what extent did the text bear the personal stamp of the author? And why has the text either faded away or lived on? How has the field itself moved on, and what has been the text's imprint on that journey? *Texts and Contexts*, then, is intended as a scholarly guide to the development of a branch of the discipline of history—to demonstrate the importance and seminal influence of individual texts in that process and, not least, to reconnect historians of the Pacific Islands to the history and historiography of their specialization.

The texts selected here tend to be older ones, but age in itself did not guarantee selection. Had that been the case, we would have automatically included Scholefield's *The Pacific: Its Past and Future* (1919),

Ryden's *The Foreign Policy of the United States in Relation to Samoa* (1933), Masterman's *The Origins of International Rivalry in Samoa* (1934), and Ellison's *Opening and Penetration of Foreign Interests in Samoa to 1880* (1936), not to mention Brookes's *International Rivalry in the Pacific Islands* (1941) and Ward's *British Policy in the South Pacific* (1948).[20] Nor did sales figures enter our calculations. Quite simply, foundational texts are the books that were once (and in some cases still are) influential in defining the parameters of particular aspects of the subdiscipline of Pacific history, revising and revisionist in their own times and sometimes beyond. So, for example, Douglas Oliver's *The Pacific Islands* (1951) was an influential and enduring general text that introduced two generations of scholars to Pacific history. Peter Corris's *Port, Passage, Plantation* (1973) altered our understanding of the labor trade in the Pacific. Dorothy Shineberg's *They Came for Sandalwood* (1967) broke ground in presenting events from a Melanesian point of view and in redirectioning subsequent research. The same, more or less, can be said of the other texts included here. The common denominator is that the texts said something new or differently and influentially *at the time* and cast a new beam of light on their subject matter that illuminated the path of later explorers.

Texts and Contexts seeks to do more. It seeks to impart a sense of what it took in those days to produce history when the technology was limited to the fountain pen and the manual typewriter, when the manuscript sources were only beginning to be made more widely available on microfilm through the Australian Joint Copying Project, and when a significant proportion of the documentation had yet to be located and retrieved by the Pacific Manuscripts Bureau. The conditions under which our predecessors worked were rudimentary and even primitive by today's standards, and a better appreciation of their books will emerge when such constraints are taken into account. To read the older texts, and to have concrete details about their authors, is to appreciate their abilities, admire their commitment to their craft, and wonder if we could have done as well in those days when the props we take for granted (photocopying, word processors, and the Internet) were undreamed of. Keith Sinclair, that irrepressible New Zealander, decided at an early age to be a writer and embarked on serious historical research during his spells of leave from the navy in war-torn London. He completed his degree after the war, but he was different from most of his fellow students in that he was there to study what absorbed him rather than merely to acquire a degree. Becoming a lecturer in history at Auckland University College, he spent summer months in Wellington as "a full-time researcher" to write *The Origins of the Maori Wars* (1957).[21] Ken Gillion and Peter Corris, who were markedly different in personality and temperament, worked diligently through an impressive array of sources for their books on labor migration. Kerry Howe spent all his spare time over a six-year period researching and writing his general history of the precolonial Pacific, *Where the Waves Fall* (1984). Gavin Souter wrote his remarkable *The Last Unknown* (1963) between journalism assignments. And Oskar Spate retooled himself for his great retirement project, *The Pacific since Magellan* (1979, 1983, 1988), in three volumes. The essays in this volume enhance our appreciation that our predecessors worked under conditions that we would find intolerable.

History is a cumulative enterprise that ought to teach humility. No one methodology or theory holds the key to the riddle that is history. Older perspectives can still be useful, and today's historical work will, in time, be displaced by others, even derided as the misguided expressions of a bygone era. Cannadine's words are salutary:

> Every generation, scholars have risen proclaiming that they have found a new key which unlocks the essence of the past in a way that no previous historical approach has ever done. Our own generation is no exception to this rule—and it will probably be no exception to this fate. For these claims have never stood the test of time. Twenty years from now, scholars will probably be concerned with something very different, and they will look with bemused amazement that our generation could believe so confidently that unravelling the "meaning" of the past was the historian's crucial and essential task.[22]

Seen in this sobering light, the foundation texts take on a different meaning. They are transitions in a never-ending cycle of reinterpretations and new understandings that stretch into the future rather than solidifying at the present. Or to modify Jim Davidson's famous waves analogy, just as waves break upon the coral-tinged shores of the South Pacific, each one overtaken by the next before its energy is quite spent, so too will Pacific Islands historiography continue to be marked by successive and merging strands of interpretation and dominant discourse. Greg Dening, whose own work is assessed here, concurs: "historians live with the certainty that someone will do the historiography of the history we write."[23]

Still, it sometimes takes an effort to appreciate that the authors of our foundational texts worked in a world that thought and acted differently from the one in which we live today. If the text has a context, so does the author. On that very theme the Australian historian Geoffrey Bolton has said: "To ignore or berate the public figures of a hundred years ago because they were insensitive to issues that we now consider important is to invite similar derision from the scholars and readers of a hundred years hence."[24] Similarly, we cannot with justice rebuke a previous generation of historians for being moved by, or reacting against, the political and intellectual climate of which they were part and for not, in consequence, being able to anticipate the intellectual fashions or moral imperatives of a future generation. Rather, we should give recognition to their achievements and build on their work, as has the Native Hawaiian scholar Jonathan K. Osorio (in this volume) with respect to Kuykendall's resolutely "old-fashioned" *The Hawaiian Kingdom:*

> I don't know a single historian of the Hawaiian Islands who has not depended on the painstaking and detailed study of government documents, foreign exchanges and letters that Kuykendall collected, organised and incorporated into his massive three volume chronicles between 1938 and 1967. I also cannot think of a single one of us who would depend on his histories as definitive nor as dependable interpretations of culture, or even believable explanations of change. Yet we should admire the task to which he committed himself.

In that spirit we offer *Texts and Contexts* as a marker of special moments in the growth and development of Pacific Islands historiography as a gauge of its varied journeys and transformations over the last half century or so.

Thirty-six separate volumes, published between 1938 and 1992, by thirty different authors, are considered in this book.[25] Sixteen of the authors are still with us, which indicates the relative youthfulness of Pacific history as a specialization. The relatively small number of deceased authors, however, might relate more to the general longevity of Pacific specialists; two of the extant authors are in their nineties (H. E. Maude and

Douglas L. Oliver). By sad coincidence, Dorothy Shineberg passed away the same day this book was accepted for publication.

Apart from Ta'unga, who was a nineteenth-century missionary (and an accidental anthropologist), the authors all trained to be academics—although two (Peter Corris and Gavan Daws) left the academy to become professional writers. Three authors were born in the nineteenth century (Ta'unga, Ralph S. Kuykendall, and W. P. Morrell). The majority of the authors were born in the 1920s and 1930s with a heavy cluster in the late 1920s and early 1930s. For the most part we preferred contributors who are "period pieces" (i.e., of much the same generation as the book or books they write about) and who know (or knew) author or authors concerned. To write about a book in the context of its times is more readily (but not invariably) achieved by someone of similar vintage, and to have personally known the author(s) is likely to provide insights otherwise not available.

Authors/Editors, in Chronological Order

Ta'unga, ca. 1818–89	Francis West, 1927–
Ralph S. Kuykendall, 1885–1963	Dorothy Shineberg, 1927–2004
W. P. Morrell, 1899–1986	K. L. Gillion, 1929–92
Andrew Sharp, 1905–74	R. G. Crocombe, 1929–
H. E. Maude, 1906–	Gavin Souter, 1929–
O.H.K. Spate, 1911–2000	Marjorie Crocombe, 1930–
Douglas L. Oliver, 1913–	Niel Gunson, 1930–
J. W. Davidson, 1915–73	Marshall D. Sahlins, 1930–
Bernard Smith, 1916–	Greg Dening, 1931–
David Lewis, 1917–2002	Gavan Daws, 1933–
Norma McArthur, 1921–84	Alan Ward, 1935–
Peter Lawrence, 1922–89	Francis X. Hezel, 1939–
Keith Sinclair, 1922–93	Deryck Scarr, 1939–
Peter Worsley, 1924–	Peter Corris, 1942–
R. P. Gilson, 1925–62	K. R. Howe, 1947–

We did consult with colleagues and have substantial correspondence to prove that there was a fairly broad area of agreement on choice of texts *according to our criteria*. There had to be a broad coverage of themes, but we made no attempt to have a representative sampling of island groups. There are two texts on Samoa and none on Tonga for reasons that relate to our definition of what constitutes a foundational text. The 1960s are most heavily represented, the very time when Pacific Islands historiography was on a production curve.

The final choice of texts is ours—with three qualifications. In two instances a text that we considered foundational got left out because we could not find a contributor. We were also constrained by publishing realities from having more chapters (e.g., on Papua New Guinea and New Zealand) and allowing the contributors a more generous word length. Third, we decided against a chapter on J. C. Beaglehole's edition of *The Journals of Captain Cook* because we were not sure that the various constraints would permit adequate discussion of such a monumental work. Otherwise the choice—and the responsibility—is ours. That said, we don't intend to spend the rest of our lives justifying the inclusions and omissions.

Brij V. Lal, Canberra
Doug Munro, Wellington

Texts: Publication Chronology

1930S

†Ralph Kuykendall, *The Hawaiian Kingdom*, vol. 1, 1938

1950S

Douglas L. Oliver, *The Pacific Islands*, 1951
†Ralph Kuykendall, *The Hawaiian Kingdom*, vol. 2, 1952
†Andrew Sharp, *Ancient Voyagers in the Pacific*, 1957
†Keith Sinclair, *The Origins of the Maori Wars*, 1957
Peter Worsley, *The Trumpet Shall Sound*, 1957
Marshall Sahlins, *Social Stratification in Polynesia*, 1958

1960S

†W. P. Morrell, *Britain in the Pacific Islands*, 1960
Bernard Smith, *European Vision in the South Pacific*, 1960
†K. L. Gillion, *Fiji's Indian Migrants*, 1962
Gavin Souter, *The Last Unknown*, 1963
†Andrew Sharp, *Ancient Voyagers in Polynesia*, 1963
†Peter Lawrence, *Road Belong Cargo*, 1964
†J. W. Davidson, *Samoa mo Samoa*, 1967
†Ralph Kuykendall, *The Hawaiian Kingdom*, vol. 3, 1967
†Norma McArthur, *Island Populations of the Pacific*, 1967

Deryck Scarr, *Fragments of Empire*, 1967
†Dorothy Shineberg, *They Came for Sandalwood*, 1967
†Ta'unga, *The Works of Ta'unga*, 1967
Gavan Daws, *Shoal of Time*, 1968
H. E. Maude, *Of Islands and Men*, 1968
Francis West, *Hubert Murray*, 1968

1970S

†R. P. Gilson, *Samoa, 1830 to 1900*, 1970
†David Lewis, *We, the Navigators*, 1972
Peter Corris, *Passage, Port and Plantation*, 1973
Gavin Daws, *Holy Man*, 1973
Alan Ward, *A Show of Justice*, 1974
Niel Gunson, *Messengers of Grace*, 1978
†O.H.K. Spate, *The Spanish Lake*, 1979

1980S

Greg Dening, *Islands and Beaches*, 1980
Marshall D. Sahlins, *Historical Metaphors and Mythical Realities*, 1981
Francis X. Hezel, *The First Taint of Civilization*, 1983
†O.H.K. Spate, *Monopolists and Freebooters*, 1983
K. R. Howe, *Where the Waves Fall*, 1984
†O.H.K. Spate, *Paradise, Lost and Found*, 1988

1990S

Bernard Smith, *Imagining the Pacific*, 1992
†deceased

Notes

1. For example, Frank Fox, *Problems of the Pacific* (London, 1912); C. Brunsdon Fletcher, *The New Pacific: British Policy and German Aims* (London, 1917); idem, *The Problem of the Pacific* (London, 1919); General N. Golovin, *The Problem of the Pacific in the Twentieth Century* (Copenhagen, 1922); Gregory Bienstock, *The Struggle for the Pacific* (New York, 1937).

2. Guy H. Scholefield, *The Pacific: Its Past and Future and the Policy of the Great Powers from the Eighteenth Century* (London, 1919); George H. Ryden, *The Foreign Policy of the United States in Relation to Samoa* (New Haven, CT, 1933); Sylvia Masterman, *The Origins of International Rivalry in Samoa* (London, 1934); Joseph W. Ellison, *Opening and Penetration of Foreign Interests in Samoa to 1880*

(Corvallis, OR, 1936); Jean Ingram Brookes, *International Rivalry in the Pacific Islands* (Berkeley, 1941); J. M. Ward, *British Policy in the South Pacific* (Sydney, 1948). See also J. W. Davidson, "The Literature of the Pacific Islands," *Australian Outlook* 1, no. 1 (1947): 63–79.

3. John W. R. Smail, "On the Possibility of an Autonomous History of Modern Southeast Asia," *Journal of Southeast Asian History* 2, no. 2 (1962): 72–102; J. D. Fage, "British African Studies since the Second World War: A Personal Account," *African Affairs* 88 (1989): 397–413.

4. J. W. Davidson, *The Study of Pacific History: An Inaugural Lecture Delivered in Canberra on 25 November 1954* (Canberra, 1955).

5. K. R. Howe, "The Future of Pacific Islands History: A Personal View," *Pacific Islands History: Journeys and Transformations*, ed. Brij V. Lal (Canberra, 1992), 229.

6. Peter Hempenstall, "The Line of Descent: Creating Pacific Histories in Australasia," in *Historical Disciplines in Australasia: Themes, Problems and Debates*, ed. John A. Moses, special issue of *Australian Journal of Politics and History* 41 (1995): 157–70.

7. Howe, "The Future of Pacific Islands History," 226.

8. See generally, Richard J. Evans, *In Defence of History* (London, 1997), 201–2.

9. Barrie Macdonald, "'Now an Island is Too Big': Limits and Limitations of Pacific Islands History," in *Reflections of Pacific Historiography*, ed. Doug Munro, special issue of *Journal of Pacific Studies* 20 (1996): 27.

10. Peter Hempenstall, "'My Place': Finding a Voice within Pacific Studies," in Lal, ed., *Pacific Islands History*, 63.

11. Macdonald, "Now an Island is Too Big"; and Teresia Teaiwa, Robert Nicole, and Alumita Durutalo, "It *Ain't* Heavy, It's Our History: Three Young Academics Talanoa," *Journal of Pacific Studies* 20 (1996): 25–27, 267–69, respectively.

12. Hempenstall, "My Place," 78.

13. Peter Novick, *The Noble Dream: The "Objectivity" Question and the American Historical Profession* (Chicago, 1988), 628.

14. Rob Pascoe, *The Manufacture of Australian History* (Melbourne, 1979); Peter J. Parish, *Slavery: History and Historians* (New York, 1989); August Meier and Elliott Rudwick, *Black History and the Historical Profession, 1915–1980* (Urbana/Chicago, 1986); John Kenyon, *The History Men*, 2nd ed. (London, 1993). The nearest equivalent in Pacific Studies is Robert C. Kiste and Mac Marshall, eds., *American Anthropology in Micronesia: An Assessment* (Honolulu, 1999).

15. For example, Marcus Cunliffe and Robin W. Winks, eds., *Postmasters: Some Essays on American Historians* (New York, 1969); Walter L. Arnstein, ed., *Recent Historians of Great Britain: Essays on the Post-1945 Generation* (Ames, IA, 1990); Stuart Macintyre and Julian Thomas, eds., *The Discovery of Australian History, 1890–1939* (Melbourne, 1995).

16. Especially in Lal and Munro's edited collections *Pacific Islands History*, and *Reflections on Pacific Historiography*, respectively, as well as Brij V. Lal, ed., *Pacific*

Places, Pacific Histories: Essays in Honor of Robert C. Kiste (Honolulu, 2004), and Ruth Fink Latukefu, "Campus, Garden, Nation," *Meanjin* 62, no. 3 (2003): 68–81.

17. David Cannadine, *G. M. Trevelyan: A Life in History* (London, 1993), xii.

18. The phrase is Ian Hamilton's, *Against Oblivion: Some Lives of the Twentieth Century Poets* (New York, 2003), 13.

19. For example, Wm Roger Louis, ed., *The Origins of the Second World War: A.J.P. Taylor and His Critics* (New York/Toronto, 1972); H. J. Allen, W. S. F. Pickering, and William Watts-Miller, *On Durkheim's Elementary Forms of Religious Life* (London/New York, 1998); Ian Jarvie and Sandra Pralong, eds., *Popper's Open Society After Fifty Years: The Continuing Relevance of Karl Popper* (London/New York, 1999); W.S.F. Pickering and Geoffrey Walford, eds., *Durkheim's Suicide: A Century of Research and Debate* (London/New York, 2000); Michael Ferrari, ed., *The Varieties of Religious Experience: Centenary Essays,* special issue of *Journal of Consciousness Studies* 9–10 (2002); [Symposium] "The Golden Anniversary of Skinner's *Science and Human Behavior,*" *Journal of the Experimental Analysis of Behavior* 80, no. 3 (2003): 311–52.

20. Little wonder that Davidson, when setting out a research agenda and a methodology on behalf of the new specialism of Pacific Islands history, was reacting against the dominance—and, as he saw it, the limitations—of conventional imperial history.

21. Keith Sinclair, *Half-Way Round the Harbour: An Autobiography* (Auckland, 1993), 100, 114, 123, 129.

22. David Cannadine, ed., *What Is History Now?* (Basingstoke/New York, 2002), xii.

23. Greg Dening, "Reflection: On the Cultural History of Marshall Sahlins and Valerio Valeri," *Pacific History Bibliography and Comment* (1988): 45.

24. Geoffrey Bolton, *Edmund Barton: The One Man for the Job* (Sydney, 2000), x.

25. To be precise, the thirty authors include the two editors of *The Works of Ta'unga* (Ron and Marjorie Crocombe).

PART I

General/Regional

CHAPTER I

Fatal Choices? Morrell's and Scarr's Imperial Histories

Jane Samson

Britain in the Pacific Islands, by W. P. Morrell.
Oxford: Clarendon, 1960.

*Fragments of Empire: A History of the Western Pacific
High Commission, 1878–1914,* by Deryck Scarr.
Canberra: Australian National University Press, 1967.
Co-published, Honolulu: University of Hawai'i Press.

THE HISTORIOGRAPHY of imperialism has always reflected the ebb and flow of Western power. Before World War II, the study of modern empires was almost entirely confined to metropolitan issues. The vast British Empire dominated a historiography that constructed colonized peoples and landscapes as the passive recipients, for good or ill, of imperial initiatives. After World War II, amid the rapid disintegration of the British Empire, new perspectives emphasized the importance of local agency and circumstances, producing "area studies" whose centers of gravity lay in Africa, Asia, or the Pacific, rather than in Europe. David Fieldhouse once described British imperial history's abrupt decentering as Humpty Dumpty's great fall, and many wondered whether to bother trying to reassemble the bits.[1]

W. P. Morrell's *Britain in the Pacific Islands* (1960) and Deryck Scarr's *Fragments of Empire* (1967) are snapshots of the transition from what I call "old imperial history" to the newer area studies approach. The Pacific history program established by Jim Davidson at the Australian National University (ANU) in the early 1950s (sometimes dubbed the Canberra school) was challenging the old imperial centers for ownership of Pacific history.[2] Kerry Howe recalls the excitement— even as late as the early 1970s—of island-centered historiography with "its apparent relevance in a post-colonial era, particularly with its concern to highlight the role of the 'other side of the frontier' in culture contact situations."[3] As Brij Lal has noted, this approach had all the hallmarks of a faith—"with a shrine (the Coombs Building at ANU), a prophet (Davidson) and an Island-oriented theology."[4] Orthodoxy was represented by culture contact research on a selected island or island group; the faithful "looked askance at those few unfortunates amongst us who had somehow chosen to deal with 'tainted' colonial topics."[5] Pacific history wanted to expand, like any missionary faith, and it was therefore necessary to emphasize the gulf between its virtues and the sins of academic heathendom.

William Parker Morrell (1899–1986) was considerably more orthodox in his thinking and approaches to history. A graduate of the University of New Zealand, Morrell took his doctorate at Oxford for a thesis on "British Colonial Policy in the Age of Peel and Russell"; it was published in 1930 under the same title and, together with an edited collection of documents published the year before, established Morrell's reputation as a historian of imperial policy.[6] More than fifty years later, Morrell's early work was still highly regarded for its span, being described as "a block-busting thesis on colonial policies of the 1840s which in its range and detail puts to shame the narrow limits of years (even months) and countries (even provinces) of . . . latter day [Oxford] D.Phils."[7] Despite being appointed to a readership at Birkbeck College, London, Morrell was not convinced that colonial history was a marketable subject in an environment where, as he put it, "historians in England generally were more interested in discussing how many oxen there were in a Domesday plough-team than they were in the history of the British empire."[8] He felt that this would prevent him getting a chair in Britain so he returned to New Zealand in 1946 as professor of history at the University of Otago.

Morrell was no critic of empire and in the preface to *Britain in the Pacific Islands*, he acknowledged the encouragement of Sir Reginald Coupland, doyen of British antislavery historians and unrepentant apologist for the benefits of British imperial rule.[9] In two important respects, however, Morrell's *Britain in the Pacific Islands* was qualitatively different from his earlier study. As well as the usual range of official sources, he consulted missionary archives. More important, Morrell was sensitive to the shifting historiography and when he began research for *Britain in the Pacific Islands* during World War II he was already determined to challenge the usual metropolitan approach to his subject. His avowed intention was to ground his study "not in Downing Street but in the islands" (vi), a radical departure from the policy-centered approach of the old imperial history.[10] The resulting book focused on the traders, beachcombers, planters, missionaries, and rogues whose uncoordinated activities drew a reluctant British government into deeper involvement in the Pacific Islands. These subaltern groups provoked the decisions made by the Admiralty, the Colonial and Foreign Offices, and, later on, the various colonial governments of Australia, New Zealand, and Fiji. Hence the book's title, *Britain in the Pacific Islands,* rather than *Britain and the Pacific Islands.*

Morrell was frank about the limitations of his research. Wartime conditions had made it difficult to consult primary documentation. For example, the Foreign Office series on the Pacific Islands was housed for some time at a country house in Surrey for safekeeping. After returning to New Zealand, he obtained a research grant for a brief visit to Fiji in 1948, and he used New Zealand–based records such as the Samoan consular collection. He regretted that the pressure of teaching and administration confined his scholarly work to the term vacations, making it impossible for him to visit other island groups or to consult Australian and New Zealand archives more extensively. Then there were the pressures of family and home. Morrell did not publish a major scholarly monograph in the twenty years between 1940 and 1960, and when a colleague remarked on this hiatus in Morrell's considerably scholarly output, his daughter responded, "You mean he got married . . . and my brother and I came along."[11] Morrell was actually writing *two* big books during those twenty years. He was also engaged in a major comparative study of mid-nineteenth-century British colonial policy, which was published in 1967.[12] The sequence of research and writing got out of kilter when Morrell put aside his Pacific work in 1951 and took a one-year fellowship in South Africa to make a push on his comparative study. It required great commitment to see the two projects to fruition, even for one as well organized as Morrell. As it happened, the original manuscript of *Britain and the Pacific Islands* was much longer, but the publisher demanded it be cut by one-third.

By the time he published his *Britain in the Pacific Islands* in 1960, Morrell was well aware of the importance of the developing field of Pacific history, and noted "a number of younger scholars holding Research Fellowships of the Australian National University" whose work was beginning to be published. He welcomed this new phase of

Pacific history, noting that the difference between various Pacific peoples and their societies was as important an ingredient as colonial policy or missionary activity.[13] On the face of it, his approach might seem to have a great deal in common with that of the Canberra school. To some reviewers, Morrell was a typical example of the new periphery-centered approach that avoided the tendency of the older historiography to find "continuity of theme by looking at the Pacific from Europe."[14] A number of reviewers regretted his incomplete and sometimes misleading research; these critics included Ethel Drus, a former member of Davidson's department who had done substantial work on Fiji herself. Owen Parnaby made the telling criticism that Morrell saw essential good in people who emerge from his own sources as villains.[15] Others noted that Morrell had not consulted recent anthropological work on historical island societies.[16] Nevertheless, Francis West declared, from ANU no less, that Morrell had written "what will be the standard work on the Pacific area for some time to come."[17]

Davidson might have been expected to disagree, yet his own review of Morrell was respectfully restrained, declaring Morrell's study to be the best available to date. Despite Morrell's failure to write Pacific history as it should be written, Davidson could still say that island peoples "still came to life in the writer's mind."[18] Other Canberra-based Pacific specialists fumed about the outsider who intruded so clumsily, as they saw it, on their domain. R. P. Gilson was particularly blunt, writing to H. E. Maude (another of Pacific history's founding fathers):

> Hell's teeth: when I think of how we have to sweat and strain and gnaw our bloody guts out trying to fathom the complexities of the island set-up, and then some joker comes along and presumes to palm off a "survey" history along the same lines. Of course, he couldn't see the whole of the literature, but why does he refuse to recognize the limitations of what he has seen?[19]

Maude wryly remarked, "Like many others who fall into the error of writing a book, he will wish that he had concentrated on gardening instead."[20]

A process of "othering" is clearly at work here. Leaving aside Morrell's preface, with its articulate summary of the limitations of his research and its generous anticipation of the fruits of the new school at ANU, some Pacific history insiders preferred to caricature what they considered to be metropolitan arrogance. This aggressive defensiveness had its short-term benefits; in the long run, however, it only served to isolate Pacific history from wider comparative frameworks.[21] Morrell's book certainly has its weak points: he would have been the first to agree that its research was patchy, especially where antipodean records were concerned. Certainly its belated appearance was unfortunate in light of the enormous changes taking place in the field. Nevertheless, there is something gratuitous about the way that *Britain in the Pacific Islands* was so severely reviewed by members of a department that itself had produced so few books at the time. Some of these reviews also give a misleading impression of the book's usefulness to Pacific scholars: W. David McIntyre visited Davidson in 1968 (the year after Scarr's *Fragments* was published) to find that *"Britain in the Pacific Islands* was the basic reference source. The starting point was always: 'What does Morrell say?'"[22]

Nevertheless, the long delay in publishing *Britain in the Pacific Islands* brought Morrell, who was in his late fifties at the time of publication, into direct competition with young Pacific historians like Deryck Scarr. A graduate student of Davidson's at ANU, Scarr was the consummate Pacific history insider. He had access to collections such as the Royal Navy–Australia Station records, which were discovered in New Zealand in 1961, and the records of the Western Pacific High Commission, then housed in Suva. These were exciting times when new things were being done, or envisaged, in Pacific Islands historiography, and there was a concomitant feeling of lost opportunity with respect to Morrell's book. Much of the research that reviewers wished Morrell had tackled in the 1940s and 1950s could now be done from microfilm housed in Canberra itself, and travel to the islands was considerably easier than it had been in the aftermath of World War II. Morrell's scholarly activities were largely confined to vacations; ANU academics at the Institute of Advanced Studies, with no undergraduate teaching and generous funding for travel, did not face such constraints. The energetic and intellectually voracious Scarr used these advantages to maximum effect; his acknowledgments in *Fragments* focus almost entirely on antipodean mentors and archives in Australia, New Zealand, and the Pacific Islands.

Drawn from his Ph.D. thesis, "Policy and Practice in the Western Pacific: A History of the Western Pacific High Commission 1877–1913," Scarr's *Fragments of Empire* discussed its subject with reference to current anthropological literature, at least with regard to Fiji. Meticulously researched and full of vignettes and anecdotes, its focus on the activities of the Western Pacific High Commission gave it a coherence that Morrell's more sweeping study had lacked. Scarr not only detailed the policies and actions of the commission and its members; he also assessed its interaction with the Pacific peoples it was meant to protect from European depredations. Scarr visited some of the islands and researched the appropriate use of genealogies, descriptive terminology, and orthography appropriate to a range of island cultures. These features were justly praised by the book's reviewers, especially by those who worked in Pacific history themselves.[23] The only complaint was that Scarr's narrative, which was dense by any standards, could swamp his readers in a flood of characters and detail.[24] Although *Fragments of Empire* was regarded as a difficult read when it came out, it is a model of clarity and simplicity compared with his more recent writings. Indeed, Scarr's colorful and opinionated style is in marked contrast to Morrell's understated wit and cautious judgments.

Scarr's most outspoken admirer was one of Britain's most eminent imperial historians, Ronald Robinson, who had also examined the Ph.D. thesis. Robinson's own work, like that of so many others in the 1960s, saw actions and agency on the periphery as vital; he regarded Scarr's contribution as part of this greater whole. There is no sense of insider/outsider distinctions in his review, which began by saying that "this volume is an example of how imperial history ought to be written and will give no small satisfaction to older scholars, if only because it shows how far the subject has been advanced in the past 20 years."[25] Robinson saw no difficulty in linking the name of Jim Davidson with that of Sir Keith Hancock to suggest an atmosphere of shared enterprise in which the interaction of metropolis and periphery would at last be explored in its full complexity.

Davidson's supervision of Scarr's thesis, and his friendship and ongoing professional contacts with British imperial specialists like Robinson, demonstrates that although Davidson denounced certain types of imperial history, he was not opposed to it in principle. For Davidson, imperial history remained of great significance—his ANZAAS presidential address in 1957 was a favorable assessment of three colonial governors[26]—and many have agreed with him. In the course of research on what he assumed to be Pacific history's neglect of imperial history, Peter Hempenstall discovered that 50 percent of the articles published by the *Journal of Pacific History* and *Pacific Studies* between 1980 and 1990 "dealt with colonial empires up to World War II, or some aspects of colonial policy or the relations between rulers and ruled."[27] Perhaps it was only a vocal minority who deemed colonial history topics to be tainted.

Recent theoretical and methodological perspectives highlight other ironic continuities between old imperial history and the early years of Pacific Studies. Scarr's extensive use of Western Pacific High Commission records and the records of the Royal Navy–Australia Station provided access to local perspectives but in a fairly limited sense. They revealed much more about the commission's interaction with Pacific Islanders than the London-based collections did, but they were still records created mainly by Europeans. Later on, Pacific specialists would address this issue by incorporating extensive island-based fieldwork, including oral history. In the meantime, we can see that both *Britain in the Pacific Islands* and *Fragments* saw the islands through mainly European eyes. The question remains: was the new Pacific history really so radically different?

This question invites others. Did Scarr's supposedly radical new approach yield results different from Morrell's? Pacific history insiders were convinced that the island-centered approach was superior to the old imperial history, yet Morrell and Scarr reach similar conclusions. Both were convinced that missionaries, traders, planters, and administrators were the real story of Britain's reluctant empire in the Pacific Islands. A parsimonious Treasury and suspicious politicians in Britain were forced to intervene in situations where "white savages" were exploiting Islanders, and where the expansionist colonial governments of Australia and New Zealand could not be relied on to respect indigenous rights. Morrell and Scarr both pronounced the accomplishments of the Western Pacific High Commission, and other imperial initiatives, to be a mixed bag of good intentions blended with insufficient resources and overwhelming economic pressures. Both noted the widespread depopulation visible by the turn of the twentieth century, and the increased talk of development for metropolitan interests (Morrell, 431–35; Scarr, 292–94). Among other things, this shift led to the acceptance of immigrant labor policies that would have dramatic long-term consequences for race relations, especially in Fiji. Like Morrell, Scarr concluded his book on a gloomy note: "By 1914, it was far from clear—except, perhaps, in Tonga—that the protectorate administrations established in the High Commission territories were of the benefit to Islanders that it had always been assumed they would be. Their effect was to weaken indigenous modes, undermine custom and cause dependence on European direction" (297).

This broad similarity between the two books was obscured by the fact that (to my knowledge) no reviewer of Scarr ever mentioned Morrell. It was as though *Britain in the Pacific Islands* had never been written. If comparisons were made, they were with the policy analysts of the 1930s and 1940s: Masterman, Brookes, and Ward. A few of Scarr's extensive footnotes acknowledge the use of Morrell as a quarry for detail, especially with regard to missionary activity, but that is all. This essay is therefore probably the first to tackle the question (pace Gilson and Maude) of how much common ground Morrell and Scarr actually shared.

Their books have also shared a common fate. *Britain in the Pacific Islands* was the work of a mature scholar. Morrell had already written books on the provincial system in New Zealand, the gold rushes, and the general history of New Zealand, but his métier was imperial history.[28] *Britain in the Pacific Islands* was a regional extension of that interest but it reflected a dated mindset when it eventually appeared. Morrell's return to New Zealand, "to run my own show," as he put it, was good for his career but disadvantageous for *Britain in the Pacific Islands*. In the 1940s, Morrell was at the cutting edge of the new "periphery" historiography, but he published *Britain in the Pacific Islands* too late to be seen as one of its pioneers. *Fragments of Empire*, by contrast, was a young man's book, and although concerned with an ostensibly backward-looking imperial topic, its iconoclastic author was more anthropologically informed and closer to local realities. Nevertheless, both books have faded away, victims of a general feeling among ANU graduates about fatally tainted imperial history topics. Anyone who anticipated a host of graduate dissertations based on these pioneering texts would have been sadly disappointed.

Nowadays a second wave of othering is creating new interpretations of historiographical traditions and new forms of insider/outsider status. Area studies have been challenged by a "return to the metropolis" in the shape of colonial discourse theory. Postmodern epistemological anxieties have undermined faith in the investigation of authentically indigenous voices; instead, there is an emphasis on colonized identities, silencing, and intellectual imperialism through metropolitan texts and discursive structures. This approach leaves little room for the indigenous agency emphasized by an earlier generation. European power is once again the only real story of empire, although we now travel by different theoretical and methodological paths to reach this traditional conclusion. There are signs of discontent with the Eurocentricity and ahistorical tendencies of colonial discourse theory, but the cutbacks and hiring freezes of the past twenty years have left the Western academy ill-equipped to produce an energetic new generation of theorists and dissenters.

In the meantime, riding roughshod over the once-cherished dichotomies of the Pacific Studies identity, Nicholas Thomas and his followers proclaim that Pacific historiography has formerly been the barren haunt of "mindlessly" empirical imperial history scholarship.[29] Thomas realizes that discourse theory can be a blunt instrument, and he is right to see similarities between the likes of Morrell and Scarr in terms of source material and epistemology. It is unclear what is mindless about their work, however. Bronwen Douglas is equally dismissive, in the pages of the new *Oxford History of the British Empire* no less, declaring that to study the British in the Pacific is "passé" unless it adopts colonial discourse theory.[30] This exclusiveness is difficult to square with Peter Hempenstall's findings concerning the wide range and enduring popularity of imperial history in Pacific journals. However, a new set of church fathers and scriptures has been proclaimed, and the usual search for heretics is on. To study imperial history in its Pacific dimension is still a fatal choice, even at a time when the academic world seems consumed by the issue of colonialism. New strategies of inclusion and exclusion determine membership in a new elect.

There is an alternative to this seemingly endless process of academic othering, renunciation and conversion. Imperial history has always provided important context for modern Pacific history; the Pacific dimension is crucial for any understanding of modern imperialism.[31] The othering of imperial history, whether by Pacific history or by a new generation of literary theorists, has thrown the baby out with the bathwater.[32] The results of this relentless exclusion are all too plain. The new *Oxford History of the British Empire* was criticized for marginalizing the Pacific (and Canada), but how could it have done otherwise when specialists in those areas have shaped their identities around a rejection of wider imperial perspectives? Indianists and Africanists remained engaged with metropolitan institutions and debates, ensuring their prominence in the new discourse studies. The long absence of the Pacific from metropolitan debate means that Pacific history conferences held in the United Kingdom, or organized from there, continue to focus mainly on Great Explorers rather than colonial regimes and practices. Debates rage about Captain Cook while the nineteenth- and twentieth-century Pacific remains mostly Terra Australis Incognita, despite the best efforts of the Sir Robert Menzies Centre for Australian Studies in London.

Perhaps the whiggish obsession with progressive historiography, whereby older approaches are denounced in favor of the latest orthodoxy, is no longer appropriate in these postmodern times. Perhaps nobody owns Pacific history, and therefore we are all free to read widely, and to take from a long conversation the scholarly insights that we find useful or challenging. Perhaps we should begin to practice the creative, transgressive bricolage we so often speak of as a feature of postmodern scholarship. E. P. Thompson was right about "the enormous condescension of posterity"; fortunately, we are beginning to understand that there are no barriers to insight beyond those we create for ourselves.

Notes

I am grateful to David Hilliard, W. David McIntyre, Antony Wood, and especially Judith Nathan (née Morrell) for helpfully commenting on an earlier draft of this essay.

1. D. K. Fieldhouse, "Can Humpty-Dumpty Be Put Together Again? Imperial History in the 1980s," *Journal of Imperial and Commonwealth History* 12, no. 1 (1984): 9–23.

2. J. W. Davidson, *The Study of Pacific History: An Inaugural Lecture Delivered in Canberra on 25 November 1954* (Canberra, 1955).

3. K. R. Howe, "The Future of Pacific Islands History: A Personal View," in *Pacific Islands History: Journeys and Transformations*, ed. Brij V. Lal (Canberra, 1992), 226.

4. Quoted in Doug Munro, "The Isolation of Pacific History," *Journal of Pacific Studies* 20 (1996): 47.

5. Howe, "The Future of Pacific Islands History," 228.

6. K. N. Ball and W. P. Morrell, *Select Documents on British Colonial Policy, 1800–1860* (Oxford, 1929); W. P. Morrell, *British Colonial Policy in the Age of Peel and Russell* (Oxford, 1930).

7. Frederick Madden, "The Commonwealth, Commonwealth History, and Oxford, 1905–1971," in *Oxford and the Idea of Empire: Essays Presented to Sir Edgar Williams*, ed. Frederick Madden and David Fieldhouse (London / Canberra, 1982), 14.

8. W. P. Morrell, *Memoirs* (Dunedin, 1979), 49.

9. On Coupland, see Madden, "The Commonwealth, Commonwealth History, and Oxford," and Ronald Robinson, "Oxford in Imperial Historiography," both in *Oxford and the Idea of Empire*, ed. Madden and Fieldhouse, 11–18, 36–38, respectively.

10. Examples include Guy Scholefield, *The Pacific: Its Past and Future and the Policy of the Great Powers from the Eighteenth Century* (London, 1919); Sylvia Masterman, *The Origins of International Rivalry in Samoa 1845–1884* (London, 1934); Jean Ingram Brookes, *International Rivalry in the Pacific Islands, 1800–1875* (New York, 1941); John M. Ward, *British Policy in the South Pacific, 1786–1893* (Sydney, 1948). See also John M. Ward, "The British Territories in the Pacific," in *The Historiography of the British Empire-Commonwealth*, ed. Robin W. Winks (Durham, NC, 1966), 200–201.

11. Quoted in W. David McIntyre, "Imperial Jubilee: W. P. Morrell's Contributions to Imperial History," *New Zealand Journal of History* 16, no. 1 (1982): 58–59. He did co-author (with D.O.W. Hall) *A History of New Zealand Life* (Christchurch, 1957). But this book was not pitched at an academic audience, and much of it had been previously published in Department of Education *Post-Primary School Bulletins*.

12. W. P. Morrell, *British Colonial Policy in the Mid-Victorian Age: South Africa, New Zealand, the West Indies* (Oxford, 1969).

13. Unless otherwise stated, the details in this and the previous paragraph are drawn from Morrell, *Memoirs;* idem, *Britain in the Pacific Islands* (Oxford, 1960), v–ix; idem, Review (of Robin W. Winks, ed., *The Historiography of the British Empire-Commonwealth*), *New Zealand Journal of History* 1, no. 1 (1967): 95; F.L.W. Wood, "W.P.M.," in *W. P. Morrell: A Tribute*, ed. G. A. Wood and P. S. O'Connor (Dunedin, 1973), xi–xii; G. A. Wood, "Morrell, William Parker (1899–1985)," in *Dictionary of New Zealand Biography*, vol. 4: *1921–1940* (Auckland / Wellington, 1998), 359.

14. Marjorie Jacobs, *Historical Studies, Australia and New Zealand* 10, no. 37 (1961): 119.

15. O. W. Parnaby, *Journal of the Polynesian Society* 70, no. 4 (1961): 512–13.

16. D. F. Crozier, *History* 46 (1961): 161–62; Francis West, *Victorian Studies* 4, no. 3 (1961): 267–68.

17. *Victorian Studies* 4, no. 3 (1961): 267.

18. *Australian Journal of Politics and History* 9, no. 3 (1963): 131–33.

19. R. P. Gilson to H. E. Maude, 25 December 1960, Papers of H. C. and H. E. Maude, MS Papers 0003, Special Collections, Barr Smith Library, University of Adelaide, General Correspondence, Series J (I am grateful to Doug Munro for sharing his notes from this collection). Gilson reviewed *Britain in the Pacific Islands* along these lines, but expressed more moderately, in *Pacific Viewpoint* 2, no. 1 (1961): 116–17.

20. H. E. Maude to Ethel Drus, 31 March 1961, Maude Papers, Series J.

21. See generally Munro, "The Isolation of Pacific History," 45–68.

22. McIntyre, "Imperial Jubilee," 65.

23. K. L. Gillion, *Historical Studies, Australia and New Zealand* 14, no. 54 (1970): 306–7; A. M. Healy, *Oceania* 41, no. 3 (1971): 151–52; John M. R. Young, *Australian Journal of Politics and History* 14, no. 2 (1968): 284–86.

24. For example, Charles S. Blackton, *American Historical Review* 74, no. 4 (1969): 134–35.

25. *Journal of Pacific History* 3 (1968): 230.

26. J. W. Davidson. "Scholarship and the Government of Colonies," *Historical Studies, Australia and New Zealand* 9, no. 28 (1957): 406–20. ANZAAS is the abbreviation for the Australia and New Zealand Association for the Advancement of Science. Davidson's address was to Section E (History). Before the founding of the Australian Historical Society in the mid-1970s, the only regular gathering of Australian and New Zealand historians was the ANZAAS Congress. So Davidson's 1957 address was a major performance and almost everyone who mattered from that part of the world was there.

27. Peter Hempenstall, "'My Place': Finding a Voice within Pacific Colonial Studies," in *Pacific Islands History*, ed. Lal, 65.

28. A bibliography of Morrell's writings (by Rosemary Hudson) is in *W. P. Morrell*, ed. Wood and O'Connor, 250–52.

29. Nicholas Thomas, *Colonialism's Culture: Anthropology, Travel and Government* (Cambridge, 1994), 61; Rod Edmond, *Representing the South Pacific: Colonial Discourse from Cook to Gauguin* (Cambridge, 1997), xi, 11; Vanessa Smith, *Literary Culture and the Pacific: Nineteenth-Century Textual Encounters* (Cambridge, 1998), 7.

30. Bronwen Douglas, "Imperial Flotsam? The British in the Pacific Islands," in *The Oxford History of the British Empire*, vol. 5: *Historiography*, ed. Robin W. Winks (Oxford, 1999), 377.

31. See introduction to *British Imperial Strategies in the Pacific, 1750–1900*, ed. Jane Samson (Aldershot, UK, 2003), xv–xxxi.

32. K. R. Howe, "Two Worlds?" *New Zealand Journal of History* 37, no. 1 (2003): 57.

CHAPTER 2

On Douglas Oliver's *The Pacific Islands*

Doug Munro

The Pacific Islands, by Douglas L. Oliver.
Cambridge, MA: Harvard University Press, 1951. Rev. ed. co-published,
New York, by The American Museum of Natural History, and Doubleday &
Co., 1961. Reissued 1962 by Harvard University Press. Reissued with correc-
tions by Doubleday as an Anchor Book, 1965. Reissued by University of
Hawai'i Press, 1975. 3rd ed., Honolulu: University of Hawai'i Press, 1989.

THERE IS a widespread belief that the first general history of the Pacific Islands was Douglas L. Oliver's *The Pacific Islands* (1951), which was only superseded a third of a century later by K. R. Howe's *Where the Waves Fall* (1984).[1] Actually, the pedigree is much longer and the genre itself has a strange history. Before 1950 there were conceivably at least three general histories of the Pacific Islands, none of which could be described as professional history. The pioneering study was *The Pacific: Its Past and Future* (1919) by the New Zealander Guy Scholefield (1877–1963). It was largely concerned with Great Power relations. The next such text was *The Story of the Pacific* (New York, 1940) by Heinrik Willem Van Loon (1882–1944), followed by *Anatomy of Paradise* (New York, 1948) by the American J. C. Furnas (1905–2001).[2] This trio of generalists was a motley crew. Scholefield's book originated as a doctoral thesis in political science at the London School of Economics, but he was essentially a journalist. The Dutchman Van Loon had a Ph.D. in history from the University of Munich. He was a popularizer whose name will be familiar to older readers as the author of *The Story of Mankind* which, like H. G. Wells' *Outline of History*, was a runaway best-seller. Furnas was also a journalist, but of more scholarly ilk than Scholefield, and, in contrast to Van Loon, his researches took him to many parts of the *29*

Pacific. Furnas's *Anatomy of Paradise* was a respectable performance for its time and well worth reading even now. A measure of its quality is the fact that *Anatomy of Paradise* shared the Anisfield-Wolf Award with none other than Alan Paton's *Cry, the Beloved Country,* for the best book on race relations published in its year—despite describing Indo-Fijians as "clamorous interlopers," among other things. Even more respectable is Furnas's biography of Robert Louis Stevenson, still in print, which a later Stevenson scholar acknowledged as one of the two "unchallenged landmarks in Stevenson studies."[3] All the same, the general histories on offer in 1950 were a statement not simply of the scholarly standards of the time but on the underdeveloped state of Pacific Islands historiography. In those amiable days of the gentleman-scholar and generalist par excellence, not one of the three authors was a specialist Pacific historian.

The trend continued in 1951 with the publication of Douglas L. Oliver's *The Pacific Islands,* on this occasion by an academic anthropologist.[4] Oliver (born 1913) earned his doctorate at the University of Vienna for a thesis (written in German) on relations between the Utu and Tutsi in present-day Rwanda. He joined the staff of the Anthropology Museum at Harvard University and unexpectedly became involved in the Pacific when, in 1936, he was assigned to a wealthy traveler who wanted an anthropologist to accompany him to New Guinea. Tiring of the company of a rich man looking for adventure, Oliver broke with the expedition and ended up on Bougainville, where he commenced fieldwork. In an academic career that has continued well into retirement, Oliver's concern with Pacific Islanders has not wavered. As well as Bougainville, he has worked in Micronesia and published major historical and ethnographic studies on Tahitians. Age ninety at the time of my writing this essay, he wishes it known that "I am still alive—thanks to daily rowing, and am now engaged in tidying up my *Ancient Tahitian Society* [3 vols., 1975] (but doubt that I'll ever find a publisher for it). Never mind; it keeps me busy."[5]

The Pacific Islands was Oliver's first book, published in his thirty-eighth year. Like W. K. Hancock's *Australia* (1930) and Keith Sinclair's *A Short History of New Zealand* (1959), it was a young man's book, oozing youthful vitality but disciplined in the sense of being well paced, carefully proportioned, and adequately researched. Those were the days when a general history and a short history were one and the same thing. This trio of short histories has a further characteristic, which Sinclair describes as "apple-treeish":

When I was about to go into production, the best advice I received was from W.K. Hancock who said "Write it under an apple tree." He meant, I think, "Don't refer continually to an index card. Do write from headings. Let the style be easy, gently flowing, perhaps breezy, but altogether apple-treeish. Let there be open skies and fresh air in the prose."[6]

In this fashion Oliver begins with the geographical and ethnographic setting ("The Islanders") before moving on to the usual suspects from across the seas—explorers, whalers, and the emissaries of that unholy trinity of commerce, the cross, and the flag, including planters, "blackbirders," merchants, miners, and administrators ("The Aliens"). The third and forth sections of *The Pacific Islands* are entitled "Metamorphosis," which accounts for the changes wrought by the aliens, and "Cataclysm and Change," on the course and consequences of World War II. Overall, Oliver puts the case that Pacific Islanders suffered vicariously from their encounters with "civilization." Not unremittingly so and the Islanders were not entirely helpless, but they definitely lost out badly and came off second best. Take, for example, the course and consequences of the sandalwood trade. Oliver acknowledges that "one-sidedness gave way as more traders began to compete and as islanders lost their first awe for anything brought in by the white demigods." But he does go on to add that the traders "chalked up a record of chicanery, violence and evil equal to the blackest chapter of colonial history" (79–80).

The approach adopted in the section on "The Aliens" follows that taken by Davidson in his seminal work on the European penetration of the Pacific, where he likened the foreign intrusion to a series of "waves breaking on the coral ringed shores of the South Seas, each one overtaken by the next before its energy is quite spent."[7] In *The Pacific Islands* there is the same passing parade of the familiar "occupational categories,"[8] from explorers through to administrators, that cut a destructive path through the island world. That is not, in and of itself, Eurocentrism but a recognition that outsiders were the most significant agents of change and that they can be usefully subdivided, for analytical purposes, according to occupation. In any case, Eurocentrism is defined by a mindset rather than by content. The succession of aliens cannot be written out of the story so the obligation is to "place the Islanders firmly at the forefront and to analyse their reactions to the various waves of Europeans reaching their islands."[9] Nor should there be reverse Eurocentrism along the lines of "explaining trade development on the Gazelle

Peninsula in terms of Tolai response to economic opportunity but without consideration of the encouragement and infrastructural support provided by Governor Hahl."[10] Oliver is not altogether successful at placing Islanders firmly at the forefront—ironically, he being an anthropologist. His interpretative thrust inhibits such a perspective: by regarding Europeans as despoilers and the Islanders as victims, the latter take a back seat and find themselves largely deprived of agency on the ground and of a profile in the text. The anthropologist Robert Borofsky makes the same links when he points out that the historian Kerry Howe's emphasis on indigenous agency in *Where the Waves Fall* (1984), as opposed to *The Pacific Islands*'s "emphasis on the changes wrought by the West," results in Howe's text containing more Islander perspectives than does Oliver's.[11]

The Pacific Islands is not only a general history but a short history. In musical terms the pace can be likened to an allegro rather than an andante. And like Furnas before him, whose *Anatomy of Paradise* Oliver greatly admired,[12] Oliver had a gift for the memorable phrase, for example: "Relieved of . . . tiresome administrative duties [by the establishment of a British protectorate], Tongans returned to the charming diversion of playing government and attending church" (133). The geographical coverage is wide-ranging but the detail is spare and selective, intended to illustrate rather than to overwhelm. It is gracefully written, in the same seamless prose that Bill Oliver (no relation) achieved in his own short history of New Zealand.[13] Like any successful short history, the sweeps of a broad brush on a wide canvas create bold contours and a clear impression. Elaboration is subordinated to the exposition of themes, and particularities are of less concern than generalizations. Conversely, the detail is sometimes too sparse, for example, the cursory discussion of Indians in Fiji (204–5)—a reflection of the problems of selection and choice that beset the genre. All in all, however, *The Pacific Islands* succeeds admirably as "a summary interpretation of a topic, intended to make it understandable."[14]

This economy of pace and scale was achieved by a cleverly thought-out organizational structure. The section on "The Aliens" is really a narrative outline of the successive waves of European penetration, while the section "Metamorphosis" elaborates the themes set out in the earlier section with reference to localities. Hence, Tonga is used to illustrate missionary activity; Hawai'i and Fiji are the sites of the "sugar revolution" and colonial rule; the Torres Strait Islands are the vehicle to discuss pearl fishing and annexation; and a wide variety of territories are used to unfold the ubiquitous "coconut civilization." The modern reader may wonder how Oliver (and Furnas for that matter) were able to write such detailed narratives on the basis of what is perceived as a slight secondary literature. Actually, the sources even then were substantial, but dispersed, ranging from anthropological accounts, travelers' tales, reminiscences of the "from my veranda" kind, official printed reports, and journal articles on health, education, and administration.[15] But there were few detailed historical works, based on solid archival research, by trained historians. A notable achievement of both Oliver and Furnas was to write substantive and flowing texts, if occasionally patchy or idiosyncratic in their coverage, despite the vagaries of the source material.

Crucially, *The Pacific Islands*' content and emphases strongly reflect the circumstances of time and place. *The Pacific Islands* was as much a contemporary statement as a strictly historical account. Its inclusions and conclusions were shaped more by the author's experiences than his anthropological training. If ever a book endorses E. H. Carr's aphorism that before you study the text, study the historian *and* the historian's wider environment,[16] it is this one. Briefly, Oliver enlisted after the attack on Pearl Harbor in 1941, and was assigned to what eventually became the United States Commercial Company (not a private enterprise, as its name might suggest, but an agency under the sponsorship of the U.S. Navy). His final assignment was the oversight of an economic survey of the Micronesian islands, to recommend to a clueless Navy how it might best go about rejuvenating the war-ravaged Micronesian economy. The survey was conducted by a team of anthropologists and Oliver, as team leader, wrote the final report, *Planning Micronesia's Future, 1946.*[17] At the very same time he started writing *The Pacific Islands,* to counter the widespread ignorance of things Pacific among the U.S. populace, and he did so in the light of his specific wartime experiences.[18]

It is no accident, given Oliver's immediate concern with the economic recovery of Micronesia, that *The Pacific Islands* is essentially a history of staples and of economic activity. It is no coincidence, given the cataclysm of war, that Oliver (as did Furnas) depicts the Islanders' encounters with outsiders in terms of dispossession and destruction.[19] Specifically, Oliver spoke of the war having "catastrophically disturbed" their lives (261). The war is the climax to 150 years of a generally negative European impact. *The Pacific Islands'* central thesis, that Islanders lost out badly through no particular fault of their own, is filtered through the lens of the recent devastation of Micronesia and the social dislocation of many Micronesian communities (and physical relocation, in some cases because their islands were test sites for nuclear weapons[20]); and Oliver concludes with the memorable passage that "if Armageddon does come to the islands, it is unreasonable to expect that the islanders will rise to the man to defend the civilization that has taken so much from them and given so little in return" (298). Considering the Cold War was settling across the globe, the implication has to be that Armageddon was a distinct possibility. Be that as it may, *The Pacific Islands* has undoubtedly had the effect of shaping public consciousness in the United States by confirming widespread notions of paradise lost and arcadia despoiled.

The Pacific Islands' influence in the public domain was reinforced by a so-called revised edition, in 1961. This slightly altered version was directed more to an undergraduate market, where it cashed in on the wave of increasing enrollments that accompanied university expansion in the 1960s. And not only in North America; it was a set text when I was introduced to Pacific history as a third-year undergraduate at the Flinders University of South Australia in 1969. It is not that *The Pacific Islands* had the field to itself and prospered only through lack of competition. In 1963, C. Hartley Grattan published his two-volume history of the Southwest Pacific. Bulky and amorphous, it was actually a series of discrete histories of Australia, New Zealand, the Islands, and Antarctica. The two cumbersome volumes' only focus, in the view of J. W. Davidson, was that they dealt with that portion of the global to the southwest of the United States and "not because they present similar problems of social change."[21] In 1978, Glen Barclay wrote a pedestrian single-volume general history that never made headway and which has pretty much disappeared without a trace.[22] By this time, however, *The Pacific Islands* itself was beginning to look shop-worn and in 1983 Jacqueline Leckie was hoping that a successor was not far over the horizon.[23]

The Pacific Islands' impact was greatest in North America and Hawai'i, where it was probably many people's only source of serious information about the Pacific Islands—as distinct from the stereotypes of the Pacific purveyed in Hollywood movies and Broadway musicals.[24]

As such, the book reinforced prevailing notions of Pacific Islanders falling victim to what later became known as a Fatal Impact in their encounters with outsiders. Alan Moorehead (or his publisher) coined the term in 1966,[25] but he was only giving a label to what remains "perhaps the single most dominant trope in the historiography of the Pacific Islands."[26] In short, Moorehead (like Oliver and Furnas) was a latecomer in an established line of descent. All three were working within a familiar tradition, articulating long-held views on the dire effects of European wickedness on an innocent island world.

There was an academic counterthrust. Just as Moorehead was being published and striking a responsive chord with a wider public, the emerging wave of Australian National University (ANU)–trained Pacific historians, the so-called Davidson school, were concertedly putting forth the contrary view that Pacific Islanders played a more positive and less victimized role in their encounters with the West.[27] Moorehead's *The Fatal Impact* was seen as a heretic text. Thus there were oppositional interpretations, each appealing to different audiences. Although the anti–Fatal Impact view cut little ice with the wider public, it meant that Oliver's interpretation started to carry less weight in specialist academic circles—although there are signs of a comeback in that a more "victim-driven view of the Pacific past" is emerging in Hawaiian and New Zealand historiography, and the latest general history of the Pacific carries the statement that the Fatal Impact theory is not "necessarily wrong."[28] Rather surprisingly, however, the mounting anthropological interest in Pacific Islanders' experiences of war, which emerged in the mid-1980s,[29] seems unrelated to Oliver's pioneering emphasis on the salience of this very subject; and in a recent major study subtitled "Micronesian Experiences of the Pacific War," *The Pacific Islands* rates not a solitary mention.[30] There was no discernable recognition that this "new" topic had been discovered, if you like, by Oliver some thirty-five years earlier—that he was the intellectual ancestor.

There is another sad postscript. Oliver was persuaded to issue a third edition, which appeared in 1989. In a Book Review Forum in *Pacific Studies*, Oliver was severely criticized for the revisions being cosmetic rather than substantive.[31] True, there had been some updating of the text as well as some additions, for example, an account of the Peruvian slave trade (98–102). But such amendments were regarded as merely decorative. *The Pacific Islands* was seen as irretrievably dated, both in content and in outlook, and Colin Newbury captured the mood when he regretfully remarked that "textbooks, unless constantly revised, should be allowed to quietly fade away." That has most certainly since happened. *The Pacific Islands'* eclipse was underscored when Moorehead, despite being preceded by Oliver, began to be seen as the referent for the Fatal Impact view.[32] The eclipse was confirmed in 1997, when *The Pacific Islands* was completely overlooked in the prestigious *Cambridge History of the Pacific Islanders*—which mistakenly identifies Kerry Howe's *Where the Waves Fall* as "the first [general history] in the field."[33] Books do drop out of sight, but not usually with such abruptness. There was a hint of a comeback when *The Pacific Islands* was cited in a couple of subsequent general works.[34] But it was too little too late, and *The Pacific Islands* has had its day. After a long reign, *The Pacific Islands* has joined the great unread.

Yet its claims on our consciousness are many—for slanting public opinion in favor of the Fatal Impact view (for which it has sometimes been severely criticized[35]); as a gauge of immediate postwar liberal/humane attitudes toward Pacific Islanders (and in that regard *The Pacific Islands* can now be regarded as a primary source); for anticipating the future upsurge of scholarly interest in the Islanders' experience of World War II; and not least for its longevity, being the standard work for almost thirty years, and an influential one at that. Oskar Spate rightly remarked that *The Pacific Islands* was "a great book in its day,"[36] and that is how it should be remembered: not for inevitably passing its use-by date but as the landmark and epochal study that it was.

Notes

I wish to thank I. C. Campbell, Peter Hempenstall, Mac Marshall, W. H. Oliver, and Tom Ryan for looking over this essay.

1. K. R. Howe, *Where the Waves Fall: A New South Sea Islands History from First Settlement Colonial Rule* (Honolulu/Sydney, 1984).

2. Guy H. Scholefield, *The Pacific: Its Past and Future and the Policy of the Great Powers from the Eighteenth Century* (London, 1919); H. W. Van Loon, *The Story of the Pacific* (New York, 1940); J. C. Furnas, *Anatomy of Paradise: Hawaii and the Islands of the South Seas* (New York, 1948).

3. J. C. Furnas, *Voyage to Windward: The Life of Robert Louis Stevenson* (London, 1951); Jenni Calder, *RLS: A Life Study* (London, 1980), viii.

4. The writing of a general history of the region by a historian went by default.

In the late 1940s and again in the 1960s, J. W. Davidson had such plans but nothing came of them. J. W. Davidson to Master, St. John's College, Cambridge, 8 March 1948; and Chief of Naval Information to Davidson, 30 August 1948, Davidson Papers, National Library of Australia, MS 5105, Box 1; "Department of Pacific History, Annual Report, 1969," 2, ANU Central Archives, 2.1.8.7.

5. Personal communication, 1 December 2003. A select bibliography of Oliver's works to 1975 is in Jean Guiart et al., *Rank and Status in Polynésia and Mélanésia: Essays in honor of Professor Douglas Oliver* (Paris, 1978), 9. Oliver's most recent book is Polynesia in Early Historic Times (Honolulu, 2002).

6. Keith Sinclair, "On Writing Shist," *Historical Studies* 13, no. 51 (1968): 427. Also idem, *Half Way Round the Harbour: An Autobiography* (Auckland, 1993), 133.

7. J. W. Davidson, "European Penetration of the South Pacific, 1779–1842" (Ph.D. thesis, Cambridge University, 1942), 313.

8. See H. E. Maude, *Of Islands and Men: Studies in Pacific History* (Melbourne, 1968), 134; I. C. Campbell, "Constructing General Histories," in *Pacific Islands History: Journeys and Transformations*, ed. Brij V. Lal (Canberra, 1992), 52.

9. K. R. Howe, *The Loyalty Islands: A History of Culture Contacts, 1840–1900* (Canberra, 1977), xi. The authors and editors of subsequent general histories of the Pacific Islands have been largely unsuccessful in finding an alternative arrangement. Indeed, one of the most recent deploys the same line of attack as that adopted in *The Pacific Islands*, with sections such as "The First Islanders," "Melanesians Microne-sians, Polynesians," "The European Trespass," "The Second Colonisation." Steven Roger Fischer, *A History of the Pacific Islands* (Basingstoke/New York, 2002).

10. Barrie Macdonald, "Forum: The Cambridge History of the Pacific Islanders," *Journal of Pacific History* 33, no. 3 (1998): 301.

11. Robert Borofsky, ed., *Remembrance of Pacific Pasts: An Invitation to Remake History* (Honolulu, 2000), 21–22, 27.

12. J. C. Furnas, *My Life in Writing: Memoirs of a Maverick* (New York, 1989), 275.

13. See W. H. Oliver, *Looking for the Phoenix: A Memoir* (Wellington, 2002), 102.

14. Sinclair, "On Writing Shist," 426.

15. See, for example, the bibliography to Felix M. Keesing, *The South Seas and the Modern World* (New York, 1942), 365–83.

16. E. H. Carr, *What is History?* (Harmondsworth, 1964), 44.

17. Douglas L. Oliver, ed., *Planning Micronesia's Future: A Summary of the United States Commercial Company's Economic Survey of Micronesia, 1946* (Cambridge, MA, 1951). A facsimile was published in 1971 by the University of Hawai'i Press, with a foreword by John Griffin. Oliver's work in Micronesia is mentioned in Robert C. Kiste and Mac Marshall, eds., *American Anthropology in Micronesia: An Assessment* (Honolulu, 1999), 23, 26, 68–69, 83, 154, 260, 390–91; Bob Strauss, *Keneti: South Seas Adventures of Kenneth Emory* (Honolulu, 1988), 304, 306; David Hanlon, *Remaking Micronesia: Discourses over Development in a Pacific Territory*

(Honolulu, 1998), 88–91; Lin Poyer, Suzanne Falgout, and Laurence Marshall Carucci, *Typhoon of War: Micronesian Experiences of the Pacific War* (Honolulu, 2001), 290.

18. There was a receptive enough audience. American mainland consciousness of the Islands was heightened by the number of U.S. ex-servicemen who had served in the Pacific theater and by such books as James A. Michener, *Tales of the South Pacific* (New York, 1947).

19. This latter point has already been made by Howe, *Where the Waves Fall*, 349–50.

20. Robert C. Kiste, *The Bikinians: A Study in Forced Migration* (Menlo Park, 1974); Stewart Firth, *Nuclear Playground* (Sydney, 1987), 1–48.

21. C. Hartley Grattan, *The Southwest Pacific to 1900* (Ann Arbor, 1963); idem, *The Southwest Pacific since 1900* (Ann Arbor, 1963); J. W. Davidson, "South-west of the U.S.A.," *Meanjin Quarterly* 23, no. 2 (1964): 204–5, 207, 209. See also J. C. Beaglehole (review of *The Southwest Pacific to 1900*), *Landfall* 72 (1964): 389, 391.

22. Glen Barclay, *A History of the Pacific from the Stone Age to the Present Day* (London, 1978).

23. Jacqueline Leckie, "Towards a Review of History in the South Pacific," *Journal of Pacific Studies* 9 (1983): 48.

24. See Sean Brawley and Chris Dixon, "'The Hollywood Native': Hollywood's Construction of the South Seas and Wartime Encounters with the South Pacific," *Sites* 27 (1993): 15–29.

25. Alan Moorehead, *The Fatal Impact: An Account of the Invasion of the South Pacific, 1769–1840* (London, 1966); Tom Pocock, Alan Moorehead (London, 1990), 272–73.

26. K. R. Howe, *Nature, Culture and History: The "Knowing" of Oceania* (Honolulu, 2000), 44.

27. A deft summary of the competing positions is provided by K. R. Howe, "The Fate of the 'Savage' in Pacific Historiography," *New Zealand Journal of History* 11, no. 2 (1977): 145–52. The defining statement of the "new" historiography was Dorothy Shineberg, *They Came for Sandalwood: A Study of the Sandalwood Trade in the South-west Pacific, 1830–1965* (Melbourne, 1967).

28. See Barrie Macdonald, "'Now An Island is Too Big': Limits and Limitations of Pacific Islands History," *Journal of Pacific Studies* 20 (1996): 27; I. C. Campbell, *Worlds Apart: A History of the Pacific Islands* (Christchurch, 2003), 8.

29. Geoffrey M. White and Lamont Lindstrom, eds., *The Pacific Theatre: Island Representations of World War II* (Honolulu, 1989), xiii.

30. Poyer, Falgout, and Carucci, *Typhoon of War*.

31. *Pacific Studies* 14, no. 4 (1991): 129–58 (reviews by Colin Newbury, K. R. Howe, Caroline Ralston, and Jean François Baré, and responses from Thomas G. Harding and Douglas L. Oliver). The only favorable academic review was by Ron Adams, *Journal of Pacific History* 25, no. 1 (1990): 128–29.

32. Brij V. Lal, "The Passage Out," in *Tides of History: The Pacific Islands in*

the Twentieth Century, ed. K. R. Howe, Robert C. Kiste, and Brij V. Lal (Honolulu, 1994), 439–40; Nicholas Thomas, *In Oceania: Visions, Artefacts, Histories* (Durham, NC/London, 1997), 44.

33. Donald Denoon et al., eds., *The Cambridge History of the Pacific Islanders* (Cambridge, 1997), 33.

34. Borofsky, ed., *Remembrance of Pacific Pasts;* Fischer, *A History of the Pacific Islands*, xiv.

35. For example, Tom Brooking, Review (of Howe, *Where the Waves Fall*), *Archifacts* no. 4 of 1984: 22.

36. O.H.K. Spate, Review (of Howe, *Where the Waves Fall*), *Pacific Studies* 9, no. 1 (1985): 166.

CHAPTER 3

Oskar Spate's Trilogy

Glyndwr Williams

The Pacific since Magellan, by O.H.K. Spate

Vol. 1: *The Spanish Lake.*
Canberra: Australian National University Press, 1979.
Co-published, London: Croom Helm, 1979.

Vol. 2: *Monopolists and Freebooters.*
Canberra: Australian National University Press, 1983.
Co-published, London: Croom Helm, 1983.

Vol. 3: *Paradise Found and Lost.*
Canberra: Australian National University Press, 1988.
Co-published, London: Routledge, 1988.

IN THIS age of collaborative scholarship, Oskar Spate's (1911–2001) three-volume *The Pacific since Magellan* stands out as a remarkable individual achievement. Written within the Research School of Pacific Studies at the Australian National University, where he had been foundation professor of geography from 1951 and director from 1967 to 1972, the work was the fruit of a lifetime's reading and reflection. In more than one way, it seemed to run against the grain of fashion. Despite belonging to an institution endowed (in those days) with generous research funds, Spate wrote his mighty triple-decker without the aid of research assistants. At a celebration of Oskar Spate's life in 2000, a colleague recalled that although he had been happy to make the services of research assistants available to other members of the school, he refused to use them himself "on the grounds that they separated the scholar from the actual *material* of the scholar."[1] Then the trilogy was, if one had to classify it, and as its title indicated, a "history," but it was written by a geographer whose best-known work was probably his *India and Pakistan: A General and Regional Geography,* first published in 1954.

40

There had been hints, of course, of the broad dimensions of Oskar Spate's interests. His collection of essays, published in 1965 under the endearing title, *Let Me Enjoy,* had as its subtitle, *Essays, Partly Geographical,* and two of the pieces included, from 1957, "Manuel Godinho de Erédia: Quest for Australia" and "Terra Australis—Cognita?," indicated an interest in the early, misty activities of European explorers in the Pacific. These essays were written during a decade when Spate was much occupied with investigations into the future of higher education in Papua New Guinea and with his famous report on the economic prospects of the Fijian people.[2] To turn to the activities of men long since dead was perhaps a form of relaxation. If so, it did not cause him to pull his punches when it came to dealing with his predecessors in the subject area, the historians G. Arnold Wood and Ernest Scott. They came under fire on several counts: no firsthand knowledge of Portuguese sources, disregard of geographical conditions, and not much expertise in the history of cartography—"maps to them are simply shapes on paper." In these criticisms we can sense what would be Spate's own approach to the history of the Pacific, and that he might be going "beyond the bounds of what most would think of as geography, seemed not to worry Oskar over much, partly because it reflected his own tendencies in the pursuit of historical causes and literary commentaries, but also, I suspect, because it demonstrated geography's intellectual qualities beyond its own discipline."[3] As he explained, he was looking for "new worlds to conquer . . . no longer as a geographer but as an historian (the two have never been far apart in my mind)."[4]

In 1972 at the expiry of his term of office as director of the Research School of Pacific Studies, Spate indicated a change of direction when he moved to the Department of Pacific and Southeast Asian History as professor of historical geography, although his own explanation was that he could hardly return to the geography department that he had founded, where he would be "either a nuisance or a nonentity." More positive influences that were turning his thoughts toward a history of the Pacific from the arrival of the Europeans up to (perhaps) World War II included a feeling of obligation to produce a large-scale work now that he was released from administrative duties, his friendship with J. W. Davidson, and—oddly, but it crops up more than once—a little-known book by F. B. Eldridge, *The Background of Eastern Seapower,* first published in 1948. It was, Spate thought, "a stimulating lead but weak on general history," and "I thought I could do better." The result of such thinking was sixteen years of "hard labour," and in the end the writing of a masterpiece.[5] He wondered at the time whether he would live to see his great project to fruition. In fact, he lived almost as long again afterward, to the dismay and sorrow of friends who saw him become a shadow of his former self.

Spate sometimes joked that the world's greatest library consisted of the books that academics intended to write but never finished. The jest nearly came home to roost when he was asked to take over the departmental headship after Davidson's unexpected death in April 1973. Spate resisted the idea, his "fundamental point" being that *The Pacific since Magellan* was giving him new life after years of tiresome administration, and he would "degenerate into a bad-tempered cranky God-professor if [he] were to lose it."[6] But he did interrupt his work in one of those acts of piety to complete and see through the press Davidson's unfinished biography of the trader and adventurer Peter Dillon.[7]

In retrospect the three volumes of *The Pacific since Magellan* emerge like massive rocks among the swirling waters of changing Pacific historiography that marked the period of Spate's time at Canberra. Those years had seen fundamental changes in Pacific history as the old concerns of imperially minded historians were replaced by the island-centered studies of scholars such as Davidson and H. E. Maude. Spate was always sensitive to the implications and nuances of their work,[8] but not all their followers gained his approval. As he put it in 1978, some were unable to "see the Ocean for the Islands." All too often they were "marooned in the tight but so safe confines of their little atoll of knowledge, regardless of the sweep of the currents which bring life to the isles."[9] His own approach was to be large-scale in concept, though often small-scale in detail. As he explained, the general theme of the work was "the turning of the greatest blank on the map, an empty immensity covering two-fifths of the water surface of the globe and crossed only by Magellan's thin line, into a network of commercial and cultural exchanges and a theatre of global competition and conflict; in short, an outline of geostrategic history of the Ocean."[10]

Spate's preface to the first volume of the trilogy, *The Spanish Lake,* set the tone for what was to follow. After pointing out the shortage of scholarly attempts to treat the Pacific "as a whole over space and through time," he went on to state that to write such a work was his objective although it would be "a history of the Pacific, not of the Pacific peoples," the latter a task he left to others. For Spate the Pacific was "a European artefact," and the first chapter of his book, "The World Without the Pacific," began with the assertion that "strictly speaking, there was no such thing as the 'the Pacific'" until after Magellan's expedition had crossed and named the mighty ocean. But for all this, Spate was totally aware that the history of the European intruders and of the Pacific peoples was a shared one. "Europeans were not in truth the first discoverers: since few even of the remoter islands of the Pacific were uninhabited when Europeans came upon them . . . the drama of exploration and exploitation was played out on an already peopled stage."[11]

Most immediately striking about Spate's approach was his broad definition of the Pacific. As he said at the commencement of his great retirement project, "Anglo-Saxon historians seem to have ignored the fact that South America has a Pacific coast," and few knew much about Russian enterprise in the North Pacific that took them down to California,[12] and this indicated the attention he would pay to the littorals of the Pacific. Then there was the scale of the unfolding work. Despite his complaints about Procrustian chopping, he would by the end have written almost twelve hundred pages. This, it is true, included end-notes, but these were an important part of Spate's writing, some of them essays in miniature, others fearful onslaughts on inadequate or boring scholars, and yet others personal reminiscences on, for example, the delights of drinking kava—as long as one did not pay too much attention to its preparation ("you don't have to be solemn to be serious," he would say). His publisher's tolerance allowed Spate to venture into farflung corners of the Pacific where few English-speaking scholars had gone before him, and where he sometimes seemed to linger a long time before emerging with some nugget of information. But above all the spaciousness of the volumes gave Spate room to exercise his writing skills, to describe, as he once said, "fascinating and bizarre episodes . . . characters noble and shady, odd and wild."[13] He could relate the story of an oceanic voyage in a way that brought out all its drama and horror, its perplexities and achievements, and he had an incomparable eye for the apt quote and for the historical parallel. As he told the harrowing story of Sarmiento's attempt to found a colony on the desolate shores of the Straits of Magellan at the ill-fated spot called Puerto del Hambre (Port Famine), he noted that the Spanish settlers were suffering and dying there at the same time as their English counterparts, the lost colonists of Roanoke, disappeared into the mists. Such scenes were a reminder of the cost of Europe's expansion into the Americas and across the Pacific, summed

up by Richard Hawkins when he wrote that the wealth of Spain overseas had been bought with "the sweet lives of multitudes of men"
(*Spanish Lake*, 291).

But there was more to Spate than the ability to tell a good story,
although that was always part of his appeal. Gavan Daws, when confronted with depressed doctoral students, had "a ready and reliable tonic
prescription to recommend"—ten pages of Oskar Spate.[14] A good narrative style was a help, but it must always have a firm factual basis. The
work that Spate perhaps held in the greatest respect was the eight-vol-
ume *Seville et l'Atlantique* by Huguette Chaunu and Pierre Chaunu, a
mighty work of statistical analysis based on almost 18,000 transatlantic
voyages. It provided Spate with both information and inspiration. The
endpapers of *The Spanish Lake* consist of a double-spread map of the
world, centered on the Pacific, but showing not—as might be expected
—the tracks of discovery vessels but trade routes. Entitled "The System of Seville and its Rivals," the map is a depiction and expansion of
the Chaunus' approach in cartographical form.[15]

It was Chaunu territory into which Spate moved at the halfway
point of *The Spanish Lake* as he considered the economic development
of Spain's Pacific empire. From Magellan to Quiros the voyages had
revealed the size of the new ocean and experienced something of the all-
important system of winds and currents, but they had come across only
relatively few of the island groups. In the South Pacific there was some
knowledge of the Tuamotus, the Marquesas, Santa Cruz, the Solomons,
and Espiritu Santo, although they were imprecisely located. Encounters
between Spaniards and Islanders were usually brief and violent, even
under commanders such as Luis Vaez de Torres. He was "stout-hearted,
competent, and loyal" toward his fellow crew members, but in dealing
with the bemused inhabitants of Espiritu Santo his "idea of an embassy
was a whiff of arquebus-shot" (*Spanish Lake*, 133, 136). Across the
North Pacific stretched a solitary European trade route, the annual
galleon voyage between Acapulco and Manila, carrying Peruvian silver
one way and eastern goods the other. The Pacific coast of the Americas
was known only as far north as California, and what lay beyond was a
matter of guesswork. The map, "Pacific Outlines 1500–1600," on the
final text page of *The Spanish Lake* shows a huge expanse of ocean
marked by only a few dots of precarious knowledge.

With the ocean still empty of Europeans, Spanish efforts at settlement, agriculture, mining, and trade took place along its margins—in

Peru, Mexico, and Chile on the ocean's eastern rim, and far to the west in the Philippines with its spider's web of Asian commercial contacts. The sea is still the essential link, but chapters such as "The Silver Tide" and "Seville and the Pacific" describe exploitation, not exploration or voyaging. Settlers, land, and labor are the dominant themes. Sections on the much-debated issue of the impact of American silver on the economies of Europe are interspersed with heartfelt comments on the depopulation of the areas conquered by Spain. As Spate was the first to point out, much of his work relied heavily on the work of specialists who had devoted themselves to the economic and social history of Spanish America, but in his hands statistics and trends became the foundation for a readable and punchy account. What appeared to many non-Spaniards to be a formidable monopoly of trade and regulation controlled from Seville was not all it seemed. The essential convoys were vulnerable to natural hazards and to foreign predators, and official statistics were not to be relied on. Spate quotes with relish the Chaunus' observation about the lading of the Manila galleon at Acapulco that if the cargo was as much as the documents indicated there would have been no room for crews, stores, or arms, and the ship would have sunk at her moorings through the sheer weight of her alleged cargo (*Spanish Lake*, 201). In the Americas Spate points out that "Spanish control was exercised from no more than three large cities—Mexico, Lima, Potosi—with a handful of second-rank towns, and thence through scores of small district centres, tiny ports, missions and mining camps, many of them wretchedly rough places" (*Spanish Lake*, 177–78). At times everything seemed to be in short supply "except bureaucracy and peculation" (*Spanish Lake*, 269). The volume finishes on a note ominous for the future of Spanish hegemony in the Pacific with the dramatic raids of Drake and Cavendish and the first Dutch approaches.

Monopolists and Freebooters has a claim to being the most original volume in the trilogy. It deals with the period from about 1600 to 1750 (with a rather awkward appendage taking developments in Spanish America to the end of the eighteenth century and beyond). The main period is, as Spate laments, "the Dark Age of Pacific Historiography," the long pause between the first European incursions of the sixteenth century and the systematic explorations of the later eighteenth century. Increase in geographical knowledge was slow and halting: Tasman's voyages toward New Holland and New Zealand and Bering's later voyages to Alaska were probably the most important. European activities were marginal in more senses than one. The Dutch in the East Indies and Japan; the Russians in Kamchatka; the Spaniards along the Pacific littoral of South and Central America—all were operating on the periphery of the great ocean and at the farthest extent of their own empires. Apart from the Manila galleon, crossings of the open ocean were still few and far between, and the only oceanic discovery voyage of much significance was that of Jacob Roggeveen, who in 1722 discovered the isolated pinprick of Easter Island, and came across two previously unknown island groups, the Societies and Samoa. It was trade and plunder, not exploration, that drew Europeans to this area, and those motives pointed to descents on known and settled coasts rather than ventures across an uncharted ocean. The Pacific caught the imagination of the Dutch, English, and French, not as a vast trackless ocean, but as the western rim of Spain's American empire. The South Sea, or Mer du Sud, that now began to exercise its fascination over buccaneers, interlopers, and fantasists was confined to the waters that lapped the shores of Chile, Peru, and Mexico.

Spate's achievement in this volume was to bring order to what at first sight was a jumble of confused activity. His evocation of the period was illuminated by telling pen-pictures of the men who sought fame and fortune along the edges of the Pacific: Vitus Bering, who perished miserably on the desolate northern island named after him, "half-buried in sand sliding down into his hollow, and begged to be left thus, for warmth"; Henry Morgan, who by contrast died prosperous, "but more in the odour of rum than of sanctity"; William Dampier, abandoned by half his crew with the taunt, "Poor Dampier, thy Case is like King James, every Body has left thee"; George Shelvocke and William Betagh, "hard liars both, though it would be as difficult as unprofitable to decide which was the more atrocious traducer"; José de Gálvez, who suffered intermittent fits of lunacy during which he thought himself to be Charles XII of Sweden, Frederick the Great, even the Deity, "in which capacity, doubtless, he projected a deep-draught canal from Mexico City to Guaymas."[16] A survey that in the hands of a less skilled writer might have become a catalogue of abortive projects and irresolute individuals came to life as connections were made across wide expanses of time and space. Thus, "Raffles was the heir of Dalrymple, Singapore the splendid reincarnation of squalid Balambangan" (*Monopolists and Freebooters*, 277). Spate was never afraid to pose the wider question, although he did not always claim to have the answer. So on the difficult matter of the balance of trade represented by the operations of the great Dutch and English companies in Asia, a single sentence took the problem beyond the realm of economics, and probably beyond solution: "Profit or loss, gain or drain, may never be accurately quantifiable even in a cash sense; and how to balance against the social evil of opium the social comfort of tea?" (*Monopolists and Freebooters*, 113).

The third volume, *Paradise Found and Lost*, presented Oskar Spate with a different set of problems. If he had found perhaps not enough scholarship on the seventeenth-century Pacific to build on, the reverse held true for the eighteenth century—the age of Cook, Bougainville, and La Pérouse, of Europe's discovery of Polynesia, noble savagery, and much more. How, I once asked him, would he deal with the massive shadow of J. C. Beaglehole falling across the Pacific seascape? That, I think, was the least of his worries. First, he had to fit in two chapters, long since promised, on "The Peopling of the Pacific" and "Oceania on the Eve." They dealt with the great diaspora of the Pacific peoples and indicated that this final volume would have a different emphasis since it would deal "with the first really substantial contacts between European and Pacific peoples" (*Paradise Found and Lost*, ix). In them Spate touched on issues concerning the origins and distribution of peoples and crops through the Pacific Islands, on the controversies about Polynesian navigation methods, and on "deliberate" versus "accidental" discovery. They presented what he described as a "much simplified, even stylised" picture of life in Oceania just before the main European arrival, and were a demonstration that for the first time in the trilogy Spate's main concern would be with ocean and islands rather than with the lands bordering the Pacific.

In structure *Paradise Found and Lost* was different from the first two volumes. Although arranged in roughly chronological order, it was in effect a series of essays. After the opening chapters Spate moved on to an analysis of the motives that took Europeans across the open ocean in the eighteenth century, set alongside a discussion of the technical means at their disposal. This was followed by two summary chapters on the European navigators—British, French, and Spanish—of the 1760s and 1770s. Then came a pause for "Comment on Cook," the central figure of the period. For Spate, Cook was, I think, a puzzle. As he put it, "beneath the surface of the exemplary professional, there were depths; but the soundings are few" (*Paradise Found and Lost*, 135). There was due acknowledgment to Beaglehole (e.g., *Paradise Found and Lost*,

134–35, 147) but Spate was writing in the period of post-Beaglehole scholarship, represented in one way by the 1978 symposium on "Captain James Cook and His Times" at Simon Fraser University—"the only conference, to my recollection, after which I left *none* of the papers in the hotel wastepaper basket" [17]—and in another by Marshall Sahlins's interpretation of the death of Cook. Gananath Obeyesekere and the full-blooded "Lono controversy" were yet to come. But Spate had his doubts about Sahlins's interpretation. He acknowledged the anthropologist's "important and richly suggestive" work, but wondered whether he had fallen into "an unwarranted cultural determinism"; and he concluded his discussion on the riddle of Cook's death not with answers but with a characteristic set of questions—"Hubris? The ineluctable acting out of the myth? Or the ascaris worm?" (*Monopolists and Freebooters,* 354n. 26, 145).

Further summaries took the story of European exploration and exploitation to the end of the century before Spate returned to essay mode with observations on scurvy and science, the Fatal Impact thesis, beachcombers and collaborators, and concepts of savagery. The comment was as perceptive as ever, but space and time, one feels, were running out. Thoughts of following the history of the Pacific into the twentieth century had long since been abandoned, but even to reach the end of the eighteenth century was a stretch as the final chapters hurried from the sea-otter trade to whaling and sealing, from settlement at Botany Bay to missionaries in Tahiti. Such activities formed the first stages of a new era in Pacific history rather than an obvious conclusion to the trilogy. The final single-page "Coda: A Prospective Epilogue" wistfully summarized the remaining course of Pacific history from the Nootka Sound dispute to tourism in present-day Polynesia, but the grand sweep of Spate's original design would never be completed. As he wrote, "Thus far, and alas, no farther ... my reach has exceeded my grasp by far" (*Monopolists and Freebooters,* ix).

In the preface to *The Spanish Lake* Oskar Spate had written that his work "will perhaps appear as a requiem for an era of historiography." It is true that it is difficult to foresee another multivolume publication written by a single scholar that spans three hundred years of Pacific history. Since the appearance of Spate's last volume in 1988, the forms of Pacific history have multiplied and diversified. It is true also that Spate founded no school of historical interpretation and methodology, but in a less formal way his successors are legion, for the story of the European arrival in the Pacific continues to fascinate. For them Spate's work—sometimes provocative, often allusive, always learned—has an enduring value. It is altogether appropriate that a scholar who combined the strengths of the geographer with those of the historian should express the aims of his task in navigational and cartographical terms.

One cannot hope to make a full survey, but one can put down judicious soundings, and one may hope to lay out one's lines with enough intelligence to bring out the main lineaments of the ocean. Put simply, the aim is a general chart, with a few insets of coasts and harbors; the objective is to give the specialist a framework of general reference.[18]

Notes

1. Donald Walker at a "Celebration of Oskar Spate's Life" at the Australian National University, Canberra, 13 October 2000 (typescript), 5. I am indebted to Alistair Couper for a record of this event.

2. O.H.K. Spate, *The Fijian People: Economic Problems and Prospects* (Suva, 1959).

3. Spate, quoted in "Celebration of Oskar Spate's Life."

4. Spate, *On the Margins of History: From the Punjab to Fiji* (Canberra, 1991), 60.

5. Quotations in this paragraph from Spate, "The History of a History: Reflections on the Ending of a Pacific Voyage," *Journal of Pacific History* 13, no. 1 (1988): 5.

6. O.H.K. Spate to Deryck Scarr [undated], Spate Papers, National Library of Australia, MS 7886, folder 7/4/2 (I owe this reference to Doug Munro).

7. J.W. Davidson, *Peter Dillon of Vanikoro: Chevalier of the South Seas*, ed. O.H.K. Spate (Melbourne, 1975).

8. Jack Golson alludes to Spate's closing address to the Second Waigani Seminar on the history of Melanesia in 1968 in which he welcomed the contributions from disciplines such as archaeology, linguistics, anthropology, human biology, and biogeography, and stressed "the importance of indigenous sources about the past, such as existed in New Guinea as elsewhere in the Pacific and throughout the world, in the form of tradition, genealogy, cosmogony and myth, which constitute an essential element in the definition of cultural identity." "Celebration of Oskar Spate's Life," 17; Spate, "Britannia, Anglia, Melanesia," in *The History of Melanesia*, ed. K. S. Inglis (Port Moresby/Canberra, 1969), 661–71.

9. Spate, "The Pacific as an Artefact," in *The Changing Pacific: Essays in Honour of H. E. Maude*, ed. Niel Gunson (Melbourne, 1978), 34.

10. Spate, "The History of a History," 6. See also Gavan Daws, "On Being a Historian of the Pacific," in *Historical Disciplines and Culture in Australasia: A Reassessment* (Brisbane, 1979), 124–25.

11. Spate, "The Pacific as an Artefact," 35.

12. "Retirement from Pacific Studies," *ANU Reporter,* 8 December 1972, 4.

13. Spate, "The History of a History," 5.

14. "Celebration of Oskar Spate's Life," 15.

15. For anyone who has admired Spate's word-juggling abilities there is something quietly amusing about the tone of schoolmasterly disapproval with which he writes that "once he breaks away from his statistics, Chaunu is always brilliant and stimulating, but sometimes carried away by epigram or lyricism." *Spanish Lake,* 309n. 53.

16. Spate, *Monopolists and Freebooters,* 243, 138, 188, 383n. 27, 300.

17. Ibid., 9; Robin Fisher and Hugh Johnston, eds., *Captain James Cook and His Times* (Canberra, 1979).

18. Spate, "Prolegomena to a History of the Pacific," *Geographia Polonica* 36 (1977): 222. At a book launch in Sydney for *Paradise Found and Lost* in 1988, I informed the gathering that Spate's trilogy had long since broken through these modest bounds. I should have known better. A few days later a letter came from Oskar referring to "your excessively kind words . . . a bit glowing even for my not inconsiderable ego." Letter from Spate to author, 27 August 1988.

CHAPTER 4

Where the Waves Fall—or, Playing the Generalist Game

Doug Munro

*Where the Waves Fall: A New South Seas Island History from
First Settlement to Colonial Rule,* by K. R. Howe.
Honolulu: University of Hawai'i Press, 1984 (as vol. 2 in the Pacific
Islands Monograph Series). Co-published, Sydney: Allen and Unwin,
1984. Reprinted 1991.

The generalist game is . . . undeniably hazardous, but it is
great fun to play. As for what success I have played it, that is
another matter. One can only do one's best, trust in God or
Clio, and get one's footnotes right.
Oskar Spate, "The History of a History," 12

A NOTABLE feature of Pacific Islands historiography is the preponderance of the scholarly monograph, the dissertation, and the specialized journal article, as opposed to the generalized text and the survey
article. These former were the stepping stones and the building blocks
of the subdiscipline as we know it today, and despite a number of general histories in more recent years, the specialist text continues to far
outweigh attempts at wider generalization. There are cogent reasons for
specialization, not least the need for detailed case studies to form the
basis for further generalization and to replace the "fondly cherished illu-
sions and stereotypes" that have gathered around Pacific history with
"more scrupulous narratives."[1] The necessity for a hard-nosed profes-
sionalism applied equally to New Zealand historiography, and in 1954
John Beaglehole

plead[ed] vehemently for technical accomplishment, for professional standards, even to the point of pedantry. I have suffered too much from an
amiable lack of pedantry in other people to be afraid of a good scholastic
layer of it over New Zealand. Our history must be unfolded by the trained
—let me say once more, by the critical—mind, and by great labour.[2]

Pacific Islands historiography received its impetus toward profes-
sionalization only a few years earlier, when J. W. Davidson began building his Department of Pacific History at the Australian National University (ANU). With the institutional backing of a university dedicated to
research and postgraduate supervision (to the exclusion of undergraduate teaching), another cohort of "pedants" grubbed away and wrote their
theses-cum-books.

Within twenty-five years there was an impressive enough range of
scholarly monographs on the Pacific Islands, which filled many of the
gaps. No longer did we have the near-absence of reliable historical
works by professional historians that confronted J. C. Furnas and Douglas Oliver in the late 1940s when they were writing their general histories of the Pacific[3] and which hampered attempts in the 1950s through to
the mid-1960s to teach the subject at tertiary institutions.[4] But did the
eventual countervailing "monograph mania" go too far, in the sense of
a commendable quest for the particular smothering an equally valid
concern for the general? One person who thought so was the New Zealander Kerry Howe, and he wrote a general history entitled *Where the
Waves Fall* (1984) to prove his point. The book did more than pull some
of the threads together; it did so in a way that reflected the islands-ori-
ented/culture contacts paradigm of the Davidson school of Pacific history with its emphasis on culture contacts and Islanders' agency.

Howe was thinking along these interpretative lines as a master's
student at the University of Auckland in the late 1960s. There, he wrote
one of the several culture contact theses (under Judith Binney's supervision) that tested, and found wanting, Harrison Wright's notion that
the Maori conversion to Christianity was a product of cultural dislocation and social demoralization. Instead, he argued that Maori became
Christian for positive rather than negative reasons.[5] Howe proceeded to
the ANU and in 1972 he presented another culture contact thesis, this
time on the history of the Loyalty Islands.[6] It is not that Howe was
against monographs in principle, and in 1979 he explained his position
in his celebrated "monograph myopia" article.[7] Conceding the contin-

ued need for detailed basic research, Howe nevertheless felt that fact-finding had become an end in itself and that Pacific Islands historiography was losing a sense of overall purpose and direction in this process of "finding out more and more about less and less." There was too much tunnel vision, as it used to be called,[8] and a corresponding lack of comparisons across the region. Pacific Islands historiography had ventured down an increasingly narrow cul-de-sac where minutiae and fact-gathering for its own sake were decidedly more important than panorama and synopsis, where the "mechanics of research" had become of greater moment than "overall direction." And Howe could only express astonishment a single general text—Oliver's *The Pacific Islands*—"should have stood alone for almost thirty years."[9]

The Davidson school had a particular interpretative thrust, or thrusts. Davidson was insistent that Pacific historians take into account the institutions and values of indigenous cultures in explaining the process of change. Dorothy Shineberg, who was Howe's Ph.D. supervisor, went further and argued in her history of the Melanesian sandalwood trade that the Islanders were less oppressed and more in control of the culture contact situation than had hitherto been allowed—actors rather than victims.[10] She took the notion of Islander agency much further than Davidson—notwithstanding his famous analogy that "the indigenous cultures of the Pacific were like islands whose coastal regions outsiders might penetrate but whose heartlands they could never conquer."[11] Shineberg's *They Came for Sandalwood* was enormously influential within—but not so much outside—the field of Pacific history. I would go so far to say that it was the single most influential Pacific history text of its generation. It set the direction of a new approach and became the paradigmatic statement of the Davidson school, which has a certain irony because Shineberg was not Canberra-trained. Whereas Davidson defined the broad contours of the new Pacific historiography in terms of culture contacts/"multi-cultural situations," Shineberg provided the specific interpretative thrust—namely, Islander agency—which Howe has followed in his own writings on culture contacts, *Where the Waves Fall* included.

And more than any other Pacific historian, Howe has confronted head-on the so-called Fatal Impact interpretation, named after the book of that title by the journalist and freelance writer Alan Moorehead.[12] This small book had a resounding popular impact. Only the first section, on Tahiti, dealt with the Pacific, but Moorehead's depiction of

Tahitians' contact with the Western world as unmitigated disaster was accorded pan-Pacific application and the notion of a Fatal Impact became deeply etched on public consciousness. One can only marvel in retrospect on Moorehead's importance to the Davidson school as a straw man—an inflated bogey, if you like. Rarely does an academic mission almost entirely pin its identity on countering a populist book written by an "amateur," especially when there were more worthy opponents—such as the geographer Grenville Price, whose *Western Invasions of the Pacific and its Continents* was written by an academic, read by academics, and in the Fatal Impact mold.[13]

It took more than usual courage to attempt *Where the Waves Fall* at all, given the potential obstacles and discouragements. By the time it was commenced, the scholarly literature had mushroomed to the extent that a single mind would struggle to absorb it all. Then there was the ambivalent attitude of the profession. When Howe went to Canberra in 1970, there was plenty of talk about the need for such a book, but no one was prepared to do it. Then there were the gainsayers who said that it could not be done and therefore should not be attempted. As Howe explained, "There was opposition in some quarters to the idea of doing it. It was claimed the time wasn't right, not enough was known about everything, and the difficulty of putting everything together."[14] Howe ignored his hidebound colleagues and got on with the job.

Where the Waves Fall is divided into four parts. First, there is a lucid and up-to-date trio of chapters on the settlement of the Pacific Islands and the nature of the pre-European-contact societies prior to the "ethnographic moments" when European explorers started recording these societies. Following is an equally lucid trio of chapters about the process of European commercial penetration and its effects, involving the familiar succession of explorers, beachcombers, traders, and missionaries—in other words, the conventional division of European arrivals into "occupational categories."[15] The bulk of the book—some 150 pages—concerns the transformation of some island groups into centralized monarchies (Tahiti, Hawaii, Tonga) and the obstacles that prevented others from following suit (New Zealand, Fiji, Samoa). The final section, on Melanesia, comprises separate chapters on the culture contacts that involved missionaries, sandalwood traders, and labor recruiters, followed by an epilogue tracing the historiographical shifts that transformed Pacific Islanders from passive victims to active participants. The latter discussion seems unremarkable in these reflexive days but historiographic musings were rather frowned upon back then. Tribal elders occasionally indulged but not the more junior members of the fraternity. In those days, one "did" Pacific history rather than talk about what it should be (which was taken for granted anyway). It was a somewhat self-satisfied field not tuned into historiography. Even now the *Journal of Pacific History,* then the mouthpiece of the Davidson school, publishes historiographic / reflective articles only occasionally.

General histories are a recognizable genre; they conform to a model, although a loose model, and they come in different shapes and sizes. The conventional image is a survey of a given topic that is fairly comprehensive in coverage but selective in supporting detail. That is to say, a general history traverses the field but with brevity, drawing on the telling aside and the revealing anecdote. As one practitioner has put it, the aim should be "to conduct the reader down some of the main roads . . . , not to furnish him with a complete and detailed map." [16] It also stands to reason, given the impossibility of mastering the totality of primary sources, that a general history is typically based on the secondary literature and contemporary printed sources, with documentary research being expected only here and there.

In some respects, *Where the Waves Fall* fits the conventional model. The judges at the 1984 New Zealand Book Awards decreed it "a very substantial work . . . which has skilfully synthesised and made sense of a previously fragmented literature on Pacific history." *Where the Waves Fall* was certainly well researched, a full six years in the making [17]— which is not surprising given the sheer quantity of secondary literature needing to be synthesized. But *Where the Waves Fall* was avowedly a partial digest of the printed sources and more recent scholarship. Howe did not set out to write "a historical encyclopaedia or reference book," but instead had "chosen to illustrate certain key themes of culture contact, rather than endlessly narrate its events" (xiv). Several greater and lesser island groups are not dealt with, including Papua New Guinea, Micronesia, and the Marquesas. The time frame is also truncated, the terminal point being the imposition of colonial rule, which could be anywhere between 1840 and 1900. *Where the Waves Fall*, then, is not what might be described as a rounded treatment of its subject, although Howe does make comparisons within the wider Pacific.

The comparative dimension is most evident in the middle sections, which comprise half the book. The six chapters deal with the attempts to form island kingdoms in the late eighteenth and nineteenth centuries and asks why "conquering kings" established unified kingdoms in Tahiti, Hawai'i, and Tonga, and, conversely, why "monarchs *manqué*" were the norm in New Zealand, Samoa, and Fiji. The short answer is that the social and political organization of these island groups was either conducive or inimical to political centralization. The other side of the equation—settler intrigue, missionary involvement, and Great Power rivalries—is given full due. Each chapter deals with a particular island group but they are far from being self-contained studies, each unrelated to the other. On the contrary, comparisons and contrasts are explicitly drawn. Moreover, given the involvement of missionaries, and especially their role in creating the island kingdoms, *Where the Waves Fall* becomes one of the few general histories of the Pacific to treat missionary activity seriously. Another by-product is that New Zealand gets reintegrated into the mainstream of Pacific Islands historiography, from which it had unaccountably become detached since the early 1970s.

Whether *Where the Waves Fall* should have strayed into the colonial period could be endlessly debated. Howe maintained there was insufficient secondary material on culture contacts to carry the story further. At a practical level, the inclusion of the colonial period would have resulted in the book doubling its size (352 pages), if the same pace and level of detail were maintained. The truncated time span of *Where the Waves Fall*, and the omission of Micronesia and mainland New Guinea, left room for Ian Campbell and Deryck Scarr (simultaneously and in ignorance of each other's activities) to write the first synoptic histories of the region as a whole since the appearance in 1951 of Oliver's *The Pacific Islands*.[18]

Arguably, the downside of Howe's precolonial time-frame was to privilege a "problematic paradigm." The interpretative thrust of *Where the Waves Fall* is a repudiation of the Fatal Impact theory. Such an approach could also be termed the Success-Story Syndrome. At the time Howe was writing, the Davidson school notion that Islanders were active agents and substantially the arbiters of cross-cultural encounters had hardened into something of an orthodoxy. The very choice of topics encouraged such tendencies. For if the focus of study was the early contact period—when Islanders held the balance of physical power and before colonial states had imposed upon Islanders' land and labor—it is indeed possible to transform Islanders from witless objects of exploitation to cerebral opportunity-maximizers who actively, creatively, and advantageously participated in the various exchanges with Europeans, and indeed who shrewdly played upon European desires and weaknesses. But there is no fairy tale ending. Islanders have not lived happily ever after. As Howe points out, the Tahitian and Hawaiian monarchies and the Samoan leaders were powerless to prevent their annexations to colonial empires (151, 176, 254); "the inability of the Fijians and settlers to regulate matters of crucial common interest left Britain little alternative but to take control" (277); "Maoris unwittingly contributed to the loss of their sovereignty" (229); and "had any of the powers wanted to annex Tonga there would have been little the Tongan monarchy could have done to prevent it" (197). Yet for all the qualifications and codicils, the emphasis (and the bulk of discussion) is on Islander agency and their success in the face of the European onslaught before they lost their independence, when a longer view would have altered the picture substantially.[19] This is not to say that Islanders were deprived of all agency under colonial rule, or that they were unable to manipulate their colonial masters—only that their agency took new permutations and tended to be opposed more systematically, and often brutally, by colonial authorities.[20]

As Sir Lewis Namier said long ago, a general history should "single out and stress what is of the nature of the thing, and not . . . reproduce indiscriminately all that meets the eye."[21] *Where the Waves Fall* certainly does not succumb to the latter, but whether it identifies the nature of the thing, given its temporal and areal definitions, is another matter. In a genial review, Oskar Spate did express unease that the omission of the Marquesas Islands may have skewed some broader conclusions: "It is not a question of 'Fatal Impact,' although Dening's *Islands and Beaches* suggests that for one group at least this might not be too strong a term. Howe's reasons for limiting his geographical scope are in principle unobjectionable, but in practice it is perhaps unfortunate that so significant a group as the Marquesas . . . should be left out."[22] Similar reservations could be expressed about the treatment of labor migration, which is largely confined to the *external* labor trade, when Solomon Islanders and Ni-Vanuatu were recruited for destinations outside their island

groups. But colonial states arrived on the scene and increasingly com-
pelled Islanders, through head taxes and labor quotas, to work on plantations within the new political borders, whether they liked it or not, for
lower wages and under inferior legislative protection. Howe mentions
this transformation of the labor trade but only in passing (342–43), which
camouflages how Islanders went from being winners to losers. Instead,
Where the Waves Fall emphasizes what Douglas Oliver has facetiously
called the "jolly, cooperative side of labor recruiting."[23] Islander agency
has its appeals, says David Chappell, "but like any chosen emphasis it
can screen out subversive data."[24]

Howe explicitly recognized, in *Where the Waves Fall* and elsewhere,
that historians' work reflects "changing intellectual assumptions" (xii),
and that "interpretations as to the fate of islanders should . . . be considered in the light of their conscious or unconscious preoccupations."[25]
This recalls Oscar Wilde's observation that "every portrait that is
painted with feeling is a portrait of the artist, not of the sitter. The sitter is merely the accident, the occasion. It is not he who is revealed by
the painter; it is the painter who . . . reveals himself." The opening and
closing few sentences in *Where the Waves Fall* go a stage further in
maintaining that the past has no independent existence beyond what the
historian imposes on it (xii): "History is what we choose to see and we
see what we are looking for" (352). Among other things, Howe sought
to dispose of the Fatal Impact theory that Alan Moorehead had popular-
ized in the mid-1960s, suggesting that acceptance of such a belief was
usually the product of European "guilt or shame" (350).[26] But if a blan-
ket application of the Fatal Impact theory is untenable (352), neither is
the idea altogether discredited. In some places there was minimal damage, in parts of Melanesia, for instance, because European contact was
slight. The damage was far greater in Tahiti, Hawai'i, New Zealand,
and the Marquesas Islands. Today the perception of many indigenous
scholars, who are responding to their own priorities and agendas, is that
their cultures suffered. Moreover, the Fatal Impact theory is far from
being dismissed out of hand in the latest general texts.[27]

Where the Waves Fall was a text of its times, conditioned by the prevailing intellectual trends and assumptions and keen to perpetuate the
prevailing orthodoxy. Published twelve years after Davidson's death, it
was not so much a "new" history but the swan song of the Davidson
school. Howe did not, nor did he set out to, set an agenda for future
research, which occasioned the lament that *Where the Waves Fall* was

"the culminating statement of an old age, not the first daring revelation of a new."[28] *Where the Waves Fall* was certainly more synthetic than original, but by no means unoriginal, striking out from time to time in new directions and incorporating the findings of other academic circles—for example, the post-Beaglehole upsurge of interest in Cook studies.[29] Unsurprisingly, *Where the Waves Fall* lives on and remains an influential text, as citation counts and its prominence in Pacific history course reading lists amply indicate.

The obvious achievements of *Where the Waves Fall* are twofold: the strength of the research upon which it is based and the clarity with which it is written. *Where the Waves Fall* demonstrates how mistaken it is to bracket general histories as once-over-lightly pieces of research and writing—not necessarily inconsequential but neither in the same league as the specialized archives-based monograph. On the contrary, general histories are in a class of their own—a specialized genre, just as general practice in medicine is recognized as a specialization in its own right, and deserving of respect.[30] It is not sufficiently appreciated that the competing technical demands of general histories—"steering a course between Scylla (factual density) and Charybdis (glib generalisation)"[31] —can be very difficult to reconcile, and especially when the database of secondary sources has reached barely manageable proportions. However, being on top of one's material and in control of the narrative flow are necessary but not sufficient conditions for a successful history text, general or otherwise. There have to be other, less tangible, qualities that are not so easy to pinpoint. Referring to the ethos of the Davidson school historiography, Howe once spoke of "the sense of discovery, excitement and ideological commitment to the region that drove its practitioners,"[32] and *Where the Waves Fall* does indeed reflect those glory days—that land of lost content that cannot come again. Capturing that ethos is the one thing above all others that makes *Where the Waves Fall* the special book that it is. It was bold and necessary, and Howe deserves all credit for making the attempt, for giving the venture so much effort and commitment. Like W. K. Hancock's *Australia* (1930), *Where the Waves Fall* was a book into which its author poured all his resources of "heart and brain."[33] Whatever else the afterlife holds in store for it,

Where the Waves Fall will always be seen as the state-of-the-art essay that so stylishly encapsulated the spirit and the ethos of the Davidson school.

Notes

I am grateful to Ian Campbell and Peter Hempenstall, whose comments on an earlier version made all the difference.

1. H. E. Maude, *Of Islands and Men: Studies in Pacific History* (Melbourne, 1968), xxi.

2. J. C. Beaglehole, "The New Zealand Scholar," in *The Feel of Truth: Essays in New Zealand and Pacific History,* ed. Peter Munz (Wellington, 1969), 251 (republication of his 1954 Margaret Condliffe Memorial Lecture). See also T. G. Wilson, "The Writing of History in New Zealand: Some Observations," *Landfall* 35 (1955): 213–33; J .C. Beaglehole, "Research in New Zealand History," *Spike* (1957): 20–25.

3. J. C. Furnas, *Anatomy of Paradise: Hawaii and the Islands of the South Seas* (New York, 1948); Douglas L. Oliver, *The Pacific Islands* (Cambridge, MA, 1951).

4. Dorothy Shineberg, "The Early Years of Pacific History," *Journal of Pacific Studies* 20 (1996): 3–4; Mary Boyd, "A Note on Pacific History in New Zealand," *Journal of Pacific Studies* 20 (1996): 17–20.

5. Harrison M. Wright, *New Zealand, 1769–1840: Early Years of Western Contact* (Cambridge, MA, 1959), 141–83; K. R. Howe, "Two Worlds?" *New Zealand Journal of History* 37, no. 1 (2003): 50. Part of Howe's master's thesis was published as "The Maori Response to Christianity in the Thames-Waikato Area, 1833–1840," *New Zealand Journal of History* 7, no. 1 (1973): 28–46.

6. Published as *The Loyalty Islands: A History of Culture Contacts, 1840–1900* (Canberra, 1977).

7. Kerry R. Howe, "Pacific Islands History in the 1980s: New Directions or Monograph Myopia?" *Pacific Studies* 3, no. 1 (1979): 81–90.

8. J. H. Hexter, *Reappraisals in History* (New York, 1963), 194–95.

9. There had actually been several contenders since 1960. They are a mixed bag but all, in their different ways, and with different degrees of proficiency, were broad surveys. But none were written within the then-dominant Davidson school, which trained almost all the professional historians of the Pacific. W. P. Morrell, *Britain and the Pacific Islands* (Oxford, 1960); C. Hartley Grattan, *The Southwest Pacific to 1900: A Modern History* (Ann Arbor, 1963); idem, *The Southwest Pacific since 1900: A Modern History* (Ann Arbor, 1963); Austin Coates, *The Western Pacific Islands* (London, 1970); Harold Brookfield, *Colonialism, Development and Independence: The Case of the Melanesian Islands in the South Pacific* (Cambridge, 1972); Ernest Dodge, *Islands and Empires: Western Impact on the Pacific and East Asia* (Minneapolis, 1976); Glen Barclay, *A History of the Pacific from the Stone Age to the Present Day* (London, 1978).

10. Dorothy Shineberg, *They Came for Sandalwood: A Study of the Sandalwood Trade in the South-west Pacific, 1830–1865* (Melbourne, 1967); also idem, "The Early Years of Pacific History," 8–9.

11. J. W. Davidson, "Lauaki Namulau'ulu Mamoe: A Traditionalist in Samoan Politics," in *Pacific Islands Portraits*, ed. J. W. Davidson and Deryck Scarr (Canberra, 1970), 267.

12. Alan Moorehead, *The Fatal Impact: An Account of the Invasion of the South Pacific* (London, 1966; New York, 1967); also *The Dictionary of National Biography, 1981–1985* (Oxford, 1990), 286–87.

13. A. Grenville Price, *The Western Invasions of the Pacific and its Continents: A Study of Moving Frontiers and Changing Landscapes, 1513–1958* (Oxford, 1963); also *Monash Dictionary of 20th Century Australians* (Melbourne, 1984), 439–40.

14. Quoted in Neil Nielsen, "Historical 'Baby' a Polemic Study," *Manawatu Evening Standard*, 10 March 1984, 6 (based on an interview with Howe shortly after *Where the Waves Fall* was published).

15. Maude, *Of Islands and Men*, 134.

16. W. H. Oliver, *The Story of New Zealand* (London, 1960), 11.

17. Nielsen, "Historical 'Baby' a Polemic Study," 6.

18. I. C. Campbell, *A History of the Pacific Islands* (Christchurch, 1989); Deryck Scarr, *The History of the Pacific Islands: Kingdoms of the Reefs* (Melbourne, 1990).

19. In the same way, my Ph.D. thesis on nineteenth-century Tuvalu would have been different in places had I known then what I know now about twentieth-century Tuvalu.

20. See, for example, Timothy J. Macnaught, *The Fijian Colonial Experience: A Study in the Neotraditional Order under British Colonial Rule prior to World War II* (Canberra, 1982); Peter Hempenstall and Noel Rutherford, *Protest and Dissent in the Colonial Pacific* (Suva, 1984).

21. L. B. Namier, *Avenues of History* (London, 1952), 8, cited in John Tosh, *The Pursuit of History*, 2nd ed. (London/New York, 1991), 137.

22. O.H.K. Spate, *Pacific Studies* 9, no. 1 (1985): 165. See Howe's review (of *Islands and Beaches*), *New Zealand Journal of History* 15, no. 2 (1981): 190–94.

23. Douglas L. Oliver, "Response," *Pacific Studies* 14, no. 4 (1991): 158.

24. David A. Chappell, "Active Agents versus Passive Victims: Decolonized Historiography or Problematic Paradigm," *The Contemporary Pacific* 7, no. 2 (1995): 304.

25. K. R. Howe, "The Fate of the 'Savage' in Pacific Historiography," *New Zealand Journal of History* 11, no. 2 (1977): 151. This is the text of the annual J. C. Beaglehole lecture, sponsored by the New Zealand Historical Association. Still in his twenties at the time, Howe is easily the youngest historian to have delivered this memorial lecture.

26. See also Pascal Bruckner, *The Tears of the White Man: Compassion as Contempt* [1983], trans. William R. Beer (New York/London, 1986).

27. Stephen Roger Fischer, *A History of the Pacific Islands* (Basingstoke/New York, 2002), xix ("No Pacific Islanders have been eternally passive victims. No Pacific Islanders have been eternally active agents either."); I. C. Campbell, *Worlds Apart: A History of the Pacific Islands* (Christchurch, 2003), 8 ("I do not accept that the so-called 'fatal impact' theory was used in the way that it was often alleged to be, nor for that matter that it was necessarily wrong.") The Fatal Impact interpretation is making something of a comeback. For example, Terence Wesley-Smith, "The Ocean in Me," and Ben R. Finney, "Playing with Canoes," both in *Pacific Places, Pacific Histories: Essays in Honor of Robert C. Kiste,* ed. Brij V. Lal (Honolulu, 2004), 72, 292–93, respectively.

28. Peter Hempenstall, Review, *Pacific History Bibliography and Comment 1984,* 44.

29. Robin Fisher and Hugh Johnston, eds., *Captain James Cook and his Times* (Vancouver, 1979); also Howe, "Tales from Several Coves," in *Pacific Places, Pacific Histories,* ed. Lal, 42–47.

30. I. C. Campbell, "Constructing General Histories," in *Pacific Islands History,* ed. Lal, 49.

31. Mary Boyd, "Canberra School History," *Pacific Viewpoint* 26, no. 2 (1985): 473.

32. Howe, "The Future," 228.

33. See Stuart McIntyre, "'Full of Hits and Misses': A Reappraisal of Hancock's *Australia*," in *Keith Hancock: The Legacies of an Historian,* ed. D. A. Low (Melbourne, 2001), 33–57.

PART II

Methodologies

CHAPTER 5

Voyagers and Navigators:
The Sharp-Lewis Debate

K. R. Howe

Ancient Voyagers in the Pacific, by Andrew Sharp.
Wellington: Polynesian Society Memoir 32, 1956; republished by
Penguin Books, 1957. Rewritten as *Ancient Voyagers in Polynesia.*
Auckland: Longman Paul, 1963; reprinted 1969.

*We, the Navigators: The Ancient Art of Landfinding in
the Pacific,* by David Lewis.
Canberra: Australian National University Press, 1972; reprinted
1973. 2nd ed. (edited by Derek Oulton), Honolulu: University of
Hawaiʻi Press, 1994.

FOR TWO hundred years Western commentators have painted a picture of the first discoverers and settlers of the Pacific Islands as fearless
sailors and skilled navigators. Such beliefs were central to the stories
that were constructed in the later nineteenth and early twentieth centuries about epic voyages to the far reaches of the ocean, notably to
Hawaiʻi and New Zealand.[1] Anthropologists referred to the early Pacific
seafarers as "Argonauts" and "Vikings."[2] The ethnographic literature
on Islanders' past navigational knowledge and maritime technology
seemed irrefutable.[3] In particular, by the 1950s, the story of the deliberate and return voyaging from eastern Polynesia to New Zealand, over
thousands of kilometers of empty ocean, was deeply embedded in New
Zealand's national mythology. It was a tale taught in schools, featured
in history books, and depicted in major art and literature.[4] It is ironic
that it was in New Zealand that these ideas and traditions were first seriously challenged.

New Zealander Andrew Sharp (1906–74) was an unlikely iconoclast.[5] Born in Dunedin, he was a Rhodes Scholar at St. John's College, Oxford. On graduating he sat the Indian Civil Service trainees' examination and was appointed a magistrate in Burma. Ill health forced him to return to New Zealand in 1932. In 1939 he embarked upon a successful career with the government Department of Internal Affairs, Prime Minister's Department, and Department of External Affairs. He had several overseas postings as a New Zealand high commissioner. In his spare time, and then during a period in the later 1960s when he was a senior research fellow in history at the University of Auckland, he wrote scholarly and well-received tomes on aspects of European exploration of the Pacific.[6] But it was his small book, *Ancient Voyagers in the Pacific*, initially published in 1956, that turned out to be one of the most provocative studies ever in Pacific history. He added material to publish "in considerable degree a new book," *Ancient Voyagers in Polynesia*, in 1963. These works changed the course of Pacific historiography, and indeed aspects of Pacific history itself, though not always in ways Sharp intended or could ever have foreseen.

Sharp's thesis on Pacific voyaging was not entirely novel. Some skepticism about Pacific navigators' abilities had been periodically aired through the nineteenth century, but it was a minority view. Sharp was the first to argue the case in detail and at length. His basic premise was that no human societies, until Westerners finally perfected the art of fixing of latitude and longitude, could readily find islands that "were more than 300 miles [555 kilometers]"[7] from the continents or from each other. "The idea of systematic exploration involves the presumption that explorers were prepared to go twice as far as any island they happened to find, and to do so many times without success . . . Above all, unless one can fix the position of the island one finds, and plot a course from it and back to it again, two-way contact is not established" (18—this and subsequent references are to the 1963 edition).

In the case of the Pacific Islands, Sharp accepted the orthodox view that they were settled from west to east, but that they were essentially one-way voyages, that is, voyages of no return. Sharp acknowledged that the early oceanic explorers "were heroes of the sea whose like may never be seen again" (32), but that even while deliberately seeking new islands, and actively trying to maintain a particular course, they had no control as to where they eventually ended up, until they spied land. The winds and currents were the ultimate determiners of location, particularly over long distances. Sharp was adamant that he was not proposing a drift theory of Pacific settlement (33–34, 71), though there were of course odd cases of helpless drift voyages. Nor did he claim that the voyagers "lacked control of their vessels or were at the mercy of the winds and waves. When they came in sight of land they could make for it. This was exploration, although the actual sighting of land, like all discovery, came of necessity by chance" (71).

The fundamental problem, as Sharp saw it, was lateral drift. No matter how deliberate an exploratory voyage may have been, or how observant its crew, there was no way to estimate the sideways movement caused by winds and currents from any intended course. Dead reckoning—the ability to judge distance along a chosen direction—thus had serious limits in practice on the empty ocean. The longer the voyage, the greater was the likelihood of lateral drift. Once a distant island was discovered, one greater than 555 kilometers away, it was impossible for the travelers to find their way back home since they could not fix where they were or where they had come from. The first discoverers of such an island were thus its first settlers.

Where Sharp was later to cause himself problems was with his rather unusual definition of navigation. Navigation is normally understood to be a practice whereby a traveler holds a desired course, or direction. Sharp argued that navigation meant the ability to hold a course to a *known* destination (33). And since an island's location could not be known until someone reached it, Sharp claimed that voyages of exploration were thus not navigated. Hence his overall conclusion that the people of the Pacific "settled their distant islands at the time they discovered them by unnavigated one-way voyages" (74). Sharp's use of the words *chance* and *accidental* also caused misunderstandings. His view was, reasonably, that any previously unknown island was obviously first encountered by chance or accident. Yet many readers came to believe that he was proposing *voyages* that were chance or accidental. The combination of the terms *unnavigated, chance,* and *accidental* was to prove confusing and detrimental.

It should not be forgotten that Sharp always stressed that "the Polynesians deserve their reputation as outstanding voyagers" (52). He readily acknowledged their ability to make return journeys over hundreds of kilometers. But he disputed that they could engage in regular two-way voyages over thousands of kilometers (53).

Sharp offered a wealth of evidence for his claims. For example, he challenged the existing arguments about the efficacy of traditional astral navigation, rightly pointing out the vagueness of the information in the literature of tradition, but, more seriously, bringing into question the assumed astronomical science behind it. He claimed that bearings taken on horizon stars can give no indication of longitudinal displacement since to an observer a star will appear at the same angle at any point on the same latitude. He advanced similar arguments for claimed use of east-west paths of the stars and the sun, and bearings relating to the Pole Star and Southern Cross.

It was the same, he said, with claims for direction finding by use of winds and ocean swells, as well as paths of migrating birds, since they too gave no clues to longitudinal displacement. Moreover, he questioned how often any reliable sightings of stars and other natural phenomena might be made, given obvious unpredictabilities such as cloud cover (day and night) and predictabilities such as difficulty seeing birds at night and stars by day.

Sharp also challenged the entrenched assumptions about the efficiency of the voyaging vessels themselves, stressing their structural vulnerability in heavy seas because they were tied together "with vegetable fibre" (56), and their relative inability to make headway while tacking into a head wind. Speedy and reliable as they might be in calm seas and running with the wind, it was a very different story against the wind and in rough conditions. Thus, in his view, while the main direction of exploration was apparently against the prevailing south-easterlies, in effect the voyagers took advantage of the occasional westerly weather patterns for their long west-to-east journeys.

Little acknowledged then, and now, are Sharp's chapters that investigated other aspects of Pacific settlement history. For example, he examined some of the so-called voyaging traditions themselves, and he found them often a product of European modification and editing over generations. He considered the "relationships of prehistoric Polynesian voyaging to the distribution of Polynesian useful plants, livestock and artefacts." He surveyed current thinking about the settlement of New Zealand, and of the overall "Polynesian migration trail" from its ancestral lands in Southeast Asia (chaps. 5–8).

Ancient Voyagers in the Pacific and *Ancient Voyagers in Polynesia* generated enormous interest. Even before the latter appeared in 1963, Sharp claimed "a hundred published notices" and "2,191 oral discussions" (6).

There was much excitement, though initially relatively little informed comment.[8] Jack Golson, then editor of the *Journal of the Polynesian Society*, noted that "few reviewers could be found, indeed, competent to assess Sharp's arguments over the full range of data which he had employed."[9] Thus in 1962 he organized a symposium of "specialists" and edited its results in *Polynesian Navigation*.[10] Of the five contributors, only one fully accepted Sharp's arguments; the remainder were variously skeptical of some though not all of what Sharp claimed.[11] By today's standards, it was all rather polite and low key.

Sharp became an increasingly controversial figure as the political and scholarly climate changed during the 1960s. The early beginnings of the modern Maori/Polynesian cultural revival, combined with a nascent postcolonialism, created an environment where Sharp would eventually be seen as committing the great sin of putting down indigenous ability. Many New Zealanders regarded his skepticism of major voyaging traditions, especially the Great Migration to New Zealand, "as a slur on their Maori co-citizens and a near-personal affront."[12] Public controversy raged. Sharp relished the fray.

Jack Golson said that the academic response was "only the tip of the iceberg of debate."[13] Nevertheless, the scholarly opposition grew tougher. New research and particularly fieldwork in the Pacific Islands, in part stimulated by Sharp's work, saw his approach deemed not only Eurocentric but also "armchair." By the 1970s criticism of Sharp had significantly hardened. Golson brought out a third edition of his symposium book in 1972, still with the original contributions, but with a new foreword and bibliographic additions indicating how far scholarship had moved since Sharp's book.[14] Another apparent nail in Sharp's coffin was computer simulation of how Polynesia was first settled, whose authors conclude that "drift or 'one-way' voyaging" could not account for the discovery of all the islands, and that at critical junctures deliberate voyaging against the prevailing winds, and not drifting, was required to find and people the islands.[15] It was a most unjust claim, because Sharp had never argued for a drift settlement; indeed, as previously mentioned, he specifically rejected that notion. But the drift tag stuck. And the fact that a computer, then regarded with some awe, proved him wrong was a crushing blow.

Put simply, his work had become unfashionable. It was not always read carefully, or not read at all. People got confused about his arguments for unnavigated, accidental, one-way voyages, and of chance findings of islands. It was all too easy to lump him into the "drifter" and "wrong" category and be scornful. He did not help his cause by never conceding an inch. His views generally became historiographically isolated and overwhelmed in the 1970s, by such publications as Ben Finney's compilation, *Pacific Navigation and Voyaging*, which reported on "new, non-armchair" research,[16] and most notably by David Lewis's *We, the Navigators*.

Nevertheless, there was one area where Sharp's arguments still held some sway, and that was with regard to the settlement of New Zealand. Thanks both to Sharp and also to David Simmons, who established that the Great Migration was largely a figment of Percy Smith's and others' imaginations,[17] there was in the 1970s and 1980s some support for the idea that the country might have been settled by the accidental arrival of even a single vessel,[18] though that is no longer the common view.[19]

David Lewis (1917–2002) was born in England, and came to New Zealand when he was two.[20] Part of his childhood was also spent in the Cook Islands. He trained as a medical doctor at Dunedin, and also Leeds, England. He was a medical officer in the British army during the war, then set up general practice in London's East End. But his real passion was adventuring. While working in London, he started sailing across and around the Atlantic, beginning in 1959 with his participation in the inaugural Single-Handed Transatlantic Race in his twenty-five-foot sloop *Cardinal Vertue*. He quit his practice in 1964 and spent three years sailing around the world with his family on the catamaran *Rehu Moana*. In the Pacific Islands, in Micronesia, he met some old men who still used traditional methods of navigation. So began his studies of this vanishing art at sea, which resulted in an appointment as a research fellow in Pacific history at the Australian National University (ANU). Although lacking formal training in history, Lewis fit extremely well into the culture and prevailing scholarly approaches of Professor Jim Davidson's department, which emphasized the importance of fieldwork and personal experience, as well as stressing the role of Pacific Islanders as active participants both in history itself and as acknowledged authorities. The result was *We, the Navigators*, published in 1972.

Lewis credited Sharp with the "salutary service in demolishing the thoughtless assumptions of [the traditionalist] school and firmly established the importance of drift and one-way voyages. Unfortunately he attempted to lay down a new orthodoxy, which virtually denied the Islanders any navigational expertise at all."[21] Lewis was impatient with Sharp and others whose "glaring misuse of book-derived nautical data made no sense at all to Pacific small-boat sailors, or . . . to anyone personally acquainted with the islands of the South Seas."[22] From 1964 Lewis published a series of scholarly articles on indigenous sailing and navigational methods that disagreed with Sharp's assessments.[23] Sharp replied in kind to these and other writers, adamantly maintaining his original position.[24] Lewis commented that Sharp "kept reiterating, in combative terms, the theories he termed his 'stock in trade as a writer.'"[25] Their different personalities and approaches to the subject fueled an acrimonious rivalry for their readers' hearts and minds. They were bound to come to blows and the bad feeling duly spilled into the public arena with a testy and essentially unhelpful exchange in the *Journal of Pacific History*.[26] Both men behaved badly. Lewis commented that his retort "particularly incensed" Sharp, who sent him one "vituperative letter" too many. Provoked beyond measure, Lewis scrawled across it "Bullshit Andrew," sent it back, and then sailed around the Antarctic in *Ice Bird*. Sharp died in 1974, before Lewis returned, lucky to be still alive.[27]

We, the Navigators was based on extensive research of historical records and fieldwork in the Pacific Islands, which included studying and applying the techniques of some remaining navigators in Micronesia like Hipour and Tevake. It countered the two key planks of Sharp's theory—that navigators could not successfully undertake two-way voyages over great distances, and that the voyaging vessels were not well suited to arduous exploration.

Lewis detailed some of the general principles and techniques of traditional island navigation. These involved a range of sophisticated practices for direction finding, which involved observing and understanding positions and movements of horizon and zenith stars, in association with seasonal wind/weather patterns. Earlier writers had claimed the navigators sailed by the stars but never adequately explained how. Lewis did. And his analysis of astral navigation made many of Sharp's observations seem most inadequate. While Sharp might have been technically correct in some of his comments on the problems of similar star angles along a line of latitude, he was correct only in so far as he assumed a European construct of latitude and longitude was the only way to navigate. Lewis showed that there were other ways of conceptualizing direction and movement, particularly by orientation using the concept of *etak*, whereby movement is visualized as the *islands* moving in relation to the vessel and to a third point, out to the side of the departure and destination islands. Further, Lewis showed that navigators could very successfully use cloud shapes and colors, swell patterns, homing (rather than migrating) birds, sea conditions, and other natural phenomena, so effectively expanding even the smallest island target. Lewis's experiences at sea taught him that the ocean was not featureless, as it might appear on a map viewed from an armchair, nor necessarily hostile. For highly trained navigators it was full of friendly, tell-tale signs.

Thus Lewis claimed that Sharp's fundamental problem of lateral drift was not a problem. Lateral displacement in practice was not necessarily uniform or consistent, and the longer the voyage the greater likelihood of self-cancellation by random drift directions. More to the point, if a vessel was consistently moved sideways off course, the navigators would be aware that this was happening and would take corrective action.

Finally, Lewis highlighted the effectiveness of the exploring vessels, emphasizing their reliability, innovative sailing technologies and practices, and capacities for up-wind sailing.

Lewis' overall conclusion was that Pacific navigators once had, and some still did have, skills to range deliberately over vast areas of ocean in search of new lands and had the ability to make safe return voyages. The islands had been explored and settled deliberately, and by a process of two-way voyaging, not by one-way journeys of no return.

Lewis' scholarship has subsequently been responsible for spurring many others to investigate Islanders' navigational techniques, and his foundational work has been endorsed by all of them.[28] Among the more recent scholars is Geoff Irwin, who has further refined arguments for a deliberate and systematic strategy of island exploration and settlement.[29]

Lewis' own efforts to put these navigational techniques "to the hard test of landfall," both on his own sailing vessels as well as on some indigenous sailing craft, were also foundational in establishing a modern tradition of building replica or prototypic Austronesian vessels and sailing them according to the old ways. Lewis was a key crew member on Jim Siers' *Taratai* expedition,[30] and perhaps most notably on Ben Finney's Hawaiian voyaging vessel *Hokule'a*, especially on its ground-breaking first voyage from Hawai'i to Tahiti in 1976.[31] Lewis sailed on numerous prototypic craft, including New Zealander Hec Busby's *Te Aurere*. Such voyaging has taken on a life of its own with many vessels now regularly sailing the ancient seaways. These craft have become symbolic of a new pan-Polynesian cultural renaissance.[32] Like the nav-igators of old, Lewis has helped pass on ancient knowledge to a new generation of Pacific peoples.

Lewis won the Sharp-Lewis navigation debate in terms of ethno-graphic understanding, practical noninstrument sailing, and historio-graphic contest. Lewis, who died in 2002, is now very much in favor and is still read. Sharp is not. What is seldom appreciated is that Sharp and Lewis had some significant points of convergence. For example, Sharp was prepared to allow reliable two-way voyaging for distances of up to about 555 kilometers. Lewis noted that "it is possible to sail from South-east Asia to all the inhabited islands of Oceania, save only Hawai'i, New Zealand, and Easter Island, without ever making a sea crossing longer than 310 miles [573 kilometers]." The argument about two-way voyag-ing might perhaps have more profitably applied to the extremities of eastern Polynesia. At the time of writing *We, the Navigators*, Lewis was himself conservative on this issue, noting how difficult it was to sail from Hawai'i to Tahiti, to Easter Island from the west, and from New Zealand to eastern Polynesia. But such potential toeholds of common ground were lost in the heat of debate and mutual bad feeling.

Also, Sharp needs at least partial redemption, particularly over the claim that he proposed a drift thesis to explain the settlement of the Pacific Islands. He did not. And it should never be forgotten that Sharp started the modern navigation debate.

The current historiography stresses the capacity of ancient naviga-tors freely to rove to and fro across the Pacific Ocean. Ironically, thanks to Sharp's challenge, there has been a reinforcement of older, Roman-tic views of epic voyages. But has the pendulum swung too far back that way? Have the inherent difficulties and challenges for the first humans to enter the remoter Pacific Ocean been minimized? Will another Sharp character emerge to provide a corrective, one perhaps based on a reassessment of the realities of sailing lonely Pacific seaways, especially with pre-European materials, without planetariums for training, and generally without modern hindsight?

Notes

1. Abraham Fornander, *An Account of the Polynesian Race, its origin and migrations, and the ancient history of the Hawaiian people to the times of Kamehameha I*, 3 vols. (London, 1878, 1880, 1885); Edward Tregear, *The Aryan Maori* (Wellington, 1885); S. P. Smith, *Hawaiki: The Original Homeland of the Maori* (Christchurch, 1910).

2. Bronislaw Malinowski, *Argonauts of the Western Pacific* (London, 1932); Peter Buck, (Te Rangi Hiroa), *Vikings of the Sunrise* (Christchurch, 1938; reprinted 1975).

3. For example, Elsdon Best, *The Astronomical Knowledge of the Maori* (Wellington, 1922); idem, *Polynesian Voyagers: The Maori as a Deep-Sea Navigator, Explorer, and Colonizer* (Wellington, 1923); A. C. Haddon and James Hornell, *Canoes of Oceania*, 3 vols. (Honolulu, 1936–38).

4. For a history of ideas about Pacific voyaging and settlement, see K. R. Howe, *The Quest for Origins: Who First Discovered and Settled New Zealand and the Pacific Islands?* (Auckland, 2003).

5. Jack Golson, "Charles Andrew Sharp (1906–1974)," *Journal of Pacific History* 9 (1974): 131–33; Russell Stone, "Charles Andrew Sharp 1906–1974," *New Zealand Journal of History* 8, no. 1 (1974): 93–94; Brian Hooker, "Andrew Sharp. A Biographical Note," 1994/2002, http://delzur_research.tripod.com/nzresearch/bibliography_andrew_sharp.htm.

6. Among the better known of these books are *The Discovery of the Pacific Islands* (London, 1960); *The Discovery of Australia* (London, 1963); *The Voyages of Abel Janszoon Tasman* (London, 1968); *The Journal of Jacob Roggeveen* (London, 1970). For a full list of his publications, see Hooker, "Andrew Sharp. A Biographical Note."

7. Sharp was probably referring to statute miles. Lewis uses nautical miles. For the sake of rough uniformity, I assume both Sharp and Lewis use nautical miles, which I convert to kilometers—one nautical mile = 1.852 kilometers.

8. For example, the New Zealand novelist and controversialist Denis Glover rubbished the idea "that the Polynesians were skilled navigators. I am with Mr. C.A. Sharp in doubting this. Skilled seamen, yes; but men cannot get longitude by squinting through holes in a coconut, and cannot navigate a boat, even haphazardly, unless they can beat to windward. However much extra-sensory perception we may wish to credit the primitives with, they never had more than the unpredictable sea would allow them." *The Dominion* (Wellington), 20 January 1960 (letter to the editor).

9. Jack Golson, ed., *Polynesian Navigation: A Symposium on Andrew Sharp's Theory of Accidental Voyages* (Wellington, 1962), 9.

10. Ibid.

11. Sharp's supporter was Captain Brett Hilder. The other contributors were G. S. Parsonson, Captain G. H. Heyen, Charles Bechtol, and G. M. Dening.

12. Golson, "Andrew Sharp," 132.

13. Ibid.

14. Golson, ed., *Polynesian Navigation*, 3rd ed. (Wellington, 1972), 7.

15. Michael Levison, R. Gerard Ward, and John W. Webb, *The Settlement of Polynesia: A Computer Simulation* (Canberra, 1973), 6.

16. Ben Finney, ed., *Pacific Navigation and Voyaging* (Wellington, 1976), 5.

17. D. R. Simmons, *The Great New Zealand Myth: A Study of the Discovery and Origin Traditions of the Maori* (Wellington, 1976).

18. Norma McArthur, I. W. Saunders, and R. L. Tweedie, "Small Population Isolates: A Micro-simulation Study," *Journal of the Polynesian Society* 85 (1976): 307–26. See also D. G. Sutton, ed., *The Origins of the First New Zealanders* (Auckland, 1994).

19. See Howe, *Origins*, 179.

20. See Lewis's autobiography, *Shapes on the Wind* (Sydney, 2000; updated edition, 2002), and my obituary to him in *Journal of Pacific History* 37, no. 1 (2003): 129–32.

21. Lewis, *We, the Navigators*, 20. All subsequent references are to the 1972 publication. Note Lewis's reference to Sharp's alleged drift ideas. Lewis also wrote a popular book on Polynesian voyaging, *The Voyaging Stars: Secrets of the Pacific Island Navigators* (Sydney, 1978).

22. Lewis, *Shapes*, 74 (quotation); *We, the Navigators*, 20.

23. Lewis lists nine articles 1964–70 in his bibliography in *We, the Navigators*, 330.

24. These are listed in Hooker, "Andrew Sharp. A Biographical Note." See also Golson, ed., *Polynesian Navigation*, 3rd ed., 164.

25. Lewis, *Shapes*, 116.

26. Sharp, "David Lewis on Indigenous Pacific Navigation"; and Lewis, "The Gospel According to St Andrew," *Journal of Pacific History* 7 (1972): 222–23, 223–25, respectively.

27. Lewis, *Shapes*, 116; idem, *Ice Bird* (Sydney, 2001 ed.), 33.

28. An extensive bibliography can be found in Nicholas J. Goetzfridt, *Indigenous Navigation and Voyaging in the Pacific: A Reference Guide* (New York, 1992).

29. Geoffrey Irwin, *The Prehistoric Exploration and Colonisation of the Pacific* (Cambridge, 1992).

30. Jim Siers, *Taratai: A Pacific Adventure* (Wellington, 1977).

31. Ben Finney, *Hokule'a: The Way to Tahiti* (New York, 1979).

32. For example, Ben Finney, *Voyage of Rediscovery: A Cultural Odyssey through Polynesia* (Berkeley, 1994); idem, "Playing with Canoes," in *Pacific Places, Pacific Histories: Essays in Honor of Robert C. Kiste*, ed. Brij V. Lal (Honolulu, 2004), 290–308.

CHAPTER 6

The Evolution of Marshall Sahlins

Michael Goldsmith

Social Stratification in Polynesia, by Marshall D. Sahlins.
Seattle: University of Washington Press, 1958.

Historical Metaphors and Mythical Realities: Structure in the Early History of the Sandwich Islands Kingdom, by Marshall D. Sahlins.
Ann Arbor: University of Michigan Press, 1981 (as ASAO [Association for Social Anthropology in Oceania] Special Publication no. 1).

MARSHALL SAHLINS (born 1930), the Charles Grey Distinguished Professor at the University of Chicago, is the highest-profile American anthropologist currently working in the field of Oceania. There is no denying his influence in theoretical areas of concern to the discipline as a whole but his final reputation is likely to rest on a number of writings on Pacific topics. Because he is an accomplished archival researcher as well as a fieldworker, his scholarship transcends anthropology and spills over into history, greatly increasing the impact his ideas have had in contemporary intellectual life.

Sahlins's main writings on the Pacific can be divided roughly into two chronological stages: those from the first phase of his work (mid-1950s to the mid-1970s), where his interests were broadly comparative, materialist, and evolutionist; and those from the subsequent phase (mid–late 1970s to the present), where his interests have stemmed from a historically informed ("processual") structuralism. *Social Stratification in Polynesia,* which stems from the earlier period, started life as his Ph.D. dissertation from Columbia University and became his first book (though its publication was delayed for some time). The seminal book from the later period, *Historical Metaphors and Mythical Realities,* was published in 1981 but had its genesis as an invited lecture to the 1979 gathering of the Association for Social Anthropology in Oceania. It is arguably his most controversial work and led to a famous debate with Princeton-based Sri Lankan anthropologist, Gananath Obeyesekere, which will be discussed toward the end of this essay.[1] Even before Obeyesekere's counterstrike, however, *Historical Metaphors* had spawned a larger critical and exegetical literature in response than *Social Stratification* and it continues to do so.

Historical Metaphors was the fruit of some earlier rethinking, in which the pivotal text in Sahlins's transition was *Culture and Practical Reason* (1976). In that book, Sahlins argued that the unproblematic distinction between nature (or environment) and culture, on which his earlier theory of adaptation depended, was itself a cultural one. This change in *theoretical* orientation was not directly mirrored by a change of *political* orientation. Sahlins has positioned himself throughout his career as a leftist intellectual. As a relatively junior academic, he opposed U.S. involvement in Vietnam, in mid-career he wrote a stinging attack on the conservative ideology of sociobiology, and more recently he has poured scorn on economist versions of development and dependency theory.[2] But the *tone* of his politics has shifted, from a straightforwardly materialist and progressive view of history to a more reactive and melancholy defense of local cultures against world systems. This is despite the fact that he eschews what he parodies as "despondency theory" (his term for dependency theory) as well as the more demoralizing and depoliticizing tendencies of postmodernism.

Social Stratification in Polynesia

I first encountered *Social Stratification* in 1968 as an undergraduate student of anthropology at the University of Auckland, where it was a required text for the second-year course on Polynesia. Of most direct relevance to local ethnographers was Sahlins's essay in formulating a theory of atoll social organization, a topic discussed in only two of the book's chapters (5 and 11). His discussion of these small-scale societies was based solely on the flimsy documentary evidence available to him in the 1950s,[3] but a decade later his ideas were helping to make sense of much richer data emerging from fieldwork undertaken in Tokelau by two Auckland lecturers, Antony Hooper and Judith Huntsman.[4]

Interestingly, by the time of *Social Stratification*'s delayed appearance as a monograph, Sahlins himself had carried out fieldwork not in Polynesia as conventionally defined but in Fiji on the island of Moala during 1954 and 1955.[5] In one of *Social Stratification*'s more cautious footnotes, he simply noted that on the basis of that field research "no facts were encountered that would seriously challenge the major hypotheses developed here" (xiii). This note displays two traits he later disowned: the scientific ethos in vogue at the time and the flatness of the prose that embodied it.

The hypotheses that guided the documentary research of *Social Stratification* stemmed from a distinction that Sahlins made between two cross-cutting aspects of social stratification. The first aspect is the *degree* of stratification, that is, the complexity of the system or the number of different kinds of ranks. The second is the *form* of stratification, that is, the sociological principles that underlie rank. Other factors being constant, the first aspect, degree, varies directly with productivity, where differences in rank are associated with "differences in function in the process of the distribution of goods. Everywhere in Polynesia, the chief is the agent of general tribal-wide distribution" (xi). On the basis of degree of stratification, Sahlins felt justified in classifying Polynesian societies into three groups: first, the most stratified (Hawai'i, Tonga, Samoa, and Tahiti); second, a complex group of less stratified societies that was itself split into two, comprising Mangareva, Mangaia, Easter Island, and Uvea (Wallis) on the one hand and the Marquesas, Tikopia, and Futuna on the other; and finally the comparatively unstratified atolls of Pukapuka, Ontong Java, and Tokelau.

The second aspect, form, underpinned a threefold categorization of Polynesian social structures. The first two such types were to be found on high islands: the ramage system, where high productivity was associated with widespread dispersal of resources, and the descent-line system, where those zones were spatially concentrated. "A ramage . . . is a nonexogamous, internally stratified, unilineal . . . descent group" (140) and the societies organized on this basis "can usually be analyzed as composed of sections of a single genealogical system [i.e., a large-size ramage] at the apex of which stands the paramount chief" (141). Most of the case studies Sahlins examined were of this type (e.g., Hawai'i, Tonga, Tahiti, Tikopia, Marquesas, Mangareva, Mangaia, and Easter Island).

The second type of social structure, the descent-line system, had not previously been discerned as a distinct category. Societies based on this system downplayed the importance of seniority based on pure patrilineal descent and instead reflected strongly localized, flexible, and ambilineal tendencies. Sahlins offered Samoa, Futuna, and Uvea as examples.

The significance of the distinction between these two kinds of social structure was that they possibly represented adaptive alternatives (201). To put it very simply, ramified systems operated where there was "a variety of scattered resource zones" that no single extended family could exploit effectively, thus leading to a kind of specialization (e.g., between coastal and inland groups) that linked them through exchanges based on genealogical connections. Descent-line systems, by contrast, would be expected "where resource areas are clustered in time and space so that a single familial group could cope adequately with the total range of available exploitative techniques" (203).

The third type of social structure encompassed the aforementioned atolls, where social organization was often historically derived from the first two but was, in any event, constrained by the resource poverty and low productivity of the atoll environment. Lack of economic surpluses encouraged a more egalitarian system but (perhaps unexpectedly) one that tended over time to become more intricate than those of the high islands. "Adaptation in social organization would move toward a multiplicity of social groups, each connected with a given productive activity or exploitation of a particular area, and to each of which every individual belongs" (236).

Sahlins summarized his arguments in a final brief chapter that trumpeted the validity of his generalizations "respecting the variable relationship between social stratification and organization and the technological adaptation of culture to the environment" (253). He urged others to develop and test the concept of adaptation. These themes loomed large in the materialist and evolutionist anthropology of the mid-twentieth century in the United States in the writings of Marvin Harris, Morton Fried, and Leslie White, all of whom Sahlins acknowledged as influences (v).

It is fair to say that contemporary reviewers who stood outside the evolutionist tradition received *Social Stratification* with more respect than enthusiasm, but at least the editors who commissioned them did Sahlins the honor of asking recognized authorities to subject his book to critical scrutiny. Among these leading scholars, Ian Hogbin and Ward Goodenough both found the hypothesized link between productivity and stratification unconvincing but praised Sahlins for providing a clear and systematic structural classification of Polynesian societies, an achievement that Raymond Firth also found "interesting" and having "the merit of clear statement." Firth, however, had "reservations" about the ramage/descent-line distinction, which led him to consider the underlying ecological correlations "rather artificial."[6] Though unconvinced by this argument as well, Goodenough found it methodologically "a valuable contribution" and backed Sahlins's criticisms of the most important alternative comparativist thesis of the 1950s, Irving Goldman's theory of status rivalry, for its lack of clarity and rigor.[7] In a dramatic exemplification of his own theory, Goldman was later to lay against *Social Stratification*'s author the most cutting accusation a left-wing materialist evolutionist could endure, that of being functionalist.[8]

I have referred to a certain flatness of the prose in *Social Stratification*. Before long, however, a different Sahlins style began to emerge, one of the more distinctive and quirky voices in contemporary anthropology. Five years after the publication of *Social Stratification*, a famous and much reprinted extension of its basic approach appeared—a nominally comparativist and materialist essay on forms of Oceanic leadership with the punning title of "Poor Man, Rich Man, Big-Man, Chief."[9] In this essay, Sahlins cites *Social Stratification* sparingly and the first footnote jokingly christens his new and looser approach the "Method of Uncontrolled Comparison." Ecological adaptation was still the primary explanatory variable but it is tempting to read Sahlins's later transition to culturalist explanations as a response to the growing recognition that differences between Melanesia and Polynesia also reflected vernacular cosmologies of power. In many respects, "Poor Man, Rich Man" represents the high-water mark in Pacific sociocultural anthropology of the kind of explanation Sahlins proposed in *Social Stratification*. Although *Social Stratification* is not as widely read as the later essay, it remains a serious and widely acknowledged statement of a particular position. The materialist and evolutionist banner, however, has since mostly been kept flying by prehistorians and archaeologists.

Historical Metaphors and Mythical Realities

Sahlins's insights in the 1963 essay and his increasing disavowal of evolutionist materialism culminated in ideas first aired in two talks delivered in 1979. One was a keynote address to the Congress of the Australian and New Zealand Association for the Advancement of Science, published as Sahlins's arguably second most famous essay, "The Stranger-King."[10] Using an approach he labels "processual structuralism" and couched in occasionally baroque language, this piece applied insights from the work of the great historical linguist of Indo-European myth and society, Georges Dumézil. Sahlins argued that Polynesian kingship represented a kind of savagery best conceptualized as originating from outside society and perpetually absorbed by locals through a variety of processes that linked history and structure.

The other 1979 talk was the ASAO Distinguished Lecture that was to appear in expanded form as *Historical Metaphors and Mythical Realities*. My earlier mention of the continuity of Sahlins's political interests, as well as their change in tone, resonates in a poignant sentence from the preface. His history, he states, "cannot claim to be Marxist, but it has the same minimum and sufficient premises: that men and women are suffering beings because they act at once in relationship to each other and in a world that has its own relationships" (vii).

He begins his monograph by questioning a persistent theoretical contrast between structure and history. The structural linguistics tradition recommends the analysis of structure by means of a synchronic approach (in which phenomena are treated as existing at one and the same moment in time, or even as existing outside time). History, on the other hand, requires a diachronic approach (in which phenomena are treated as existing in and through time).[11] On this view, structural anthropology has no business with history. For Sahlins, however, the theoretical rigor that this exclusion brings risks the loss of "what anthropology is all about," which is to say "practice—human action in the world" (6). How, then, to reconcile structure and history? By showing "that history is organized by structures of significance" or, to put it another way, "ordered by culture"; and, further, by showing how "in that process, the culture is reordered." The introduction closes with the question, "How does the reproduction of a structure become its transformation?" (8).

Sahlins answers with the provocative assertion that Hawaiian history repeats itself as event only after its initial appearance as myth, in which individual persons take on the character of their ancestral leaders and collective identity. Historical accounts of the explorer Vancouver's attempts to convert a Hawaiian chief to Christianity in the late eighteenth century turn out to reenact a myth based on "annual ritual alternation of the gods Lono and Ku" (11). Lono was the god of peace, fertility, and productivity, who reigned during the four-month period called the Makahiki; Ku, the god of warfare and human sacrifice, held sway the rest of the year. The opposition between them reflected a division based on original reproductive powers in the maternal line and the violent transgressive usurpation of those powers by an invading male (the "stranger-king" of Dumézil's theory, to which Sahlins makes reference in *Historical Metaphors*, 14).

All this sets the stage for a "cosmological drama" (17). The Hawaiian interpretation of the arrival of Captain Cook in early 1779 at the big island of Hawai'i equated Cook with Lono. Sahlins claims that this view was not only well attested in the historical record but also expressive of cultural logic. During the Makahiki, priests carried an image of Lono on a clockwise circuit of the island, which happens to be the direction in which Cook's ships circumnavigated the island before he landed at Kealakekua Bay. Moreover, the ships ran parallel to, and at roughly the same speed as, the shore-bound procession. Kealakekua happened to be the site of an important temple devoted to Lono where, according to tradition, his circuit of the island began and ended each year (18–22). The rituals by which Cook was received and one of his sailors was buried, the fact that the British were allowed to take away the temple's wooden fence and images to use as fuel, the gifts made by the British of tools and other objects made of iron, the enormous hospitality (in terms of food and sexual services) provided by the Hawaiians, Cook's fortuitous announcement that he would leave soon as the Makahiki came to an end and that he would return in a year's time—all of these events brought together a historical sequence and a ritual calendar.

The time of Ku was at hand, as represented by the recent arrival of Kalaniopu'u, the paramount chief of Hawai'i. The cosmological drama was confirmed by the ships' departure on schedule. Unfortunately for Cook, his ships returned a week later because one of them had sprung a foremast. The cool welcome they received, in contrast to the earlier exuberant one, showed that Cook had disturbed the ritual categories. Incidents of theft and violence by the locals increased and chiefs could not be persuaded to keep their subjects under control. Cook's premature return posed a threat to the resurgent power of Ku and, when he tried to take Kalaniopu'u hostage as a bargaining chip for the return of a stolen cutter (ship's boat), a hostile group attacked and killed him. Some of his remains were handed over to the stunned British survivors while others were later claimed to have been incorporated into the cult of Lono.

The death and subsequent installation of Cook as a cult figure fit with Hawaiian ideas about chiefly succession and the absorption of dead chiefs into local genealogies by conquering ones. Through a complex system of historical transformations, Kamehameha, the chief who was to establish unified and dynastic control over the Hawaiian archipelago by the end of the eighteenth century, took this absorption a step further by seeking a special connection to the British monarchy and welcoming British trade. Thus was "the theory of the Makahiki transposed by the death of Cook into a register of practice" (27). The trade goods introduced into this world, as well as the earlier objects exchanged between Cook's voyagers and the locals, became a way of reinforcing and reshaping the hierarchical separation between chiefs and commoners (29–31 and chap. 3, "Transformation").[12] Embroiled in notions of tapu, changes in the status of chiefs also led to a transformation of relations between different lines of chiefs, between men and women, and between Hawaiians and outsiders. It was this detailed reinterpretation of the evidence in terms of an imputed Hawaiian version of mytho-history that went beyond the existing historical accounts by J. C. Beaglehole and Gavan Daws.[13] Sahlins's approach turns the spotlight back on Western forms of historical thought as themselves irreducibly cultural modes of understanding.

Sahlins's short monograph clearly addressed issues of concern to historians of Hawai'i as well as to those who wanted to understand the importance of cultural difference in early encounters between Western explorers and Pacific peoples. Not all specialists in the region agreed with his interpretations, but the debate did not stray much beyond the pages of regional journals.[14]

What brought *Historical Metaphors* to wider attention was Obeyesekere's famous attack on the idea of the apotheosis of Captain Cook. Obeyesekere, a Sri Lankan anthropologist whose own field research had been carried out in South Asia, was new to Pacific Studies but drawn into the argument by what he saw as a fallacy. The view that Hawaiians had received Cook as the god Lono struck Obeyesekere as a Western fantasy routinely found in explorers' accounts of their reception by "natives." Were such notions inventions, he asked, "based on prior 'myth models' in Europe's antecedent history"?[15] All the trappings of veneration toward the white explorer could be explained in terms of universal standards of economic and political rationality.

In support of his surmise that Cook was not Lono he pointed to the fact that the great navigator was made to take part in rituals *honoring* Lono. At best, then, Cook was installed as a chief, and his deification, if it took place at all, occurred *after* his death, not before. Now Obeyesekere conflates two issues here: whether deification occurs before or after death and whether it occurs to an insider or an outsider. His interpretation of the latter (that, on the basis of South Asian evidence, outsiders are rarely if ever deified) is probably influenced by caste-like notions of purity, which aim to defend the boundaries of the group against pollution; for Sahlins, however, the Polynesian logic of hierarchy works in an opposite fashion, by allowing or even requiring chiefs, conceived as "outside" society, to achieve power.

Conclusion

No brief description of this debate can convey the passion and even anger of Sahlins's responses to Obeyesekere's criticism. Indeed, in two recent essays,[16] Sahlins has launched a further attack on Obeyesekere's thesis that narratives of "savage" cannibalism are another fabulist form of Western obsession with natives, whose main role is to fulfill certain fantasies of colonizing cultures.[17] Despite the fact that Sahlins dismisses Obeyesekere's contributions as "artificially maintained controversies," there seems little doubt that he in turn will continue to fuel the antagonism if provoked.

Will one of these two anthropological heavyweights score a knockout? Most Pacific specialists see Sahlins as leading on points because of his superb command of rhetoric in argument, his vast erudition in the Hawaiian and Fijian historical archives, and his grasp of the ethnographic context based on his own fieldwork. These are formidable strengths. Even in the unlikely event that he has to concede on some matters of interpretation, there is little chance of him throwing in the towel to his younger and taller opponent.

Two lessons, then, can be drawn from the evolution of Marshall Sahlins over the half century of his career so far. The first is that he commits himself passionately to the arguments he puts forward and defends them vigorously when he believes that his views have been misrepresented or that his attackers have not put in the training and preparation that he has. The second is that he is perfectly capable of changing the grounds of his argument, as the clear theoretical differences between *Social Stratification in Polynesia* and *Historical Metaphors and Mythical Realities* reveal. And yet such major rethinks may occur no more than once in a lifetime. Almost a quarter of a century after he reached the pinnacle of materialist explanation and then turned to a new way of understanding Pacific cultural history, the present-day Sahlins shows no signs of undergoing a theoretical conversion similar to the one he went through then. If he ever does so, my reading of his work's trajectory suggests that he will do so not by publicly disowning his earlier stance but by moving to a new position on his own terms and in his own time. There will be no concession speech.

Notes

1. Gananath Obeyesekere, *The Apotheosis of Captain Cook: European Myth-making in the Pacific* (Princeton, 1992); Marshall D. Sahlins, *How "Natives" Think: About Captain Cook, For Example* (Chicago, 1995).

2. Sahlins, "What is Anthropological Enlightenment? Some Lessons of the Twentieth Century," *Annual Review of Anthropology* 28 (1999): i–xxiii; and the revised version of this essay published as "On the Anthropology of Modernity; or, Some Triumphs of Culture over Despondency Theory," in *Culture and Sustainable Development in the Pacific*, ed. Antony Hooper (Canberra, 2000).

3. See Niel Gunson, "An Introduction to Pacific History," in *Pacific Islands History: Journeys and Transformations*, ed. Brij V. Lal (Canberra, 1992), 12.

4. Antony B. Hooper, "Socio-Economic Organization of the Tokelau Islands," VIIIth Congress of Anthropological and Ethnological Sciences, *Proceedings*, vol. 2. (1970), 238–40; Judith Huntsman and Antony Hooper, *Tokelau: A Historical Ethnography* (Auckland, 1996).

5. Sahlins, "Production, Distribution, and Power in a Primitive Society," in *Cultures of the Pacific*, ed. Thomas G. Harding and Ben J. Wallace (New York, 1970), 78–84 (originally published in 1960); idem, *Moala: Culture and Nature on a Fijian Island* (Ann Arbor, 1962).

6. Ian Hogbin, *Oceania* 30, no. 1 (1959): 79–80; Ward Goodenough, *Journal of the Polynesian Society* 68, no. 3 (1959): 255–58; Raymond Firth, *American Anthropologist* 63, no. 3 (1961): 610–12.

7. Irving Goldman, "Status Rivalry and Cultural Evolution in Polynesia," *American Anthropologist* 57, no. 4 (1955): 680–97.

8. Irving Goldman, *Ancient Polynesian Society* (Chicago, 1970), 23, 481. This accusation rests on a major progressive political criticism of functionalism, that it upholds and justifies continuity over change by treating societies ahistorically. Given Sahlins's concern for evolutionary change, the charge is unconvincing but it still would have stung.

9. Sahlins, "Poor Man, Rich Man, Big-Man, Chief: Political Types in Melanesia and Polynesia," *Comparative Studies in Society and History* 5, no. 3 (1963): 285–303.

10. Sahlins, "The Stranger-King: Dumézil among the Fijians," *Journal of Pacific History* 16, no. 3 (1981): 107–32.

11. The founding text for the synchrony/diachrony distinction is Ferdinand de Saussure's *Course in General Linguistics* (New York, 1959, but first published in French over forty years before).

12. See also Sahlins, "The Political Economy of Grandeur in Hawaii from 1810 to 1830," in *Culture through Time: Anthropological Approaches*, ed. Emiko Ohnuki-Tierney (Stanford, 1990), 26–56.

13. J. C. Beaglehole, "The Death of Captain Cook," *Historical Studies, Australia and New Zealand* 11, no. 43 (1964): 289–305; Gavan Daws, "Kealakekua Bay Revisited: A Note on the Death of Captain Cook," *Journal of Pacific History* 3 (1968): 21–23.

14. See, for example, Steen Bergendorff, Ulla Hasager, and Peter Henriques, "Mythopraxis and History: On the Interpretation of the Makahiki," *Journal of the Polynesian Society* 97, no. 4 (1988): 391–408; Christine Ward Gailey, "Categories without Culture: Structuralism, Ethnohistory and Ethnocide," *Dialectical Anthropology* 8, no. 3 (1983): 241–50; Marshall D. Sahlins, "Captain Cook at Hawaii," *Journal of the Polynesian Society* 98, no. 4 (1989): 371–423.

15. Gananath Obeyesekere, *The Apotheosis of Captain Cook: European Myth-making in the Pacific* (Princeton, 1992), 8.

16. Sahlins, "Artificially Maintained Controversies: Global Warming and Fijian Cannibalism," *Anthropology Today* 19, no. 3 (2003): 3–5; idem, "Artificially Maintained Controversies (Part 2)," *Anthropology Today* 19, no. 6 (2003): 21–23.

17. Obeyesekere, "British Cannibals: Contemplation of an Event in the Death and Resurrection of James Cook, Explorer," *Critical Inquiry* 18, no. 4 (1992): 630–54; idem, "Cannibal Feasts in Nineteenth-Century Fiji: Seamen's Yarns and the Ethnographic Imagination," in *Cannibalism and the Colonial World*, ed. Francis Barker, Peter Hulme, and Margaret Iversen (Cambridge, 1998), 63–86; idem, "Narratives of the Self: Chevalier Peter Dillon's Fijian Cannibal Adventures," in *Body Trade: Captivity, Cannibalism and Colonialism in the Pacific*, ed. Barbara Creed and Jeanette Hoorn (New York/Dunedin, 2001), 69–111; idem, "Comment: Cannibalism Reconsidered," *Anthropology Today* 19, no. 5 (2003): 18.

CHAPTER 7

Revisioning the Pacific:
Bernard Smith in the South Seas

Tom Ryan

European Vision and the South Pacific, 1768–1850: A Study in the History of Art and Ideas, by Bernard Smith.
Oxford: Clarendon, 1960. Oxford: Oxford University Press paperback, 1969. New Haven: Yale University Press, 1985. Sydney: Harper & Row, 1985. New Haven: Yale University Press, 1989. Melbourne: Oxford University Press, 1989.

Imagining the Pacific: In the Wake of the Cook Voyages, by Bernard Smith.
Melbourne: Melbourne University Press, 1992.

BORN IN Sydney in 1916, Bernard Smith is today widely considered to be Australia's preeminent art historian and a major cultural theorist.[1] While working as a school teacher and artist during the late 1930s and early 1940s, he came under the influences of surrealist aesthetics and communist politics, especially as mediated by refugee intellectuals from Hitler's Europe. During this period his principal literary inspirations were the Bible, Marx, and Toynbee; it was their different takes on history, especially of its unfolding over long durations, that most impressed him.[2] As an academic and writer through the next half century, Smith produced numerous historically oriented studies of Australian and modernist art, which broadly can be divided into two periods of publishing activity.[3] His most acclaimed achievement, however, is *European Vision and the South Pacific 1768–1850: A Study in the History of Art and Ideas,* first published in 1960 and a work that has continued to grow in stature and influence in the four decades since its original appearance. It is the history of this text, and of its companion-piece, *Imagining the Pacific: In the Wake of the Cook Voyages,* published in 1992, and the contexts in which they were produced and have been consumed, that are the main concerns of the present essay.[4]

European Vision and the South Pacific had its beginnings in Smith's very first publication, *Place, Taste and Tradition: A Study of Australian Art since 1788*. The latter emerged from his early 1940s work as a public arts educator, but it is equally linked to the broader context of World War II Australia, when Britain's hold on its former colony was being replaced by Australian national assertiveness and the growing influence—military, political, and cultural—of the United States. Of the shift from one text to the other, Smith noted in *European Vision:*

> This book arose, in the first instance, from an inquiry into the origins of European art in Australia begun 15 years ago and published in 1945. That inquiry revealed the need to investigate the beginnings of European art in the south Pacific more fully; beginnings which may be traced from 1768 when professional artists first began to voyage in the South Seas. How did they see this new world of the Pacific? Did their entry into it stimulate thought and affect in any way traditional forms of expression? Such questions, it seemed to me, were worth asking. (v)

Though not overtly a politicized text, Smith has since described *Place, Taste and Tradition* as being written from a historical materialist perspective and as having "good claim to being the first Marxist art history of a nation state."[5] As its title indicates, "place" was a central trope in his intellectual armory from the start. However, rather than simply following the conventional interpretations of Australian art as either pale reproductions of European originals or as thoroughly local productions, his concern was the dynamic but unequal relations between Australian and European art—that is, in a wider frame, the processes of cultural exchange between metropolis and periphery. Art, like other cultural forms, Smith argued, is socially produced, quite unpredictable, invariably hybrid, and never really original, especially when cultivated in the hothouse of imperialism. If art in colonial Australia was predominately European in derivation, so too European art and thought were irretrievably affected by contacts with the Antipodes. And whereas art in Europe had often been entangled with religion, in Australia its initial reference point was science.[6]

Only in 1945, when the University of Sydney abandoned its insistence on Latin as a prerequisite, was Smith able to begin formal study in the humanities—specifically in undergraduate English, history, and classical archaeology.[7] The following year he applied for a British Council scholarship, proposing to study "the English contribution to the beginnings of art in Australia"; eventually he was informed that the Courtauld Institute of Art in London would accept him for the 1948–49 year as a nonacademic student to "work on a piece of research on eighteenth- and nineteenth-century British art."[8] At the Courtauld he attended courses on European art history given by, among others, Antony Blunt and E. H. Gombrich. In a lecture by the latter, he was struck by the throw-away phrase "all art is conceptual," for Smith, who until then had accepted uncritically the conventional notion of "the innocent eye," Gombrich's comment was "a revelation . . . [which] unwittingly provided me with a paradigm that seems to have guided my work for the next two years, though I was quite unaware of it at the time." A week later, while studying the original drawings of Parkinson and other artists who had traveled with Cook, he noted in his diary: "Considerable variation in the original sketches and the engravings made from them." It was the differences that now interested him; clearly they were not due to a lack of ability to copy accurately.[9]

In his quest to find the work of early British artists who had traveled to Australia and in the Pacific, Smith made contact with Rex Nan Kivell, an expatriate New Zealander and connoisseur of early drawings and paintings relating to the South Seas, and R. A. Skelton, the British expert on Cook's voyages of exploration.[10] He also decided—since "all art is conceptual"—to start from the beginning, by looking at the earliest European ideas about the Southern Hemisphere, particularly the concept of the Antipodes. That is, a long view of history—as with the Bible, Marx, and Toynbee. Antony Blunt, director of the Courtauld, approved this project and sent Smith to the Warburg Institute to see Rudolf Wittkower, an expert on medieval teratology, who in turn endorsed Smith's direction and passed him to one of his colleagues, Charles Mitchell. Realizing that Smith's lack of Latin would prevent serious engagement with medieval notions of the Southern Hemisphere, Mitchell encouraged him to return to the art historical scholarship of the early modern period, beginning with the writings of Panofsky, and personally introduced him to Ernst Gombrich. Thus it was that Smith came back to something like his original project.[11]

By late March 1949 the essay that was to become "European Vision and the South Pacific" was taking shape. Soon afterward, through Mitchell, a letter arrived from J. W. Davidson, a New Zealand scholar of the Pacific then based at Cambridge University—a letter which, to quote Smith, "in one sense, changed the course of my life." Davidson had agreed to edit a supplementary volume to accompany fellow New Zealander J. C. Beaglehole's planned three-volume Hakluyt edition of Captain Cook's journals. The supplementary (or fourth) volume would involve general essays on the historical, geographical, and ethnological aspects of the voyages; an assessment of their relation to eighteenth-century science and philosophy; and a section on bibliographies and catalogues. Smith was invited to compile a catalogue of art from the three voyages—to be finished in a year or so. At first reluctant to take on such an unscheduled task, Smith agreed on condition that he be allowed also to write an essay on Cook's artists. But the project turned out to be much more complex than anyone had foreseen, and the intended fourth volume was eventually abandoned and replaced by Beaglehole's proposal for a biography of Cook.[12] Rather than being a quickly finished bit-part to a supplementary text, Smith's allotted tasks took four decades to complete and ultimately resulted in three large volumes, *The Art of Captain Cook's Voyages* (1985–87), written in collaboration with Rüdiger Joppien.[13]

Having had his scholarship extended for another year, Smith continued his researches in the British Museum Library, The Natural History Museum, the National Maritime Museum, the Public Records Office, the Royal Commonwealth Library, the London Missionary Society headquarters, and Castle Howard in Yorkshire. The finished essay was published in the *Journal of the Warburg and Courtauld Institutes* in 1950.[14] Little read outside of European classical and postclassical art history circles, it nevertheless laid the foundation for his influential book *European Vision and the South Pacific*.[15] Smith has recently summarized his essay as follows:

> My central concern was to define the ways in which scientists made use of art to document and support their findings; and what followed from this conjunction of scientific curiosity and aesthetic vision during the late eighteenth and early nineteenth centuries. I began by looking at the instructions given to navigators on far voyages, and the degree to which the artists taken on such voyages succeeded in carrying them out. I concluded that as far as the documentation of plants, and the provision of coastal profiles as aids to navigation were concerned, the artists *did* succeed in providing the scientists with what they desired: faithful records of nature.

Smith stresses this final point, noting his concern that some commentators have misinterpreted him as arguing that European depictions of un-European things are "inevitably distorted; or worse, that faithful, objective, representation of non-European places and cultures is not possible." Such misreadings of his views are dismissed by Smith as "fashionable nonsense":

> What I did argue was that whenever aesthetic categories such as the picturesque, exotic, or sublime became involved they tended to affect objective description. That is to say artists, to the degree that they were artists, brought an aesthetic vision with them and applied it, sometimes consciously, sometimes unconsciously, to what they saw before them.
>
> Such preconceptions operated most powerfully when it came to recording indigenous peoples. When Cook sailed on his first voyage a current view was that Patagonians were giants. But Banks in his descriptions, and Buchan and Parkinson, the artists he took with him, were able to correct this false notion and provide evidence that Patagonians were of normal size. Thus the enlisting of artists on scientific voyages was vindicated.[16]

Technically accurate drawings for scientific purpose were, however, a quite different thing from engravings produced as illustrations for aesthetically fashionable books aimed at "people of taste." Drawings by Buchan of the natives of Tierra del Fuego, for instance, were never published until Smith himself published them in 1950 and the 1980s. Yet some of Buchan's drawings had served as the basis for illustrations by the famous English engraver Bartolozzi, who re-presented the Fuegans as "noble savages." A somewhat different transformation occurred in respect to Tahiti, where Banks had given classical Greek names to individual Tahitians based on their personal attributes. Moreover, the country itself was seen by early European visitors as an Arcadia, though the elaborate mortuary rites observed there reminded them that death was also a constant presence. In the hands of the engravers back in England, however, such considerations were translated into depictions of Tahitians in the context of the powerful trope of "death in Arcadia."

Smith's essay also contrasted the traveler's vision with those of the convict and the missionary. Thus, the Pacific, as seen by the likes of Banks, "was transformed through the eyes of the exiled convict, Thomas Watling, and the Reverend Thomas Haweis." In this way the noble savage trope—which had earlier been traced by scholars like Lovejoy and Boas back to Greek antiquity—was transformed into the trope of the ignoble savage. The latter concept, as it related to late-eighteenth- and early-nineteenth-century European art and literature, Smith insists, was very much his own invention. His essay concluded with considerations of how the missionary endeavor encouraged ideas of progress and civilization in the Pacific, and how as a result the ignoble savage was in its turn transformed into a degraded figure of fun.[17]

On his arrival back in Australia in early 1951, Smith returned to his employment in the Art Gallery of New South Wales, and the following year completed his bachelor of arts degree at Sydney University. Having resigned his membership of the Australian Communist Party prior to his departure for Britain, and given up on "real existing socialism" after a visit to Czechoslovakia, politics was no longer a significant distraction: he was now a professional art historian.[18] In 1954–55 Smith was a doctoral scholar at the Australian National University (ANU), under the supervision of J. W. Davidson, and lecturing part-time in art history at Melbourne University. Because of "Mr Smith's previous extensive research experience in the general field of his course, [and] his having already carried out a year's research on the margins of his PhD topic, as evidenced by publications," he was not required to meet the usual three years' residency requirements as a research student. The title of his thesis was "The Study of European Art and Ideas of Contact with the Pacific, 1768–1851" and, on its submission in early 1956, J. C. Beaglehole (Wellington) and Charles Mitchell (London) were appointed as external examiners.[19] It was, effectively, the draft manuscript for his book, *European Vision and the South Pacific, 1768–1850.*

The year 1956 saw also the publication of a second important essay by Smith in the *Journal of the Warburg and Courtauld Institutes.*[20] It radically contradicted the orthodox view of the origins of Coleridge's *The Rime of the Ancient Mariner* by arguing that the poem's principal inspiration had been William Wales, chief astronomer on Cook's second voyage. While researching the paintings of Hodges in the Mitchell Library, Smith had chanced upon Wales's journal manuscript and meteorological observations, and noted that after the voyage he had become mathematics teacher at Christ's Hospital, London. Knowing that Coleridge had been a pupil there around the same time, Smith surmised that Wales must have introduced him to Pacific literature and stories, a theory substantiated by Smith's discovery of parallels between the log and the poem.[21] For the next four decades, nevertheless, Coleridge scholars largely ignored this exposition of the links between Cook's greatest voyage and Coleridge's noblest work—a situation that began to change only after the essay was republished in 1992 in Smith's second major South Seas–focused work, *Imagining the Pacific: In the Wake of the Cook Voyages*.[22] Interestingly, the Coleridge essay is the only one of the ten essays in this collection that dates specifically from the first rather than the second phase of Smith's art history career, and which is on a literary rather than a visual theme.

Broadly speaking, the essays in *Imagining the Pacific* are arranged chronologically, beginning with the pre-Cook period and concluding with reflections on the great explorer's posthumous reputation. Prior to the piece on Coleridge are chapters on the development in Europe of types of artwork within which "the Pacific was imaged and imagined"; the context within which "scientific" art played its subordinate but significant role in the European penetration of the Pacific; the effects of the empirical naturalism associated with travel, science, and topography on the conventions of European classical naturalism; the consequences for both Europe and the Pacific of the imposition of "an alien European *genre*, portraiture, upon the peoples of the Pacific"; and the impact of Pacific light and atmosphere upon the art of William Hodges, and his leading place in the history of *plein-air* landscape painting. Then, after the Coleridge essay, come chapters dealing with the ways an apparently "documentary art" of Pacific peoples was fashioned to serve ideological purposes; the relevance of Edward Said's notion of "orientalism" for understanding European perceptions of the Pacific; the role of the model of ancient Greece and Greek civilization in shaping the "primitivism" central to Europe's early imaginings of the Pacific; and, finally, the variety of political ends and ideological purposes "Captain James Cook" was unwittingly obliged to serve in the decades after his death.

Each of the essays in *Imagining the Pacific* provides a critical summary of, or an eloquent intervention in, a key thematic in the culture history of early European perceptions of the Pacific. But, equally, each develops an idea or ideas originally raised or hinted at, a third of a century earlier, in *European Vision and the South Pacific*. Most important, Smith's overriding concern for broad historical spans rather than specific events or epochs, for the continuities as much as the discontinuities of history, is mirrored in the praxis of all his writings about the South Seas. Over the years some critics have found his thinking about Australian and Western art variously too revisionist, too Marxist, too humanist, too modernist, too Hegelian.[23] But such arguments lose traction when translated across to his Pacific-centered writings.

From its first publications in the 1960s, *European Vision and the South Pacific* was welcomed by a broad audience. The paperback edition proudly highlighted a prediction from the flagship British anthropology journal *Man* that "students of taste, art historians, literary scholars and anthropologists ... will long honour and use this book"; next to it was a quote from a review by the historian J. C. Beaglehole in the *New Zealand Listener,* stating that the book "really helps us, who live in the Pacific, to see our world as part of the world at large." Smith himself has said that it was mainly anthropologists and geographers, rather than art historians, who first appreciated this particular work—and there is undoubtedly a basis to his observation. But with its several re-editions during the 1980s, in both Australia and the United States, with colored illustrations and enlarged format, *European Vision and the South Pacific* was claimed by a fresh generation of scholars and students, many of them working in new academic fields such as postcolonial theory, travel literature, and cultural studies.

This process gained further momentum with the publication in 1992 of *Imagining the Pacific.* Reviews of this work were overwhelmingly positive: while it was invariably seen as a "sequel" to *European Vision and the South Pacific,* and lacking the dramatic impact of its predecessor, it was nevertheless considered to be a worthy and novel undertaking.[24] Then in 1996 a conference was held in Canberra to honor Smith's work, and particularly "his extraordinary book *European Vision and the South Pacific.*" In an introduction to the collection of essays that emanated from this forum, Nicholas Thomas described the latter text as having been "published twenty years too early," and as having been appreciated more by general readers than scholars "until Edward Said's *Orientalism* appeared in 1978, stimulating what was to become a pervasive interest in topics such as Orientalism, primitivism, colonial culture and the representation of otherness."[25]

An even more expansive summary of Smith's wide influence and ongoing relevance was provided recently by the cultural theorist John Frow, in a review of Peter Beilharz's insightful study of the man and his oeuvre:

The central piece of work, the one that ultimately defines Smith's stature, is *European Vision and the South Pacific*. It is, in the first place, one of those major works of learning that transform or even establish a field of study, and its strengths lie in part in its use of the ordinary craft tools of the historian to open up an archive, to organise the vast amounts of material it contains and to develop a bold and original thesis by way of patient argument and meticulous documentation . . . But this history of vision has a further and broader context, that of the systematic extension of European imperialism through the Pacific in the eighteenth and nineteenth centuries, and of the structures of seeing and imagining—the categories of understanding, especially the primitivisms, hard and soft—that Europeans bring to bear in their dealings with the peoples and landscapes of the Pacific, and that they both modify and fail to modify in the process of encounter and exchange. Here Smith crucially anticipates Said's theses on Orientalism, and has had an enormously fruitful influence on histories of first contact in the Pacific.[26]

Bernard Smith must, therefore, be judged a *revisionist* in the very best senses of that word: as one who forced changes in our understanding of early contacts and interactions between Oceanic and Occidental peoples, and, especially, as *the* writer who initiated a seismic shift in the theorization of how and to what effect Pacific lands and their indigenous inhabitants were *visually represented* by early European artists and scientists in the great theater of encounter that was, and still is, the South Seas.

Notes

1. For an overview of Smith's oeuvre, see Peter Beilharz, *Imagining the Antipodes: Culture Theory and the Visual in the Work of Bernard Smith* (Cambridge, 1997). See also entries on Smith by Chris Wallace-Crabbe, in *The Oxford Companion to Australian History*, ed. Graeme Davidson, John Hirst, and Stuart Macintyre (Melbourne, 1998), and by Peter Beilharz, in *Dictionary of Cultural Theorists*, ed. E. Cashmore and C. Rojek (New York, 1999). A comprehensive intellectual biography of Smith is currently being written by Patricia Anderson.

2. Smith's early years are the focus of two finely crafted autobiographies, *The Boy Adeodatus: Portrait of a Lucky Young Bastard* (Ringwood, 1984), and *A Pavane for Another Time* (Melbourne, 2002).

3. For the first period, see especially *Place, Taste and Tradition: A Study of Australian Art since 1788* (Sydney, 1945), *Australian Painting, 1788–1960* (Melbourne, 1962), and Bernard Smith et al., *The Antipodean Manifesto: Essays in Art and History*

(Melbourne, 1959). For the second phase, see particularly *The Spectre of Truganini* (Sydney, 1980), *Modernism's History: A Study in Twentieth Century Art and Ideas* (Sydney, 1998), and Bernard Smith and A. Wheeler, eds., *The Art of the First Fleet and Other Early Australian Drawings* (Melbourne, 1988).

4. See also Rüdiger Joppien and Bernard Smith, *The Art of Captain Cook's Voyages* (vols. 1–2, Sydney, 1985; vol. 3, Sydney, 1987); Andrew David with Rüdiger Joppien and Bernard Smith, *The Charts and Coastal Views of Captain Cook's Voyages* (vol. 1, London, 1988; vol. 2, London, 1992; vol. 3, London, 1997); and W. Eisler and Bernard Smith, eds., *Terra Australis: The Furthest Shore* (Sydney, 1998).

5. *Pavane*, 124–25.

6. Beilharz, *Antipodes*, chap. 2.

7. *Parvane*, 145–46.

8. Ibid., 154–58.

9. Ibid., 240–41.

10. Ibid., 241.

11. Ibid., 245–48.

12. Beaglehole's three edited volumes appeared between 1955 and 1967 as *The Journals of Captain James Cook*, while his *Life of Captain James Cook* was published (posthumously) in 1974.

13. *Pavane*, 282–83.

14. "European Vision and the South Pacific," *Journal of the Warburg and Courtauld Institutes* 13 (1950): 66–100.

15. *Pavane*, 370–71.

16. Ibid., 371–72.

17. Ibid., 372.

18. Ibid., 448, 459–60.

19. Minutes of the Board of Graduate Studies, Australian National University: 18 September 1953; 26 March 1954; 20 January 1956, ANU Central Archives (thanks to Doug Munro for providing this information). See also S. G. Foster and Margaret M. Varghese, *The Making of the Australian National University, 1946–1996* (Sydney, 1996), 199, 200.

20. "Coleridge's *Ancient Mariner* and Cook's Second Voyage," *Journal of the Warburg and Courtauld Institutes* 19 (1956): 117–54.

21. Bernard Smith, personal communication, 26 November 2003; idem, *Imaging the Pacific: In the Wake of Cook's Voyages* (Melbourne, 1992), x–xxi.

22. In particular, because a New Zealand–based researcher, Bill Whelan, delivered a paper on the topic at the 4th International Coleri held in England in 2000.

23. For example, Richard Haese, *Rebels and Precursors: The Revolutionary Years of Australian Art* (Ringwood, 1981), 151–56; Ian Burn, Nigel Lendon, Charles Merewether, and Ann Stephen, *The Necessity of Australian Art: An Essay about Interpretation* (Sydney, 1988), 39–53, 62–75; Rex Butler, "Australian Art History and Revisionism," *Pre/dictions: The Role of Art at the End of the Millennium* (Welling-

ton, 2000), 177–85; Fay Braeur, "Hegelian History, Wölfflinean Periodization and Smithesque Modernism," *Art History* 24, no. 3 (2001): 449–57. I am grateful to Deborah Cain for advice on the wider art historical contexts of Smith's career.

24. For example, reviews by Paul Carter, *Journal of Historical Geography* 20, no. 1 (1994): 81–86; K. R. Howe, *Journal of Pacific History* 29, no. 2 (1994): 242; Adrienne L. Kaeppler, *Eighteenth Century Studies* 28, no. 1 (1994): 158; John Frow, *UTS Review* 2, no. 1 (1996): 182–85; Harry Liebersohn, *Journal of Modern History* 68, no. 3 (1996): 617–19.

25. Nicholas Thomas and Diane Losche, eds., *Double Vision: Art Histories and Colonial Histories in the Pacific* (Cambridge, 1999).

26. *Meanjin* 56, nos. 3/4 (1997): 497–99.

CHAPTER 8

More Celebrated than Read:
The Work of Norma McArthur

I. C. Campbell

Island Populations of the Pacific, by Norma McArthur.
Canberra: Australian National University Press, 1967.

FOR A generation the name Norma McArthur was the device to terminate any discussion on population issues in the Pacific. Such was her authority that although she offered her work as a challenge, it was received as a declaration that historians were unable to either question or emulate. In the history of culture contact, population trends ought to have been a central question because nothing can be more fundamental to the history of a community than its physical survival. Yet historians during the Davidson-dominated decades were preoccupied with the more familiar themes of trade, conversion, the politics of centralization, and the incursion of European authority.

Population questions were prominent during what might be called the "pre-Ph.D." era. Nineteenth-century observers were ubiquitously convinced of a terminal and inevitable population decline; labor employers and recruiters continually sought new reservoirs to tap; colonial officials sought to establish the facts and searched for remedies to the observed or supposed decrease. Some scholars tried with more or less rigor to ascertain and understand the trends.[1] By the time of World War II the perception of population had changed: decline had ceased; numbers had leveled off before contemporaries had realized it, and were rapidly increasing. By the 1950s they were rising sharply, driven by increasing rates of infant survival and improved childhood health, so that the population problem now became one of excess rather than deficiency.

This was the point at which Norma McArthur (1921–84), a demographer at the Australian National University (ANU), entered the scene. A proposal had been made to hold coordinated censuses for a number of territories across the Pacific in 1956, standardized for data as well as time of execution. McArthur was an adviser to the project, and analyzed the data that would give governments reliable baseline information as well as an understanding of the principles that would determine future population trends. Fundamental to such explanation was understanding population structure. McArthur's importance is that she brought mathematical rigor to these questions. She established data not just for 1956 but placed that data against the context of population history that seemed so empirically secure as well as mathematically sophisticated that there was nothing historians could do but cite her. In its final form, this work was not published until 1967, as *Island Populations of the Pacific*, but her work was known to colleagues long before then. With this book the population question was closed to the "new" Pacific historians almost as soon as it was opened.[2]

Island Populations was not written primarily for historians, but the historical sections covered the demographic history of the major archipelagos (Fiji, Tonga, Samoa, Cook Islands, and French Polynesia) since first European contact, attempting to establish population sizes, the subsequent changes in size and structure, and the reasons for these changes. McArthur's basic theme was that "if enough were known about these populations at various times in their history, there would be no need to invoke the psychological reasons which Pitt-Rivers and others believed responsible for the supposedly universal decline in island populations." Not only was population decline not universal, but where it did occur it could be attributed not to "a ubiquitous inferiority complex" but to "shattering epidemics . . . which through age selective mortality, left its age structure distorted." In asserting this she laid down a challenge: her hypothesis, she said, was not proven, but "the case is put and it is for you to judge" (xvi).

Each chapter begins with a brief sketch of the archipelagic contact history, followed by a discussion of precensal estimates, including the means by which they were made. Sometimes, as in the case of Fiji, these were made by a count of villages over a certain stretch of coast line, an estimate of the numbers associated with each, to give a density per coastal mile, multiplied by the total coast line length, with a proportion added to allow for the possibility of an inhabited interior. Such a method is tolerable for small islands, but the larger the island the greater the likelihood of error, and it is totally inappropriate for islands such as Viti Levu (2–4). Elsewhere, Samoa and Cook Islands, for example, the early estimates are mainly missionary estimations, made with varying degrees of formality and rigor. The reader is thus very properly prepared early on to be skeptical about early estimates. Discussion of them with their circumstances and rationale follow. McArthur's accounts are prudent and seem faithful to the sources. A recurring theme of these early estimates, however, is that they were made cautiously and conservatively, by reflective men who generally thought that they were more likely to overestimate than underestimate the sizes of populations. When they revised their estimates downward, or revised their predecessors' estimates downward, McArthur was apt to infer that the incidence of population decline was overstated, even imagined. Reports of abandoned agricultural areas and decayed village sites she did not accept as evidence of reduction so much as of mobility (5; also Samoa chapter).

This rigorous pruning of population estimates does not seem to have been ideological. Rather, it was methodological, merely the operation of a scientist's Occam's razor, and a refusal to make claims for which there was not adequate evidence. McArthur accepted assertions of population decrease where she had documentary evidence—or at least reports of sufficient antiquity—for epidemics, thus discrediting earlier nonepidemic theories. This was her intention, but it was also her assumption, and one made convincing for historians by her status as a scientist and her reputation for rigor. Her hallmark method was to recalculate mortality rates by calibrating one category of data against another, leading invariably to the conclusion that the deaths from epidemics were overestimated by contemporary or near-contemporary reporters (7–11). Extrapolating from the known subsequent population, McArthur revised the pre-epidemic population estimates downward (11). For subsequent enumerations, she exposed the uncertainties of the counting and the inexactitude of the methods used, to demonstrate that the impression of precision given by historical numbers was misplaced. The result was a consistent trend in her work toward lower estimates rather than higher ones, and for lower rates of decrease (from smaller initial populations) than more dramatic ones (100–102). There follow discussions of the features of demographic change, and particularly the point at which numerical decline gave way first to stabilization, and then to increase (26–37).

Crucial to these discussions is an understanding of the mechanics of population change. In particular, whether the effect of epidemics may be more severe in the long term than the immediate would depend on the variables of each case:

> Provided the age structure of this diminished population was favourable to rapid increase, it might have regained its former size before the next lethal outbreak ... Had the age structure of the population been altered by the early epidemic mortality ... its recovery even under favourable conditions, would have been slow. (6)

Alternatively, after an epidemic the appearance of population recovery could in fact be the result of lower death rates because the deaths of the aged had been advanced perhaps a few years by the epidemic. The fewer deaths in those postepidemic years might mask a period of fewer births to the extent that population might actually increase (29). Obviously growth of this kind could not be sustained for long, and hence the importance of understanding the dynamics of the changes. On other occasions, the population might fall in years free of illness. This is because a previous epidemic had distorted the population structure, thus diminishing that population's reproductive potential. In other words, if an epidemic had reduced the number of girls approaching reproductive age, then the number of births would be reduced until the next cohort of female children (albeit a reduced one) came to maturity (30). There are reasons for thinking that mortality of some historical epidemics (both directly and indirectly) had this effect (30–31). After the point of stabilization was passed, the rates of increase of population were likewise responsive most of all to structural changes: increasingly as infant survival rates improved, so the reproductive capacity a couple of decades farther on was enhanced. Population trends were also susceptible to the direct effects of migration either inward or outward, but the most significant variable was the size and fertility of the young adult female population.

Besides reports of epidemics, other sources of demographic data, in particular the information given to census officials and the records of registration of births and deaths, were subject to wide margins of error throughout the first half of the twentieth century. It is possible to calculate the incidence of such errors on internal evidence, but such estimates provide only minima, and the effect on demographic trends and processes remained uncertain (46–50).

A salutary aspect of McArthur's rigorous skepticism is the conclusion that the population changes did not follow uniform trajectories. For each island group she went to the sources closest to the events, scrutinized the reports, evaluated their reliability, and constructed the trajectory of population change that could be most strongly supported by the evidence. For French Polynesia, for example, McArthur's conclusion that "the most optimistic estimate for Tahiti's population at the time of their discovery . . . would be in the vicinity of 35,000 and probably less" is an extrapolation from more reliable later figures, in conjunction with the general pattern of observation over a lengthy period and the manifest inadequacy of assessments by the earliest visitors (260). The evidence supports a steep decrease by 1797, mainly through epidemics, but assisted by war and infanticide, so much so that there was a marked imbalance of the sexes (a female deficit) until 1848 with obvious implications for reproductive capacity. In the Marquesas the opacity of the vague and contradictory data can be illuminated a little from an apparently reliable set of data from 1889, which shows a deficiency in the size of the 1870s birth cohort. There are a number of possibilities, including a deficiency in the size of the parent cohort for those years.

Tahiti was the eponymous example for the whole Pacific, shaping historians' perceptions. It had always had a central place in Pacific Islands historiography in the pre-Davidson era because of its primacy in exploration, mission, commercial, and imperialist history. It was the focal and metonymic image of the encounter between the decadent, sophisticated West and the quintessence of primitivism. In proportion that Tahiti fed the Fatal Impact interpretation, McArthur's revision of Tahitian populations estimates was crucial in reconstructing the counterhypothesis. She seemed to prove that the impact had not been fatal, or not so fatal that Tahitian depopulation was more than a temporary artifact of altered population structure, partly due to indigenous causes. The argument was perfectly judged in time and tenor to fit the outlook of the Davidson school with which McArthur's working life was virtually coextensive.

In her conclusion, McArthur explained the meaning of over three hundred pages of close, detailed argument. It was evident that different things were happening to population sizes in the two half centuries either side of 1900. The striking feature of the later period is the very great increase in size, with the overall population trebling (345). Except for the extreme cases of Fiji and Marquesas, the nineteenth-century populations changed little in the previous half century. Data before about

1850 were so unreliable and inconsistent that attempting to define con-
tact-moment sizes was pointless (346). Nevertheless, it was probable that
in some cases populations dropped "following European contact, but
not necessarily because of it" (346). Introduced diseases certainly were
a factor in the southern Cook Islands, for example, but this was by no
means universal.

The critical point in McArthur's argument was apparently overlooked by most who have cited her work: an epidemic will not cause
sustained population decline unless it affects the age or sex structure of
the population in specific ways. Thus it is less important how many people were killed than which ones were. For a population to halve in thirty
years at an even rate, an annual decline of one percent would suffice if
given a start by a few epidemics fairly close together. Probable rates of
infanticide could achieve the sustained decline (347–48). When additional factors like war and famine are considered, it becomes very difficult to know whether these or imported diseases were more responsible
for depopulation: any factor causing a deficiency in births over a given
period will have later and possibly extended consequences for population sizes; the addition to that of small population losses caused by even
low-impact epidemics could create a surplus of deaths over births. In
the absence of full data sets, there is what some might find an uncomfortable degree of the hypothetical in this argument, but the point is that
death has multiple causes and not always uniform results. Depopulation
is multifactorial. The 1918 influenza pandemic is instructive: Western
Samoa is the notorious case of high mortality, but not only did the population size recover quickly; according to McArthur, "Tahiti's is the
only population which clearly shows the imprint of the epidemic in its
age structure . . . and there is no trace in the Western Samoan population" (353). Finally, since even twentieth-century governments had difficulty establishing accurately the size and structures of their populations, how much less could one have confidence in earlier estimates?

It may be imagined that McArthur was both gratified and disappointed with the response to the book. Reviewers generally lauded her
work. Her sometime colleague, Gerard Ward, called it "the definitive
statement on Pacific populations" and considered her challenging
remark about her case not being proven to be "perhaps too cautious."[3]
Even Ward, however, was more concerned with the numerical data
than with the argument, which he mentions without scrutinizing. Other
reviews were generally complimentary, and endorsed her specific data

and her overall argument about the significance of age-selective mortality.[4] Island historians following her accepted her estimates of population sizes at first contact, and relied on her for reporting the trajectory of nineteenth-century populations and playing down the Fatal Impact. None took up her interpretative framework, and many of them appear to have ignored her work altogether. None engaged her in written debate. Many seem to have regarded her book as definitive, and since the issue was thereby closed, her arguments seem to have been regarded as of no further interest.

Among reviews, one stood out for its willingness to take up McArthur's challenge.[5] Peter Pirie challenged her skepticism of missionary population estimates, building a case out of a remark she made about the Samoan estimate of 1845 by missionaries, yet his own inference from this estimate is merely that it is "a useful guide to the order of magnitudes involved." This is hardly different from McArthur's own conclusion, but the implication is that her use of evidence was loose and her argument predetermined. In fact, her argument does not rely exclusively on these data, or on data of this sort, and her skepticism is shaped by the overall pattern of data obtained for nineteenth-century Samoa. The second fatal flaw he saw in her work was the apparent contradiction that while fertility and fecundity were strong enough for Samoans to maintain their population against the losses by disease and warfare, in the era before contact the same fecundity without heightened mortality was sufficient merely to keep the population stable in precontact times. The answer is that population growth is not determined solely by biological potential, but by social and political considerations—that is, by deliberate control of fertility. The third apparently fatal flaw was monocausality in the case of the Marquesas, where the decline was attributed to the age-structural ripple effect of the great famine of the early years of the nineteenth century. This, too, is unfair to McArthur, whose discussion of the Marquesan data is detailed but shows no clear pattern. The point was not that the ripple effect was a single and sufficient cause, but that such an event was bound to have some long-term effect, "but whether [the diminution] was a consequence of the famine . . . , or the almost incessant internal conflicts, or mortality from introduced diseases . . . seems impossible to unravel from the evidence now available" (348).

Pirie found a fourth fatal flaw: McArthur overlooked some epidemiological possibilities, in particular, the loss of fertility associated with the endemicity of certain new but not immediately fatal diseases (gon-orrhea and syphilis) and the contribution to death rates of slow-acting diseases such as tuberculosis. The point is a fair one, but not so the charge that McArthur neglected the concept of biological isolation. Sim-ilarly, the cumulative effect of successive or simultaneous infections can have serious consequences in the absence of major recorded epidemics. In this, however, Pirie seems to recommend McArthur should adhere to a disease explanation when she has no evidence. Yet repeatedly, she asserts that the evidence is inadequate to explain the apparent popula-tion effect, and also that the population reports are themselves so inse-cure that the presence of disease (or other causes) cannot be inferred from them.

Pirie himself seemed to want to make an intellectual leap from pos-sibilities to tentative probabilities with his own alternative to McArthur's minimalist estimates. This was the possibility of long-term ecological cycles in which populations alternately expanded and contracted with possibly quite large amplitudes. In a provocative but understated chal-lenge to McArthur's expressed intention, he wrote that there might indeed be a psychological contribution to depopulation "in view of the close relationship now [1968] known to exist between physical and men-tal health." This point is not developed and in the end he accused McArthur of dismissing her earliest observers as "fools, knaves or liars." The allegation is unjust.

Implicit in this review was an approach to the population question that would arise much later, but in the meantime historians of the Pacific were content to take McArthur on trust and let her have the last word. In his magisterial *Ancient Tahitian Society*, Douglas Oliver admitted that "Dr. McArthur's treatment of the few eyewitness estimates is so detailed and authoritative that I am left with little more to do than echo her findings."[6] Many other studies cite her book in their bibliographies, without any other citation and often with no discussion of indigenous populations.[7] Others cite the book, and have passing references to pop-ulations, but do not engage her ideas and often do not even mention the details.[8] Others for whom her work might have been considered rele-vant make no mention of it at all.[9] Deryck Scarr in one general text seems to endorse her work, but in another takes her conclusions so much for granted as not to mention her.[10] Kerry Howe cited her, used her, was clearly influenced by her, and considered not only that she had proven her case, but that she was a cornerstone of the anti–Fatal Impact thesis.[11]

Less convinced by the anti–Fatal Impact orthodoxy, Campbell did not cite her, referred to her obliquely, used her figures, but did not adopt her argument; in a different work he made no mention, but later gave her an index entry and discussed her ideas with some dissent, but made no bibliographic citation.[12] Donald Denoon purportedly took up the issues, but he clearly considers her merely a "pioneer" of the field, and asked, for example, why populations declined when there were no epidemics.[13] Overall, McArthur was either ignored by historians or became an authority to be cited rather than a scholar to be either argued against or applied.

While the silence on McArthur was perhaps because her arguments were very much in tune with the intellectual currents of her own time and place, demography later became the subject of excited debate as the result of the work of a scholar distinctly not so in tune. David Stannard's book on Hawaiian population caused a storm of both indignant and measured response,[14] as well as enthusiastic acceptance among activist Hawaiians. Whereas McArthur's case was built on a careful and closely calibrated study of evidence relating directly to postcontact populations, Stannard took an ecological approach, incorporating issues of productivity, carrying capacity, growth rates, and historical accounts of Hawaiian industry and cultivation. He presented a very powerful argument that there were no economic, mathematical, or physiological reasons why the precontact population of Hawai'i should have been as low as the 100,000 to 200,000 that had become the accepted estimate, let alone for the reported and unpublished inclination of McArthur that it was even lower.[15] Since there was the capacity for the population to be much larger, and in the absence of reliable estimates, Stannard challenged the orthodoxists to come up with evidence that it was not. The best response was Andrew Bushnell's, which was that if there had been such a large population, then the massive number of deaths necessary by 1803, and the epidemics needed to cause them, could not have escaped the attention of the frequent visitors of the 1790s.[16] The absence of evidence became interpreted as evidence of absence; whatever the logical inadequacy of the syllogism, Bushnell's counterchallenge had a compelling force.

Stannard's response to earlier critics, in a Book Review Forum in *Pacific Studies,* was more germane to McArthur's thesis than his original argument.[17] The issue was whether populations could collapse fast enough to account for 800,000[18] becoming only 142,000 by 1824. By

McArthur's reasoning, it seems unlikely. In a later publication Stannard demonstrated that it could, citing mission evidence of sharp declines in various localities in the 1820s and later. Not only were deaths numerous and not confined to the elderly, but relative or absolute childlessness had become common. The fertility of the Hawaiians dropped not just because of age-selective mortality but because of disease-induced infertility among those who lived. This was a variable that did not enter into McArthur's calculations. Simultaneous or near-simultaneous infections caused more severe morbidity and mortality than single infections, and evidence for such multiple infections was abundant. As if this were not enough, stress or depression has also been shown to depress fertility. He concludes, "The vast majority of what should have been the native peoples' natural replacements simply were not born—and most of those who were born did not live long enough to reproduce."[19]

The implications of Stannard's conclusions are profound. Much of McArthur's argument about population sizes was based on assumptions of epidemics being periodical, and that if death rates were elevated in intermediate years, they were not so much larger than birth rates to justify rejecting the evidence for lower initial populations. This is not to say that her reconstruction of populations for most of the nineteenth century is incorrect, but in many cases there was quite a considerable gap of years between first contact and first literate foreign residents. In Samoa no one could make credible reports of population size or density until about 1840, but there had been fairly steady if not numerous contacts since the beginning of the century, and the first significant contact in 1787; in Tonga likewise there was enough contact from the 1790s before the arrival of permanent missionaries in 1826. The same is true of Tahiti and even more so for the Marquesas. If populations could collapse as fast as Stannard argues, then the first-contact populations were very likely much larger than McArthur's estimates, and the role of disease was more important than she thought. This does not impair her points about the capacity of populations to recover from single epidemics, or about the importance of age-selective mortality, nor does it weaken her suggestion that there are other things besides disease that contribute to long-term population declines. It does show, however, that her work can no longer be regarded as definitive: there is more evidence to be added to her database for the understanding of the early impact of Western contact on island populations.

It would seem unthinkable to revive Pitt-Rivers and Rivers,[20] whose work on population has been oversimplified and derided as reducing the causes of depopulation to "psychological" factors or a "sense of inferiority" arising from the encounter with Western civilization. But if McArthur's arguments can be revisited and reassessed, so can these earlier works. Indeed, while McArthur wanted to differentiate herself from them, in many ways they anticipated her own arguments especially about the importance of population structure for understanding the effect of specific events and for long-term trends. Similarly, Denoon's essay "Pacific Island Depopulation"[21] is anticipated in important respects by both Rivers and Pitt-Rivers. Their arguments were that population change is often multifactorial, indeed, that single events were unlikely to have much effect. They certainly contested the orthodox view that disease was the simple and sufficient cause, and stressed cultural and psychological conditions. Stannard and Kunitz,[22] and even in places McArthur herself, do not seem to be far from the same position.

Yet McArthur implies that not only did Pitt-Rivers and others believe psychological causes to be responsible, but she even suggests that that was the common and popular belief, making her role the reinstatement of disease at the same time as she sought to diminish the scale of depopulation. In this respect she fit perfectly into the ANU perception of Pacific history as it developed in the 1950s and 1960s: that on the one hand inflated the perception of the Fatal Impact and on the other derided earlier scholars as deluded if not fanciful. In doing this, ANU scholars claimed both a moral dignity and an intellectual superiority by contriving differences between themselves and their predecessors.

Though not often cited, McArthur's findings became a fundamental if subliminal tenet of the thinking of the ANU school, so effective that when after thirty years scholars looked again at population issues, they seemed to regard McArthur as the starting point for further research. It is likely that she will suffer the fate of being shifted from orthodoxy to obscurity by the passions engendered by revived population debate just as her generation disregarded earlier work in the passions aroused by the Fatal Impact thesis, which is perhaps more current now than ever before. As to the main purpose of *Island Populations of the Pacific*, historians have not yet turned their attention to the study of mid- to late-twentieth-century population movements, and when they do, McArthur's data will prove invaluable as the baseline for the beginning of the new era of Pacific Islander migration.

Notes

1. W.H.R. Rivers, ed., *Essays on the Depopulation of Melanesia* (Cambridge, 1922); G. H. Lane-Fox Pitt-Rivers, *The Clash of Culture and the Conflict of Races* (London, 1927); Stephen Roberts, *Population Problems of the Pacific* (London, 1927).

2. This was not McArthur's only publication of relevance to be cited by historians. But it is her major work, the one on which her reputation principally rested, and the one most referred to. For her complete bibliography, see D. E. Yen, "Norma McArthur: A Personal Postscript," *Journal of Pacific History* 19, no. 1 (1984): 60–63. See also Ann Moyal, *Breakfast with Beaverbrook: Memoirs of an Independent Woman* (Sydney, 1995), 125, 132–33.

3. R. Gerard Ward, *Journal of Pacific History* 3 (1967): 230–31.

4. For example, Jane Hainline Underwood, *American Anthropologist* 71, no. 1 (1969): 172–73; Philip Snow, *Geographical Journal* 135, no. 1 (1969): 110.

5. Peter Pirie, "Polynesian Populations: Review," *Australian Geographical Studies* 6 (1968): 175–81.

6. Douglas L. Oliver, *Ancient Tahitian Society*, vol. 1: *Ethnography* (Honolulu, 1974), 529–30n. 7.

7. Peter France, *The Charter of the Land: Custom and Colonization in Fiji* (Melbourne, 1969); Noel Rutherford, ed., *Friendly Islands: A History of Tonga* (Melbourne, 1977); Greg Dening, *Islands and Beaches: Discourses on a Silent Land. Marquesas, 1774–1880* (Melbourne, 1980); H. E. Maude, *Slavers in Paradise: The Peruvian Labour Trade in Polynesia, 1862–1864* (Canberra, 1981); Elizabeth Wood Ellem, *Queen Salote of Tonga: The Story of an Era, 1900–1965* (Auckland, 1999).

8. Colin Newbury, *Tahiti Nui* (Honolulu, 1980); Philip Houghton, *People of the Great Ocean* (Cambridge, 1996); Donald Denoon et al., eds., *The Cambridge History of the Pacific Islanders* (Cambridge, 1997); J.A.R. Miles, *Infectious Diseases: Colonising the Pacific?* (Dunedin, 1997).

9. Noel Rutherford, *Shirley Baker and the King of Tonga* (Melbourne, 1971); Sione Latukefu, *Church and State in Tonga: The Wesleyan Methodist Missionaries and Political Development, 1822–1875* (Canberra, 1974); Caroline Ralston, *Grass Huts and Warehouses: Pacific Beach Communities of the Nineteenth Century* (Canberra, 1977); John Young, *Adventurous Spirits: Australian Immigrant Society in Pre-cession Fiji* (Brisbane, 1984); David Routledge, *Matanitu: The Struggle for Power in Early Fiji* (Suva, 1985); Edwin N. Ferdon, *Early Tonga as the Explorers Saw It, 1616–1810* (Tucson, 1987); Nicholas Thomas, *Marquesan Societies: Inequality and Political Transformations in Eastern Polynesia* (Oxford, 1990); David A. Chappell, *Double Ghosts: Oceanian Voyagers on Euroamerican Ships* (Armonk, NY, 1997); Brij V. Lal and Kate Fortune, eds., *The Pacific Islands: An Encyclopaedia* (Honolulu, 2000).

10. Respectively, Deryck Scarr, *The History of the Pacific Islands: Kingdoms of the Reefs* (Melbourne, 1990); idem, *A History of the Pacific Islands: Passages through Tropical Time* (Richmond, UK, 2001).

11. K. R. Howe, *The Loyalty Islands: A History of Culture Contacts, 1840–1900* (Canberra, 1977), x, 145; idem, *Where the Waves Fall* (Sydney, 1984), 351.

12. I. C. Campbell, respectively, *A History of the Pacific Islands* (Christchurch, 1989); idem, *"Gone Native" in Polynesia: Captivity Narratives and Experiences from the South Pacific* (Westport, CT, 1998); idem, *Worlds Apart: A History of the Pacific Islands* (Christchurch, 2003).

13. Donald Denoon, "Pacific Island Depopulation: Natural or Un-natural History?" in *New Countries and Old Medicine*, ed. Linda Bryder and Derek Dow (Auckland, 1995), 324–39.

14. David E. Stannard, *Before the Horror: The Population of Hawai'i on the Eve of Western Contact* (Honolulu, 1989), with critical responses by Eleanor C. Nordyke (105–13) and Robert C. Schmitt (114–21) and a reply by Stannard (122–46). Two reviewers strongly opined that Nordyke and Schmitt had simply fallen back on their old arguments rather than engaging with Stannard's evidence. Robert V. Wells, *Journal of Interdisciplinary History* 21, no. 9 (1990): 159–60; Patricia Nelson Limerick, "The Multicultural Island," *American Historical Review* 97, no. 1 (1992): 121–35.

15. Stannard, *Before the Horror*, xvi.

16. Andrew F. Bushnell, "'The Horror' Reconsidered: An Evaluation of the Historical Evidence for Population Decline in Hawaii, 1778–1803," *Pacific Studies* 16, no. 3 (1993): 115–61.

17. *Pacific Studies* 13, no. 3 (1990): 255–301 (reviews by Terry L. Hunt, Ann F. Ramenofsky, Francis L. Black, and Lynette Cruz and J. Kalani English, and response by David E. Stannard).

18. This was Stannard's estimate for the purposes of debate; he arrived at the figure by consistently taking the conservative end of the range of possibilities for growth and sustainability factors. His argument overall supports a case for an even higher estimate. For example, *Before the Horror*, 37.

19. David E. Stannard, "Disease and Infertility: A New Look at the Demographic Collapse of Native Populations in the Wake of Western Contact," *Journal of American Studies* 24, no. 3 (1990): 350.

20. See note 1, above.

21. Denoon, "Pacific Islands Depopulation."

22. S. J. Kunitz, *Disease and Social Diversity: The European Impact on the Health of Non-Europeans* (Cambridge, 1994), as represented by Denoon.

CHAPTER 9

Two Pacific Biographies:
Hubert Murray and Father Damien

Francis West

Hubert Murray: The Australian Pro-consul, by Francis West.
Melbourne: Oxford University Press, 1968.

Holy Man: Father Damien of Molokai, by Gavan Daws.
New York: Harper and Row, 1973. Paperback reprint, Honolulu:
University of Hawai'i Press, 1984.

FIFTY YEARS after Jim Davidson's inaugural lecture, very few Pacific historians have published biographies, as distinct from sketches. This lack may reflect assumptions about the role of an individual in history. Some of the great and good among British historical scholars in the 1950s and 1960s warned historians off biography: it was simply not history. Sir Lewis Namier condemned biography because historians lacked essential qualification in normal and abnormal psychology. Sir Geoffrey Elton dismissed biography because focus on an individual life entailed a false perspective on its times and relied on out-of-date theories in another discipline: psychology. By contrast, in America William Langer, as president of the American Historical Association, was setting the next assignment for historians in 1957: they must acquire mastery of "the coldly penetrating calculus" of psychoanalysis.[1] Pacific historians, already in need of interdisciplinarity with social anthropology to understand Melanesian and Polynesian cultures in contact with the European one, might well hesitate over biography when faced with yet another discipline.

Twenty-four years after Davidson's lecture, his successor Gavan Daws, noting that historians of the Pacific "have not produced much in the way of biography," observed that in reading the lives actually published "it becomes clear that among biographers there has been next to no interest in trying to account in psychological terms for the ways in which their subjects lived their lives in the Pacific."[2] Only four "schol-arly" biographies were listed by Bronwen Douglas in her 1999 survey of British Pacific historiography: *Hubert Murray*, the first to be pub-lished in 1968; lives of two other colonial governors, William Macgregor (1971) and John Thurston (1973, 1980); and of a trader, Peter Dillon (1975).[3] Gavan Daws's *Holy Man*, published in 1973,[4] was excluded from her list by Oxford's British imperial brief.[5] All five biographies were island-orientated, but their authors were Europeans writing of a European, although aware that Islanders were not a passive factor. Of the five, only Gavan Daws explicitly invoked psychoanalytical concepts to explore a life. Neither Roger Joyce with Macgregor nor Deryck Scarr with Thurston devoted much space, still less discussion, to the early years of their protagonists, although the first four or five years of life, in Freudian theory, determined later personality. In *Hubert Murray* (5) I explicitly declined psychological speculation since there survived no reliable evidence for his early childhood, while later evidence showed a consistency between the private and the public man that suggested con-scious, not unconscious, motives for his actions.

Daws, via Cushing Strout, accepted Erik Erikson's ego-psychol-ogy:[6] an individual's "thoughts, feelings and actions can be understood as a process over time of an unconscious effort—*in conjunction with con-scious aims*—to achieve his own identity."[7] He was concerned with the motives, conscious and unconscious, which led Europeans to the South Seas. In the case of Father Damien de Veuster, youngest son of a Bel-gian small farmer, he described what his subject believed was a divine vocation to devote twenty-five of his forty-nine years of life to Catholic missionary priesthood in Hawai'i, the last sixteen in the lonely, dread-ful conditions of the leper settlement of Molokai. Daws wrote biogra-phy as psychohistory. Murray, classically educated at Oxford, the bar-rister son of a prominent Irish-Australian pastoralist and politician, by contrast had chosen to go to British New Guinea as chief judicial offi-cer when a man of settled personality at the age of forty-three (15–34), and, despite conditions of life he disliked, to remain as governor of the colony Australia renamed Papua for the uniquely long term of thirty-three years. In neither his private nor his public papers were there symp-toms of the unconscious psychosexual and psychosocial drives assumed in psychoanalytical theory.

Murray's official papers were made available by Paul Hasluck, min-ister for territories, before the fifty-year archival limit then in force. His private papers survived in Australian libraries, letters and memorabilia in his family's possession, and parallel archival collections of papers of contemporary politicians, ministers, and public servants in Australia and in Papua, some still alive to supply oral testimony. It was possible to know how Murray saw his world, how contemporaries saw him and it, what they thought, said, and did *at the time,* as distinct from retrospective recollections in oral testimony and in his own published writings. "The Murray policy" meant peaceful penetration to establish with a minimum of bloodshed law and order throughout Papua—paramountcy of Papuan interests over European in land, labor, and development policies. Evidence for Murray's policy was clear, but that for its impact in any particular Papuan group was less so. For, apart from his own observation on judicial circuit or tours of inspection, Murray depended on reported observations by his officers; he and they might or might not be right in their perception of Papuan societies. His government anthropologist, F. E. Williams, from the mid-1920s studied a few Papuan societies and social anthropologists—Bronislaw Malinowski, Margaret Mead, Reo Fortune—published field studies of others, but, as Williams told Murray in 1925, "we know little, but the native knows less of us" (218). With few intensive field studies of differing areas, Murray's biography did not fully cover the practice, as distinct from the policy, of Murray's government that had been eulogized by an earlier biographer, Lewis Lett.

According to Lett, Murray was the only man alive to whom Australian governments could have turned in 1907 to realize their aspirations in Papua, every phase of whose life had prepared him for such a role.[8] To Lucy Mair, familiar with colonial policies in Africa and quoting Lord Hailey's judgment on Murray, to John Legge, familiar with both Fiji and Australian colonial policy, Murray's was simply benevolent police rule; James McAuley, a poet teaching government at the Australian School of Pacific Administration, added that Murray's published reports were high-grade advertising matter rather than factual reportage.[9] But none of these writers had access to the unpublished official and nonofficial papers—indeed, only one of them, Legge, was a historian and only Lett, a long-time resident of Papua, had direct personal knowledge of Murray, their main source being Murray's printed *Annual Reports* to the Australian parliament, his own published works, and contemporary newspaper article reports of him and Papua.

The myth—that Murray on taking office had a clearly thought-out policy—vanished in my biography. In its place was the portrait of a man who in 1906 believed his first duty was to Europeans whose enterprise would develop a resource-rich territory (122). Papuans must be protected from incidental ill-treatment, but native land and labor must be made available to Europeans if Papua were ever to dispense with the annual Australian subsidy. Only at the end of 1912 did Murray see that possibility, and turn to the distinctive policy that came to bear his name. Pacification of the whole of Papua was the first step, using the 1890s methods of Macgregor: patrols by European officers with an escort of armed native constables, village constables being appointed to maintain government influence and to report offenses against Native Regulations that covered every aspect of Papuan life. Only in 1918 did development of Papua by Papuans become an objective. Native plantations were then established to grow cash crops to provide, through native taxation, resources for native hospitals, medical assistants, and subsidies to missions' elementary and technical schools. From 1923 village councilors were appointed to facilitate communication between government and Papuans destined to become peasant proprietors within village communities, not as individuals, which policy aimed to preserve. In 1929, village councilors might sit as assessors to advise resident magistrates on sentences under European law, for Murray perceived no native customary law that could be codified (230–31). Always with very limited resources in money and men, to lift Stone Age people to the level of contemporary Filipinos, said Murray in 1939, might take a hundred years (257); meanwhile, he expected the "dreary round of arrest and imprisonment" to continue (253).

The biography had a mixed reception. Lucy Mair, an established scholar in the field of African and Papuan administration, thought it "likely to be the definitive biography, being neither idolatry nor iconoclasm but judiciously evaluating Murray in the context of his times"[10] John Legge, another established scholar who had written on Fijian and Papuan administration, objected to the chronological and thematic balance of the book. He pointed to its concentration on Murray's administration up to the 1920s and to the unbalance that came from its arrangement by chapters that seemed chronological, but actually discussed issues of colonial rule running across the whole of Murray's governorship, failing adequately to cover its last decade. In consequence, the development of Murray's feelings and thoughts was obscured by a mass of administrative detail. Why, for example, was little said of his unsatisfactory first marriage of forty years? Legge recognized the case for concentrating on the innovative years of Murray's governorship up to the 1920s, but the result was a lack of satisfying biographical detail. He had a valid point. In my earlier research on Norman administrators in Anglo-Saxon-Danish England—alien rulers, as were colonial administrators, in a cross-cultural situation[11]—personalities are unknowable, but the actions of the justiciar, the king's "other self," were a matter of record. With Murray, biographical details were included when they seemed relevant to administrative history, and to fill out the portrait, a companion volume of Murray's letters was needed to reveal the man.[12] A canon of medieval scholarship still applied: what mattered was what was important to the man's past, not what was important to the present. Hence an imbalance: pioneering interested Murray; established routine did not (275). Nevertheless Legge deemed the final judgment "gentle and just" with no extravagant claims for Murray's native administration, which my epilogue compared with that of notable British governors: Gordon in Fiji, Lugard in Nigeria, Cameron in Tanganyika (263–76).[13]

European academics working in the new University of Papua New Guinea were less kind, with the exception of Charles Rowley, the professor of political studies at the University of Papua New Guinea.[14] Kevin Green, an archivist, considered that I had corrected many "false judgements" about Murray but had added little new information either about the persons or the place he administered.[15] Peter Biskup suggested that Murray used the work of others to claim credit for originality.[16] Hank Nelson emphasized gaps between Murray's policies and their implementation.[17] In a historiographical essay nearly twenty years later, Roger Thompson quoted these, but not Mair's and Legge's reviews, asserting that Murray had been set up on a pedestal almost as high as Lett's.[18] But the major challenge, not to scholarship but to values, came from Murray Groves, an anthropologist, who denounced Murray's administration, "such as it was," as stagnant, paternalistic, meddlesome, and uncreative, neither enlightened nor progressive even in its own time compared with the British in Africa and Asia.[19] Plainly, I should have included the Mandated Territory of New Guinea and the neighboring British Solomon Islands Protectorate, unfavorable compared by contemporaries with Murray's Papua, in the concluding discussion of African and Fijian governorships.

The context of *Hubert Murray* was decolonization, and it was easy, if anachronistic, to condemn Murray for failing in the 1920s and 1930s to prepare Papuans for independence forty years later. He could also be accused of racism. Had I not ignored the infamous White Women's Protection Ordinance of 1926, which prescribed the death penalty for sexual attack on a European woman but afforded no such protection to Papuan women?[20] I should have mentioned the ordinance, if only because Lett had described Murray's anger over its passage, but it was not important to Murray in the mid-1920s in the same ways as it was to Murray Groves and Amirah Inglis in the late 1960s and early 1970s. The historian, thundered Groves, "has every right, by condemning the values of past generations, to affirm and strengthen the values that he holds dear in his own."[21] His point—history should not be concerned to understand the world as it was, but to help to change it—was the antithesis of a medieval historian's creed: we study the past on its own terms, not ours, to establish what was important to them, not to us; otherwise we repeat the errors of Whig history in distorting the past into a reflection of the present.[22]

That the balance of *Hubert Murray* was weighted toward a history of his administration rather than his personal life was noted by another experienced historian, Geoffrey Bolton, who wrote that I was "not of that school of biographers who write of the tempests within a man's breast, the forces of darkness which hound him," concerned with the mainsprings of character "but only what can be documented with tolerable accuracy."[23] In declining psychoanalytical speculation (5), *Hubert Murray* came under Gavan Daws's stricture: Pacific biographers who "have contented themselves—when they have gone in at all for psychological discussion of their subjects—with commonsense remarks of an informal sort."[24] Individual life histories were "looked at as particular embodiments or exemplifications of a large concrete or general interest to be served." All biographers "have been guided by 'psychological' hunches," but the "question now is whether things might be usefully pushed further, whether in fact biography written as psychohistory might not be a responsible as well as an interesting way of approaching Pacific history." He recognized the methodological difficulties of fragmentary data to assemble patterns rather than any great covering law, but nevertheless Eriksonian ego-psychology could be used as a means "of thinking one's way into the specific situation of . . . a person, so far as the evidence can support it" in order to achieve "heightened sensitivity to the intersections . . . of family-centred difficulties with social and cultural history, for they interact and resonate with each other." Gavan

Daws found Cushing Strout's approach "an attractive enough working basis for attempting biography as psycho-history."[25]

The life of Joseph (in religion, Damien) de Veuster, youngest son of a Flemish farmer and his devout wife, had attracted much pious hagiography,[26] but no psychological explanation in terms of family relationships intersecting with rural Catholic culture and the social history of leprosy in the later nineteenth century. Daws disliked the word *leper*, although that was the usage of Damien and his contemporaries, preferring *Hansen's' disease*, after the discoverer of the bacillus that caused it (xi). Its dreadful, incurable symptoms, the isolation of its victims, he described at length in order to explain how "le bon petit gros Damien" (26), certain of his vocation as a missionary priest of the Congregation of the Sacred Hearts of Jesus and Mary, isolated himself in the leper colony of Kalaupapa on Molokai in the Hawaiian islands, himself contracting the disease in 1878 and dying there in 1889 at the age of forty-nine. Damien was neither a fluent nor a frequent letter writer to his family (50), although significant papers survived in mission archives, in the records of the royal Hawaiian government, and in the material collected for his Cause as a candidate for beatification and sainthood in the Roman Catholic Church. The case for Father Damien's sanctity became a matter of international controversy when he was publicly denounced by an American Protestant minister in Honolulu, Dr. Charles McEwen Hyde, as "a coarse, dirty man, headstrong and bigoted" who had gone to Molokai without orders, had no hand in reforms and improvements, and was impure in his relations with women (12). Robert Louis Stevenson, living in Samoa, publicly defended Damien, a strong handyman who could himself build mission churches, meditate, and mortify himself to be at one with Christ (11–13, 25). How to explain this poorly educated holy man whom his superiors and colleagues found very difficult to work with, who regarded Hawaiians as wicked, promiscuous children?

Daws used psychoanalytical concepts to interpret the life of a man whom many of his contemporaries in Europe regarded as "the most benign of imperialists" (9) and most Catholics as a saint. Damien's father was conventionally religious, but his pious mother gave her daughter Eugenie to the Ursuline nuns and, when she died of typhus, replaced her with her younger sister, Pauline. Auguste, in religion Fr. Pamphile, a brother three years older than Damien, became a priest of the Congregation of Sacred Hearts at Louvain. Damien had played with his brother at being a hermit, took to sleeping on a hard board, not a bed, and in

1858 told his parents that it was "my turn to choose the road I will walk" (21). Not well-educated enough for priesthood without further study at the Picpus house in Paris, on his brother's persuasion he became not a Trappist monk but a postulant of the Sacred Hearts. Hearing the vicar apostolic of Tahiti preach, he became convinced of his vocation to be a missionary, and when his Order was short of workers in Hawai'i asked to go after his brother, who had been chosen, fell ill with typhus. His Superior was less than pleased. What mattered to Damien, wrote Daws, was that he was going and Pamphile was not; he was no longer a follower of his brother. Although he does not make his psychological theory explicit, Daws's explanation assumes both the Oedipus complex and sibling rivalry as driving forces, and adds a self-image: Damien measured himself against the Jesuit missionary Saint Francis Xavier, beside whose portrait he had himself photographed (58). In Hawai'i, where he was ordained priest after less than a year's study at Ahuimanu College, Damien believed that Pamphile, now a theologian at Louvain, was evading responsibility, whereas he, like Christ alone and scorned at the point of death, believed himself "transformed into Christ crucified" among his lepers and, contracting the disease, wished "to be dissolved and to be with Christ" (117).

Another psychoanalytical concept, *thanatos* or death-wish, is implicit in Daws's description of Damien's profession into his Order: prostrate in solemn silence before the altar under a black mortuary pall, amid ritual insistence on the overmastering presence of death (26). And in the leper settlement at Molokai death was always present. Father Damien, quarreling with two priests successively sent to join him, was regarded by his superiors in Honolulu as too demanding, too quick to want things his own way, ill-bred, and lacking common sense. "Personal drives of the most powerful sort produce a version of religious duty unpalatable to those responsible for a prudent equilibrium with the institution" (249). They also marked Damien's relations with Hawaiians. Praying to achieve the spirit of humility, he dismissed traditional Hawaiian medicine as nonsense: "I am a missionary in a corrupt, heretical, idolatrous country" (35). He foresaw "the eternal unhappiness of some who would not obey me" (119), using sweet words, harsh words, thunder, and charity, but also a big stick to break up dances that led to immorality. His duty to God was to save souls who were otherwise damned, but most of all to save his own.

To a nonbeliever, Father Damien invites secular explanation. He may have had no doubts that he was fulfilling God's will for him, but psychoanalytical theory explained personality by Freud's id-psychology of early infancy and Erikson's own ego-psychology of later life, as with Martin Luther.[27] When Daws was writing, psychohistory, with psychobiography as a subfield, was taking institutional shape: an International Psychohistorical Association and an Institute for Psychohistory with its own press and journal, and a less dogmatic but still Freudian Group for the Use of Psychology in History.[28] Psychohistory was "the interdisciplinary study of why man has acted as he has in history, prominently using psychoanalytical principles."[29] Gavan Daws avoided the often arcane psychohistorical jargon that led Frank Vandiver, biographer of Generals Stonewall Jackson and "Black Jack" Pershing, at the 1982 Texas Committee for the Humanities conference, to describe psychobiography as "mired by motivation" in the effort to graft psychological and social sciences onto biography, thus "warping the art."[30] Daws nevertheless implicitly accepted Freudian concepts in explaining Father Damian. Although he avoided the determinism that reduced motivation to a single factor—for example, psychosexual development in infancy— he asserted that "we all have our Oedipus complexes," and came close to explaining Damien by sibling rivalry with Father Pamphile (31, 44). He accepted a psychoanalytical explanation of holiness, as his predominantly Catholic reviewers pointed out.

Daws was faced, wrote the reviewer Nelson Algren, with the mystery of personal integrity, which he unsentimentally described without really attempting to resolve.[31] Another, A. J. Hamilton, complained that Daws did not employ some of the more available psychohistorical tools to explore the peasant-ascetic quality of Damien, adding that Daws became tedious because of his difficulty in grasping Catholic tradition.[32] As a history of leprosy in the late nineteenth century that exposed "the imperialistic and social thinking of the period," the book attracted the attention of only two historical journals, both of them Pacific regional, not major European ones, both reviewers being Jesuit priests. Fathers John Eddy and John Bernard McGloin agreed that the author had been judicious in tackling the mystery of personal integrity in an essentially private man, but the mystery remained. Why, asked Eddy, did Damien's awful circumstances sanctify rather than destroy him; was he seeking a cross rather than accepting one? All the Catholic reviewers seem implicitly to assume that a nonbeliever can never explain the mystery of holiness, while a Freudian explanation was ruled out by their Church.[33]

Twenty-seven years after *Holy Man* another biography of Father Damien appeared, followed by his Beautification by Pope John Paul II, at the urging of Mother Teresa, in Brussels in 1995, after the necessary posthumous miracle had been accepted as genuine. Daws's biography was cited only once by Richard Stewart, a Catholic professor of medicine, to correct a factual error: Damien's mother did not die, clutching his photograph to her breast, of shock on hearing his leprosy.[34] The implicit ego-psychology explanation in *Holy Man* was ignored, the mystery of faith, including miracles, proclaimed.

After *Holy Man*, Daws went on to look at five secular Europeans, all from disturbed childhood and family backgrounds, rejected by their own societies and driven to discover themselves and achieve recognition in the South Seas.[35] He still used Erikson's ego-psychology as defined by Cushing Strout: "human beings grow stage by stage into the world," which "for better or worse prepares the individual for an outer reality made up of human traditions and institutions which utilise and thus nourish his developing capacities, attract and moderate his drives, respond to and de-limit his fears and fantasies, and assign to him a position in life appropriate to his psychological powers." He quoted Erikson: "We cannot even begin to encompass a human being without indicating for each stage of his life cycle the framework of social influences and of traditional institutions which determine his perspectives on his more infantile past and on his more adult future."[36] Yet Erikson's work on Martin Luther has not been accepted as good historical scholarship, even by psychohistorians.[37] It has never been accepted by historians of the Reformation period like Geoffrey Elton, while to a philosopher of science like Karl Popper, by the canons of scientific explanation, psychoanalysis was "pseudo science."[38]

After *Hubert Murray*, Arnold Toynbee invited me, as son-in-law and literary executor, to write the life of Hubert's younger brother, Gilbert Murray, OM,[39] who left a mass of personal papers and an unfinished autobiography. Some of this evidence had been available for Hubert Murray. But in writing the life of his brother, from the same family background, close in age, similarly educated at school and at Oxford, their different careers and apparently different personalities—man of action, man of ideas—entailed reconsideration of the usefulness to a historical biographer of psychoanalytical theories. In the absence from the mass of ultimate evidence of repeated patterns of behavior revealing unconscious drives—no Oedipus complex, no sibling rivalry—anti-Freudian,

Darwin-derived birth-order theory seemed to offer a better explanation of siblings who established individual niches.[40] With much more evidence available for the lives not only of the two brothers but of their parents, half sisters, and a half brother born of the same father but of different mothers, genetic inheritance and shared family background seemed more useful than psychoanalytical theory to explain personality. In a context of continuing discoveries in microbiology—DNA, the genetic code—hard science made the Freudian unconsciousness an unnecessary hypothesis. A Nobel Laureate physiologist, Sir Peter Medawar, declared "doctrinaire psychoanalytical theory . . . the most stupendous confidence trick of the twentieth century."[41]

As history, *Hubert Murray* and *Holy Man* provide a record of what two Europeans did and said. Both men were agents of change in the Pacific; their actions were part of that history. But the focus was on indigenous reactions, not on Islanders and their societies as themselves actors and initiators of responses, the focus of later Pacific historians.[42] As biography, *Hubert Murray* seems pre-Freudian conventional, while *Holy Man* seems "new" psychohistory. But fashions change. In 1982 only one of the participating historical biographers at the Texas Conference on biography thought Erikson's psychology had anything to offer history, while the others regarded psychobiography as doubtful because of its reductionist explanation. At most it was a pointer to unconscious motives.[43] *Hubert Murray* and *Holy Man* raise the same issues, still figuring in the ongoing debate: nature or nurture? This is false, because exclusive, alternative. Theory aside, *Hubert Murray* and *Holy Man* both document the role of accident, chance, or luck in the human life.

Notes

1. L. B. Namier, "History: Its Subject Matter and Tasks," *History Today* 32, no. 3 (1952): 160–62; G. R. Elton, *The Practice of History* (Sydney, 1967), 134–35; William L. Langer, "The Next Assignment," *American Historical Review* 63, no. 2 (1958): 283–84. There are useful discussions of psychohistory by W. F. Mandle, "Psychology and History," *New Zealand Journal of History* 2, no. 1 (1968): 1–17; Richard Ellmann, "Freud as Biographer," *The American Scholar* 53, no. 4 (1984): 465–78; Reed Whittlemore, *Whole Lives: Shapers of Modern Biography* (Baltimore, 1989), 79–116; Robert Skidelsky, *Interests and Obsessions* (London / Basingstoke, 1994), 410–20.

2. Gavan Daws, "'All the Horrors of the Half Known Life': Some Notes on the

Writing of Biography in the Pacific," in *The Changing Pacific: Essays in Honour of H. E. Maude,* ed. Niel Gunson (Melbourne, 1978), 297.

3. Bronwen Douglas, "Imperial Flotsam? The British in the Pacific Islands," in *Oxford History of the British Empire,* vol. 5: *Historiography,* ed. Robin W. Winks (Oxford, 1999), 372n. 26, 373n. 33.

4. *Holy Man* has since been published in Dutch, French, German, and Korean editions. *Pater Damiaan: de heilige man van Molokai* (Lannoo, 1983); *Nous autres lépreux: Le Père Damien de Molokai (1840–1889)* (Paris, 1984); *Damian De Veuster: Den Aussätzigen ein Aussätzuger geworden* (Freiberg, 1988); *Mundungi songja Damian: Father Damien of Mokokai* (Seoul, 2001), respectively.

5. The long lead time between submission and eventual publication resulted in several more recent biographies pertaining to the British Pacific being omitted from Douglas's list. For example, Brij V. Lal, *A Vision for Change: A. D. Patel and the Politics of Fiji* (Canberra, 1997); Robert D. Kiste, *He Served: A Biography of Macu Salato* (Suva, 1998).

6. H. Lawton, *The Psychohistorian's Handbook* (New York, 1988), 26, 48, citing Erikson's theory that ego identity develops through life, not just in childhood as per Freud's id-psychology, as a "real innovation," which Strout cautiously accepted.

7. Daws, "All the Horrors," 298–99.

8. Lewis Lett, *Sir Hubert Murray of Papua* (Sydney, 1949), 93.

9. L. P. Mair, *Australia in New Guinea* (London, 1948); J. D. Legge, *Australian Colonial Policy: A Survey of Native Administration and European Development in Papua* (Sydney, 1956); J. P. McAuley, "The Distance Between the Government and the Governed," *South Pacific* 8 (1954): 815–24.

10. *Journal of Commonwealth Political Studies* 8, no. 1 (1970): 77–78.

11. Francis West, *The Justiciarship in Anglo-Saxon England, 1066–1232* (Cambridge, 1966). I explored the analogy in "A Colonial History of the Norman Conquest," *History* 84, no. 274 (1999): 219–36.

12. Francis West, ed., *Selected Letters of Hubert Murray* (Melbourne, 1970).

13. *Historical Studies* 14, no. 53 (1969): 106–9.

14. *Quadrant* 13, no. 4 (1969): 73–75.

15. *New Guinea* 4, no. 2 (1969): 77.

16. *Australian Book Review* 8, no. 5 (1969): 88–89.

17. H. N. Nelson, "Hubert Murray: Private Letters and Public Reputation," *Historical Studies* 14, no. 56 (1971): 612–21 (reviewing *Selected Letters of Hubert Murray*).

18. Roger M. Thompson, "Hubert Murray and the Historians," *Pacific Studies* 10, no. 2 (1986): 82–83.

19. *Journal of Pacific History* 4 (1969): 235.

20. Amirah Inglis, *"Not a White Woman Safe": Sexual Anxiety and Politics in Port Moresby, 1920–1934* (Canberra, 1974), 87, repeats Murray Groves's criticism; they ignore the fact that rape of a Papuan woman was punished under the Native Regulations. See Edward P. Wolfers, *Race Relations and Colonial Rule in Papua New Guinea* (Sydney, 1975), 40n. 1, 56–58.

21. *Journal of Pacific History* 4 (1967): 235–36.

22. Francis West, *Biography as History* (Sydney, 1973), 6–7.

23. *Australian Journal of Politics and History* 15, no. 2 (1969): 141.

24. Daws, "All the Horrors," 297.

25. Ibid., 297–98. Cushing Strout, "Ego Psychology and the Historian," *History and Theory* 7, no. 3 (1968): 281–97.

26. John Farrow, *Damien the Leper* (London, 1937), printed with a *Nihil Obstat* by the Catholic devotional publisher Burns, Oates and Washbourne, bibliography 232–33.

27. Erik H. Erikson, *Young Man Luther: A Study of Psychoanalysis and History* (New York, 1958).

28. Lawton, *The Psychohistorian's Handbook*, 7.

29. Ibid., 5.

30. John F. Veninga, ed., *The Biographer's Gift: Life Histories and Humanism* (College Station, TX, 1983), 37. A reasoned and moderate defense is William McKinley Runyan, *Life Histories and Psychobiography: Explorations in Theory and Method* (New York/Oxford, 1982).

31. *Critic* 32, no. 76, in *Book Review Digest, 1973* (New York, 1974), 298.

32. *America* 129, no. 131, in *Book Review Digest, 1973*, 298.

33. John Eddy, *Journal of Pacific History* 9 (1974): 221–23; John Bernard McGloin, *Pacific Historical Review* 43, no. 4 (1974): 614–15.

34. Richard Stewart, *Leper Priest of Molokai: The Father Damien Story* (Honolulu, 2000), 298.

35. Gavan Daws, *Dream of Islands: Voyages of Self-discovery in the South Seas—John Williams, Herman Melville, Walter Murray Gibson, Robert Louis Stevenson, Paul Gauguin* (New York, 1980).

36. Daws, "All the Horrors," 298.

37. Lawton, *The Psychohistorian's Handbook*, 49.

38. Elton, *The Practice of History*, 25n. 2; Karl Popper, *Conjectures and Refutations: The Growth of Scientific Knowledge* (New York, 1968), 35. One of the few historians to express enthusiasm for *Young Man Luther* was W. K. Hancock, *Attempting History* (Canberra, 1969), 26–27 and n. 23.

39. Francis West, *Gilbert Murray: A Life* (London, 1984).

40. Frank J. Sulloway, *Born to Rebel: Birth Order, Family Dynamics and Creative Lives* (New York, 1996).

41. P. D. Medawar, "Victims of Psychiatry," *New York Review of Books,* 23 January 1975, 17.

42. K. R. Howe, "Pacific Islands History in the 1980s: New Directions of Monograph Myopia?" *Pacific Studies* 3, no. 1 (1979): 81–90.

43. Veninga, ed., *The Biographer's Gift*, 37, 56, 82–83, 99–100, 110–11.

PART III

Activities

CHAPTER 10

The Missionary Position: *Messengers of Grace* and *The Works of Ta'unga*

Hugh Laracy

Niel Gunson, Messengers of Grace: Evangelical Missionaries in the South Seas, 1797–1860, by Niel Gunson.
Melbourne: Oxford University Press, 1978.

The Works of Ta'unga: Records of a Polynesian Traveller in the South Seas, 1833–1896, edited by R. G. and Marjorie Crocombe, with annotations by Jean Guiart, Niel Gunson, and Dorothy Shineberg.
Canberra: Australian National University Press, 1968 (as vol. 2 in the Pacific Islands Series). Paperback reprint, Suva: Institute of Pacific Studies of the University of the South Pacific, 1984, 1992.

MOST OF the Europeans who have played a significant part in shaping the lives of Pacific Islanders since the turn of the nineteenth century may be conveniently divided into several occupational categories. Of these probably none has been more influential or more voluminously commented on or more variously interpreted than "the missionaries"— the envoys of Christian churches and congregations who came to the Pacific dedicated to spreading knowledge of their religious beliefs and practices and of winning new adherents to them. The basic impulse for this activity lies in the biblical injunction "Go ye into the whole world and preach the gospel to every creature" (Mark 16:15). Christianity is an inherently proselytizing creed. The historical response to those motivating words of Christ, though, has always been conditioned by circumstances of the temporal order. So, too, has been the response of the recipients—and of the resisters. Yet Christianity in one form or another, as well as creating a major area of convergence with the world beyond the Pacific, has also become a profound and pervasive element of indigenous identity and culture throughout most of the islands of Oceania. As *127*

if to illustrate that statement, the Samoan national rugby football team—
Manu Samoa—includes a chaplain, along with coaches and a physio-
therapist, in its nonplaying support staff. In the same vein, the New Zealand team, which was composed of Polynesians, huddled in the middle
of the playing field in a prayer of thanksgiving after winning the Hong
Kong Sevens rugby tournament in 2003. At another level, the Tongan
coat of arms carries the legend "God and Tonga Are My Inheritance"
while in Fiji in 1987, following the obscenity of a military coup led by
Colonel Rabuka, who was also a Methodist lay-preacher, the usurpers
of democratic authority sought to make Christianity the state religion,
even though half the population was non-Christian.[1]

Given the importance of missionaries among the "agents of
change," and not only for the effects they wrought but also for the fact
that they left a singularly rich archival record of their observations and
experiences and activities, it is scarcely surprising that missionary studies should feature prominently among the corpus of work produced in
the Pacific History Department of the fledgling Australian National
University (ANU). The process that led systematically to that end began
in 1956 when J. W. Davidson, the founder of the department, awarded
a doctoral scholarship to Walter Niel Gunson (born 1930). A University
of Melbourne graduate interested in Non-Conformist Protestantism and
in genealogy, among much else, Gunson undertook research on the first
three generations (1797–1860) of Protestant missionaries to penetrate
the South Seas.[2] Of special concern to him were those of the London
Missionary Society (LMS), to which he had a family connection and
which was conspicuously important in Polynesia. His thesis was completed in 1960 and in 1962, after a spell of teaching history at the University of Queensland, he was appointed to a research post in Davidson's
department. In this position he was also expected to supervise further
doctoral theses mainly, although not exclusively, on missions.[3] His other
major interest, which stemmed from his work on missionaries, was traditional Polynesian society.[4]

The firstfruits of that responsibility were theses by David Hilliard on
Protestant missions in the Solomon Islands (1967), by Sione Latukefu on
the Methodist mission in Tonga (1968), and (informally, for he was not
the official supervisor) by myself on Catholic missions in the Solomon
Islands (1970).[5] Reworked versions of these theses were subsequently
published in 1978, 1974, and 1976, respectively.[6] There is an irony in

these dates in that Gunson's thesis, which those writers had all read closely and which exemplified the style and the standards that he had enjoined on his protégés, was not itself published until 1978. At the same time it was not unfitting that the master should be preceded by the acolytes, the Messiah by John the Baptist (in triplicate!). Besides, Gunson, aided now by his book, *Messengers of Grace: Evangelical Missionaries in the South Seas, 1797–1860*, continued to guide researchers in mission history. Among his own students were Norman Douglas on Mormon missions (1974), David Wetherell on the Anglicans in Papua New Guinea (1974, published 1977), Andrew Thornley on the Methodists in Fiji (1979), Geoff Cummins on the Methodist missionary J. E. Moulton in Tonga (1980), Diane Langmore on European missionaries in Papua (1981, published 1989), Graham Hassall on religion and nation-state formation in Melanesia (1990), and Fele Nokise on indigenous Samoan missionaries (1992).[7] Like his earlier students, various of the latter found careers in academic teaching and research, maintaining and extending the interest in missions that he had fostered in them.

Messengers of Grace was widely, quickly, and authoritatively acknowledged as an outstanding piece of scholarship. Thus Charles Forman, professor of missions at Yale University, began a review of it with the following comments:

> The study of the history of Christian missions has gained greatly in depth and sophistication in recent years. There have been important writings dealing with the work of missionaries in China, India and Africa, including some careful analyses of particular mission stations. But nowhere has there appeared a study of a whole region which is at once so detailed and so broadly encompassing as the present work by Niel Gunson.[8]

Gunson begins his book with a brief chronological survey of missionary settlement in the Pacific. In this he acknowledges a Spanish Catholic presence in parts of Micronesia (dating from 1668) and a brief Catholic sortie into Tahiti (1774–75), but his subject is the first sustained, widespread, and pace-setting assemblage of missionary operations. This phenomenon was also coherent in that its personnel were British and Anglophone and largely drawn from the artisan class and that theologically they were inclined to Calvinism. His analysis of them is sociological and intellectual rather than denominational. Thus, although the London Missionary Society drew its envoys from the Congregational churches and the Methodists were Wesleyans, his concern is to explore the common ground they shared rather than to define them by membership of discrete organizations.

Logically, if the forces that were brought to bear on Pacific Islanders by these people, and to which they responded so profoundly, are to be understood, the starting point had to be the missionaries themselves and the religious and social matrix from which they emerged. The particular impulse that commonly spurred missionary activity, Gunson notes, was the religious experience of revival, of "new birth" in the spirit, of conversion to a life of holiness, of manifest virtue, and of a wish to spread the knowledge of God. Many of his evangelicals had already served as home missionaries before venturing abroad. Few of them, though, had much theological education or, indeed, any form of higher learning until after 1830, when training at religious academies (as they were commonly styled) began to be prescribed for prospective missionaries. Stamina, zeal, and practical skills were deemed to be quite adequate, and more appropriate than erudition, for instructing the "ignorant heathens" of the South Seas, although that did not prevent many of the missionaries from developing as savants, especially in local languages.

From "The Missionary in the Making" Gunson then turns to "The Missionary in the Field." Here he discusses their lives in the new worlds that they had entered upon: their material and financial circumstances, developments in—and challenges to—their religious thinking and sense of vocation, their leisure activities, and, finally, their notion that the people they had come to save were intrinsically depraved. But the latter were still redeemable because with the literal interpretation of the Bible that prevailed among theologians in the period before 1860 they were seen as sharing in the common origin of humanity: "the miraculous creation of Adam and Eve and the repeopling of the world after the deluge by the Japhetic, Semitic and Hamitic races." They may have lapsed from the original ideals of the race, which had been best preserved among the European peoples (Japhites!), but traces of their earlier nobility and possession of religious truth could still be discerned, especially in the Polynesians (Semites!) among whom Gunson's subjects were mostly employed. Hence the missionary effort involved helping them reclaim their heritage. By this approach to anthropology the darker peoples of the Pacific (the Melanesians) and elsewhere were deemed to be disadvantaged by the curse of Ham (who was said to have insulted his father Noah) and thereby to be less readily convertible. Such beliefs,

Gunson observes, "depended very largely on a particular conception of history," and thereby encouraged many missionaries to collect indigenous myths and traditions and to record customs (206).[9] Much of the research of subsequent anthropologists and historians would be immeasurably impoverished, and the ordinary curiosity of many people—including Pacific Islanders—would remain unassuaged were it not for the information thus recorded by these pioneer "field workers," whom many writers have simplistically misrepresented as cultural vandals.

Having identified and explained just who the missionaries were, Gunson finally describes them in action in part 3, "The Missionary as a Social Force." Here they are dealt with as preachers, as teachers, as healers, as advisers in affairs of state, and as church builders. This is also the dimension of the subject within which they interact most closely with and are most dependent on Pacific Islanders, who have been the objective of, and who give focus and meaning to, all that has gone before in the book. Here island societies are being transformed, with the active but calculating cooperation of the Islanders, who now become distinctly important in the story. Particularly significant are those who themselves become involved in the work of evangelization. It is a notable merit of the book, therefore, that in appendixes naming his envoys of the gospel, and noting their personal details and places of ministry, he includes a comprehensive list of the "South Sea Islander Missionaries" who began to be recruited for the work of redeeming their people as early as 1820. Desirable as it might be, it is also a tribute to the remarkable effort of painstaking research in unpublished papers that such a full list, which even then is not complete, could be compiled. Portentously, it has subsequently become the starting point for doctoral research on Tahitian missionaries by one who is himself a Tahitian pastor, Rev. Marama Gaston Tauira.

On a broader front, *Messengers of Grace* has the further distinction of transcending the narrow confines of a monograph. It resonates afar. Forman comments that

> a study like this reveals the inadequacy of most generalizations about missionaries. The treatment here shows the variety of views on the relation of evangelization to civilization, on the relations of Christians to warfare, on the introduction of western clothing. The complexity of missionaries' relation to the political scene is also brought out and the quite different positions which different missionaries took are made clear. We see some

missionaries, especially in the early days, dwelling in thatch huts with dirt floors and dressed in rags, while others, especially in the later time, had comfortable houses, good clothing and local young people as servants.[10]

Plurality, variety, individuality: and that is only among Gunson's people. It correlates with, though, and is reinforced by the conclusions that might be drawn from Kenelm Burridge's wide-ranging ethnographic study of the missionary phenomenon itself, to the effect that invoking stereotypes contributes little to our understanding of the actors or of the activity.[11]

While recognizing that Pacific history needed to be nesocentric ("Islands-centered" was the vogue term under Davidson's aegis), Gunson's work also reflects the need to set his topic solidly within the European context from which it derived, and which supplied the momentum that led the missionaries to make an impact in the Islands. One outcome of this is an essay on John Williams of the LMS. The outstanding figure among the evangelical missionaries, Williams features extensively in *Messengers of Grace*. He initiated the mass conversion of the Samoans (among whom he is venerated). But it was as an adventurer, sailor, author, hero, and martyr—matters that attracted particular attention in Britain—that his subsequent general notability is based. Killed on Erromanga in Vanuatu in 1839, he secured an enduring reputation that served to draw the attention of far distant populations to the Pacific and to stimulate their piety and encourage their support for missions.

Subsequently Gunson's essay on "John Williams and his Ship" has been emulated by at least two other commentators writing on the enduring symbiosis set up between Europe and the Pacific through the publicity engendered by the killing of a missionary. David Hilliard has shown how the killing of the Anglican bishop John Coleridge Patteson on Nukapu near the Solomon Islands in 1871 generated a wave of fervor that not only attracted material resources and personnel to the Melanesian Mission but has made him a continuing source of religious inspiration. I have done something similar for Pierre Chanel.[12] A French missionary belonging to the Catholic society of the Marists, Chanel was killed by the chief of the island of Futuna, near Tonga, in 1841. The politics of Futuna that led to Chanel's death were intricate, but for a new religious organization looking for recognition and for the Catholic Church in France at odds with the French government his death was a godsend. Both could claim him as a hero, and present him as glorifying both Church and State. In 1954 Chanel was canonized and named as patron saint of Oceania. In another religious constituency that was a rank already long held by John Williams, the name of whose ship, *Messenger of Peace*, is alluded to in Gunson's title.

From similar source materials to those on which he based his John Williams essay, Gunson was also able to deal with more explicitly indigenous topics, for example, the Mamaia movement. This was the reaction of a large section of the Tahitian population in the years 1826–41 against the religion to which they had so recently converted and a rejection of those who had brought it. The events that marked the Mamaia, together with the ideas that informed it, are presented in a coherent and rounded manner that does not deny the rationality of its devotees, even though their opponents dismissed them as fanatics. Published in 1962, that essay, too, is distilled into *Messengers of Grace*, enhancing the tone of mature scholarship.[13] So, too, does an exploration of the family of William Henry, who came to Tahiti as a missionary in 1797. Published in 1970 in *Pacific Islands Portraits*, an epiphanic volume for Davidson and his lieutenants, it told of Henry's descendants who had spread widely across the South Pacific in a range of occupations. One of them was his mixed-blood granddaughter, Teuira Henry, who in 1928 published *Ancient Tahiti*, a foundational account of traditional Polynesian culture.[14]

In the synthesis of European and Pacific elements that mark Gunson's book is contained another point that should be made explicit. It is that he presents what may be read as a comprehensive refutation of the dated, but not yet dead, contention that indigenous people rather than expatriates in some way "own" Pacific history.[15] He shows that both parties contributed to a set of crucial events and processes that shaped that history, a history that would largely be unknowable in any detail or subtlety without missionary records—and the application of scholarly expertise to interpret them. "The past" cannot be owned but is part of the common inheritance of whomsoever is interested in it. That is also a view that the Tongan scholar Latukefu supported when he deplored the fact that "racism has driven some prominent Pacific scholars to believe fervently that outsiders should play no part in historical research in the Pacific."[16] Though strident, the voices of obscurantism, fortunately, have been and are few. Gunson's work, which reveals so much of the Pacific past, shows why this should be so.

Both the making and the writing of history, though, are sweepingly cooperative enterprises. Within the context of the present discussion, this observation is attested by a book composed from the writings of a nineteenth-century Cook Islander that was published a decade before *Messengers of Grace* and that richly complements Gunson's text. This is *The Works of Ta'unga: Records of a Polynesian Traveller in the South Seas, 1833–1896*. It is invaluable as a rare (but not unique) account of the activities, observations, and thoughts of an early convert to Christianity who himself became a missionary, working to plant the gospel according to the LMS in New Caledonia and later in Samoa.

Ta'unga (his name is the local version of the New Zealand Maori word *tohunga*, meaning "priest") was born in the district of Ngati Au on Rarotonga, the son of a chief named Teariki Taia, about 1818. In 1828, Charles Pitman arrived from Tahiti and established a mission at Ngatangiia village. There Ta'unga attended school and quickly came under the missionary's influence. He adopted the new religion and learned to read and write in his own language. One of the most persuasive weapons in the missionaries' armory, literacy was proving to be highly attractive to Pacific peoples. For his part, Ta'unga proved so apt a pupil that in 1832 he was dispatched to take classes for the children of Titikaveka village. From this point his involvement with the mission intensified and in March 1842 he was one of a party of Rarotongan mission teachers that set off in the barque *Camden* for Melanesia (then known in missionary circles as Western Polynesia). For the next four and a half years he was engaged in the pioneering work of primary evangelism in New Caledonia, mainly on the Isle of Pines and on Lifu and Mare in the Loyalty Islands, and from 1847 until 1879 he was involved in consolidating the growth of the church among the people of Samoa.

That career alone entitles Ta'unga to a significant mention in the history of his times, but he secured an indelible place for himself there by writing about what he saw and did. Whenever he had the chance, he says, he put on paper in his own language "what I saw with my eyes, heard with my ears, felt with my hands" (xv). Over almost sixty years he produced about sixty manuscripts (letters, memoirs, reports) of history, ethnology, and autobiography. Of these enough survived, scattered in various repositories, to make a modest-sized volume when published in 1968. It was the second volume in the unhappily defunct Pacific History Series, under the general editorship of Davidson's lieutenant, H. E. Maude, which provided an outlet for the publication of original manuscripts.

Collecting Ta'unga's writings was undertaken by Ron Crocombe (a former Ph.D. student in Davidson's department) and his wife Marjorie, herself a Cook Islander, who translated them into English. Many notable works of scholarship have commenced in unexpected circumstances, not least *The Works of Ta'unga*. As the Crocombes explain, they had ordered photocopying from the Polynesian Society and a Ta'unga manuscript was included by accident. Fascinated by the man and what he was describing, they spent another five years locating further Ta'unga manuscripts and preparing them for eventual publication—"a labour of love," as they describe it, "fitted into weekends as well as during field-trips for other purposes" (xv–xvi). Having located almost thirty different Ta'unga manuscripts in repositories as far away as the New York Public Library, the Crocombes arranged and linked them with connecting commentary to produce a chronologically coherent narrative.

Ta'unga was well served by his editors. He thus emerges in the historiography of the Pacific as a rich source of information. His is also, of course, notable as an indigenous voice and while, as in his letters to Pitman about New Caledonia, he shows little sympathy for traditional customs and beliefs he is at the same time displaying his own conception of the Christianity he is so committed to promoting. That is itself an element of history, and is indicative of a mentality that was far from unusual among Pacific Islanders making the momentous transition from one system of spirituality to another; the implications of exchanging one set of sanctions and fundamental beliefs for another are profound. Very similar sentiments, mingling audacity and aspiration, are also to be found in the biography of Joeli Bulu, a Tongan pastor who worked in Fiji and who was overwhelmed by the transcendent appeal of Heaven; he wished "to live among the stars."[17] Given what was at stake, there was, and could not be, much room for compromise. That is likewise the case with Maretu, another Cook Islands teacher, but one who worked among his own people, and whose extensive memoirs were also translated and edited by Marjorie Crocombe. The title under which they were published, *Cannibals and Christians*, epitomizes the stark way in which the process of religious change was seen by many of those intimately involved in it. Ta'unga was not alone in his attitudes.[18]

The Works of Ta'unga was enthusiastically received, even if some reviewers did warn that Ta'unga's self-censorship and somewhat Eurocentric attitudes diminish the value of his writings as truly representing an indigenous voice.[19] There is no doubt, however, that the book has made a lasting impact. First, the Crocombes placed the native pastor firmly in the center of the historiographic stage, and ensured henceforth that Ta'unga and his colleagues would receive their due for being pivotal in the spread of Christianity. Before *The Works of Ta'unga*, it was insufficiently appreciated that the introduction and consolidation of the new *lotu* was not the work of European missionaries alone, but of a veritable army of native pastors. Now there was no excuse for not knowing. Second, the Crocombes' edition of *The Works of Ta'unga* has, at least implicitly, spawned a large historiography on the pastor phenomenon, almost a genre in its own right.[20]

The Crocombes would be the first to acknowledge that they were not alone in bringing Ta'unga's works to light. They were fortunate in being able to draw on the expertise of leading subject specialists to provide annotations, elucidating Ta'unga's text where such was required. Thus Jean Guiart, an anthropologist, enhanced precision and detail by identifying people and place names in New Caledonia, while two colleagues of the Crocombes in Davidson's department also collaborated generously. One was Dorothy Shineberg, the author of a definitive history of the sandalwood trade in southern Melanesia, who helps place Ta'unga's stay in that area within the general contact history of the period—just as Shineberg's access to the Ta'unga material before its publication assisted her own work.[21] The other was Niel Gunson who, comments Maude, "illuminated many obscure passages in the text from his unrivalled documentation of mission documentation" (xi).

Finally, it seems apposite to observe that the collaborative high-quality scholarship involving Guiart, Shineberg, and Gunson is not a reflection on *The Works of Ta'unga* but a commendation. As Maude again notes:

> Biased as Ta'unga often is by his own beliefs, he has nevertheless given us the first detailed description of Melanesian society that we possess, and even if imperfect by the standards of modern professional ethnography, it cannot be ignored by future students. (xii)

Those words retain the force they had when first penned. The missionaries who crowd Gunson's pages could scarcely have guessed that, among much else, their labors would produce the first Polynesian anthropologist.[22]

Notes

1. Sione Latukefu, *Church and State in Tonga: The Wesleyan Methodist Mission-aries and Political Development, 1822–1875* (Canberra, 1974), 253; Brij V. Lal, *Broken Waves: A History of the Fiji Islands in the Twentieth Century* (Honolulu, 1992), 317. See generally Winston Halapua, *Tradition, Lotu and Militarism in Fiji* (Suva, 2003).

2. W. N. Gunson, "The Missionary Vocation as Conceived by the Early Mis-sionaries of the L.M.S. in the South Seas and the Extent to which This Conception Was Modified by Their Experiences in Polynesia, 1797–1839" (master's thesis, University of Melbourne, 1954).

3. Niel Gunson, "An Introduction to Pacific History," in *Pacific Islands History: Journeys and Transformations*, ed. Brij V. Lal (Canberra, 1992), 1–13.

4. For example, Gunson, "Sacred Women Chiefs and Female 'Headmen' in Polynesian History," *Journal of Pacific History* 22, nos. 3/4 (1987): 139–72; idem, "Understanding Polynesian Traditional History," *Journal of the Pacific History* 28, no. 2 (1993): 139–58.

5. Davidson was a firm believer in the value of experience. For this reason, he did not want Gunson to supervise a thesis on Catholic missionaries. Neither was my supervisor, Dorothy Shineberg, a Catholic, but she was an area specialist, and was thus qualified to look after my work.

6. David Hilliard, *God's Gentlemen: A History of the Melanesian Mission, 1849–1942* (Brisbane, 1978); Sione Latukefu, *Church and State in Tonga;* Hugh Laracy, *Marists and Melanesians: A History of Catholic Missions in the Solomon Islands* (Canberra, 1976). We were all given the early opportunity to display our wares in J. W. Davidson and Deryck Scarr, eds., *Pacific Islands Portraits* (Canberra, 1970).

7. Norman Douglas, "Latter-Day Saints Missions and Missionaries in Poly-nesia, 1844–1960" (Ph.D. thesis, Australian National University, 1974); David Wetherell, *Reluctant Mission: The Anglican Church in Papua New Guinea, 1891–1942* (Brisbane, 1975); Andrew Thornley, "Fiji Methodism, 1874–1945: The Emergence of a National Church" (Ph.D. thesis, ANU, 1979); Geoff Cummins, "Missionary Chieftain: James Egan Moulton and Tongan Society, 1865–1909" (Ph.D. thesis, ANU, 1980); Diane Langmore, *Missionary Lives: Papua, 1874–1914* (Honolulu, 1989); Graham Hassall, "Religious and Nation-State Formation in Melanesia: 1945 to Independence" (Ph.D. thesis, ANU, 1990); U. F. Nokise, "The Role of the LMS Samoa Missionaries in the Evangelisation of the South West Pacific, 1839–1930" (Ph.D. thesis, ANU, 1992). Thornley and Latukefu have both acknowledged their indebtedness to Gunson's supervision. Thornley, "On the Edges of Christian His-tory in the Pacific," *Journal of Pacific Studies* 20 (1996): 178–80; Latukefu, "The Making of the First Tongan-Born Professional Historian," in *Pacific Islands History*, ed. Lal, 24.

8. Charles W. Forman, *Journal of Pacific History* 14, nos. 3/4 (1979): 184. See also the review by John Broadbent, *Journal of Pacific Studies* 4 (1978): 95–98.

9. For a pertinent study of theories of Polynesian origins, see K. R. Howe, *The Quest for Origins: Who First Discovered and Settled New Zealand and the Pacific Islands?* (Auckland, 2003).

10. Forman, *Journal of Pacific History*, 185.

11. Kenelm Burridge, *In the Way: A Study of Christian Missionary Endeavours* (Vancouver, 1991); see also my review in *Journal of Pacific History* 29, no. 2 (1994): 254–55.

12. Niel Gunson, "John Williams and his Ship: The Bourgeois Aspirations of a Missionary Family," in *Questioning the Past*, ed. D. P. Crook (Brisbane, 1972), 73–95; David Hilliard, "The Making of an Anglican Martyr," in *Martyrs and Martyrologies*, ed. Diana Wood (Oxford, 1993), 333–45; Hugh Laracy, "Saint-Making: The Case of Pierre Chanel of Futuna," *New Zealand Journal of History* 34, no. 1 (2000): 145–61.

13. W. N. Gunson, "An Account of Mamaia or Visionary Heresy of Tahiti, 1826–1841," *Journal of the Polynesian Society* 71, no. 2 (1962): 209–43.

14. Niel Gunson, "The Deviations of a Missionary Family: The Henrys of Tahiti," in *Pacific Islands Portraits*, ed. Davidson and Scarr, 31–54.

15. See Doug Munro, "Who 'Owns' Pacific History: Reflections on the Insider/Outsider Dichotomy," *Journal of Pacific History* 29, no. 2 (1994): 232–37; Michael Monsell-Davis, "Entangled Stories: Personal, Local and Global Histories," *Journal of Pacific Studies* 20 (1996): 188–97.

16. Latukefu, "The Making of the First Tongan-Born Professional Historian," 28.

17. Joeli Bulu, *The Autobiography of a Native Minister in the South Seas, translated by a missionary* [Lorimer Fison], ed. G. Rowe (London, 1971).

18. Maretu, *Cannibals and Converts: Radical Change in the Cook Islands*, ed. Marjorie Tuainekore Crocombe (Suva, 1983). Related works includes Marjorie Crocombe, *If I Die: The Life of Ta'unga* (Suva, 1976); Ron and Marjorie Crocombe, eds., *Polynesian Missions in Melanesia: From Samoa, Cook Islands and Tonga to Papua New Guinea and New Caledonia* (Suva, 1982).

19. Gavan Daws, *Journal of Pacific History* 4 (1969): 228; Peter Biskup, "The Cook Island Chronicler," *Australian Book Review* (February 1969): 73; G. S. Parsonson, *New Zealand Journal of History* 5, no. 2 (1971): 201.

20. Examples of scholarly work on pastors, in addition to the Crocombes', include John V. Broadbent, "Attempts to Form an Indigenous Clergy in the Catholic Vicariate's Apostolic of Central Oceania (Wallis, Futuna, Tonga) and the Navigators' Islands (Samoa and Tokelau)" (Ph.D. thesis, Louvain University, 1976); Nancy Morris, "Hawaiian Missionaries Abroad, 1852–1909" (Ph.D. dissertation, University of Hawai'i, 1987); Doug Munro and Andrew Thornley, eds., *The Covenant Makers: Islander Missionaries in the Pacific* (Suva, 1996); Semisi Nau, *The Story of my Life: The Autobiography of a Tongan Methodist Missionary who Worked at Ontong Java in the Solomon Islands*, ed. Allan K. Davidson (Suva, 1996); Raeburn Lange, *The Origins of the Christian Ministry in the Cook Islands and Samoa* (Christchurch, 1997);

Michael Goldsmith and Doug Munro, *The Accidental Missionary: Tales of Elekana* (Christchurch, 2002); Nokise, "The Role of the LMS Samoa Missionaries." See also Doug Munro and Andrew Thornley, "Pacific Islander Pastors and Missionaries: Some Historiographic and Analytical Issues," *Pacific Studies* 23, nos. 3/4 (2000): 1–31.

21. Dorothy Shineberg, *They Came for Sandalwood: A Study of the Sandalwood Trade in the South-west Pacific, 1830–1865* (Melbourne, 1967).

22. The Crocombes asked that their royalties from *The Works of Ta'unga* be set aside to establish a fund for Pacific Islander students. This was the germ of the idea that resulted in the Te Rangi Hiroa Prize. See the Papers of H. C. and H. E. Maude, Special Collections, Barr Smith Library, University of Adelaide, MSS 0003, Series I/34 (I owe this information to Doug Munro).

CHAPTER 11

Of Islands and Sandalwood: Shineberg, Maude, and the Hidden History of Trade

Bronwen Douglas and Doug Munro

They Came for Sandalwood: A Study of the Sandalwood Trade in the South-west Pacific, 1830–1865, by Dorothy Shineberg.
Melbourne: Melbourne University Press, 1967. French translation by André Surleau, *Ils étaient venus chercher du santal*. Nouméa: Société d'Etudes Historiques de la Nouvelle-Calédonie, 1973.

Of Islands and Men: Studies in Pacific History, by H. E. Maude.
Melbourne: Oxford University Press, 1968. Paperback edition, Suva: Institute of Pacific Studies of the University of the South Pacific, 1991.

JIM DAVIDSON and Harry Maude are linked in the origin myth of Pacific history as partners in its development as a recognized subdisciplinary specialization at the Australian National University (ANU). Davidson was the field general scanning the horizon for new opportunities, intellectually curious and wide-ranging, drawing new troops by his strength of personality. Maude was the loyal lieutenant, manning the fort and building the foundations for future conquests. That is an accurate enough depiction from an institutional standpoint. Intellectually, however, Harry Maude and Dorothy Shineberg are the more natural pairing, as exemplars of the new island-oriented historiography and more specifically for establishing what Davidson facetiously referred to as the "yo-ho-heave-ho school of history"—that is, they wrote about trade and traders rather than the conventional Pacific themes of politics and missions. Shineberg's *They Came for Sandalwood*, published in 1967, was the first detailed study of a Pacific Islands trade. Maude's *Of Islands and Men*, published the following year, was broader ranging—a collection of previously published essays containing substantial chapters on trade, but embracing other themes. Together, they set an outstanding standard of documentary research, so necessary for the difficult retrieval exercises involved in the study of trade and traders. As well as breathing life into the subject, they expanded the historiographic frontier. These were two of the outstanding books to emerge from the Davidson era and to leave indelible marks.

Born in 1906, Henry Evans Maude began his career in the British colonial service, commencing in 1929 as a cadet and culminating as resident commissioner of the Gilbert and Ellice Islands Colony from 1946 to '48.[1] This was followed by a frustrating seven years directing research on social development at the newly formed South Pacific Commission, culminating in his appointment to the Australian National University (ANU) Department of Pacific History in 1957 as a senior research (later professorial) fellow. Although Maude had published in anthropological journals, he was not, in conventional terms, sufficiently credentialed for an academic appointment. But the unconventional Davidson, the participant historian par excellence, sought to turn Maude's vast experience to academic purpose and brought him to Canberra to write about the people he had once administered.[2] In his way, the shy and self-effacing Harry Maude realized a lifelong ambition to enter the academic world. He channeled his energies initially into writing a series of specialized journal articles, many of which were gathered together in 1968 by Oxford University Press under the title *Of Islands and Men*.

It was a mixed bag, demonstrating Maude's catholicity—although he doubted whether the selection of essays, made by his publisher, was a fair representation of his best work.[3] As well as chapters on the Spanish and post-Spanish discovery of the islands of the Central Pacific, there were two others on the *Bounty* mutineers and their descendants. They are landmarks of the careful scholarship that typifies the book as a whole. A stand-alone chapter, "The Colonization of the Phoenix Islands," is a somewhat sanitized account of Maude's involvement in a scheme to resettle land-hungry Gilbertese, resulting in Britain's final imperial extension. It is an example of "participant history" that was designed to conceal rather than to reveal: at no stage did Maude mention that the primary motivation was to thwart U.S. designs on the Phoenix Islands and that the impoverished Gilbertese provided the pretext for what in fact was an exercise in preemptive imperialism. That said, Maude genuinely believed in the virtues of the scheme for the Islanders: he had been pressing for resettlement since the 1931 census, and the concern about American interest in the region gave him the opportunity to put the scheme into practice.[4] A further chapter, "Rarotongan Sandalwood," is about a speculative venture in 1814 to collect sandalwood, only for the sandalwood to turn out to be a worthless misidentification. The ensuing debacle was a violent affair that illustrated only too clearly the perils and mutual misapprehensions of early cross-cultural encounters. More so than the other essays mentioned thus far, "Rarotongan Sandalwood" conveys Maude's concern for a more island-oriented historiography that would place Islanders center stage and, in turn, would have the almost therapeutic effect of giving the (then) colonized peoples of the Pacific a sense of self-worth "through a proper sense of pride in their history" (xviii–xix). More specifically, "Rarotongan Sandalwood" is a critical contribution in the combined historical use of European and indigenous materials, both written and oral. Maude had always been troubled by the limitations of European documentation as a basis for writing Pacific history and how they could be transcended by the use of materials of Islander provenance. He now put this concern to the test. The essay was co-authored with Marjorie Tuainekore Crocombe, herself from Rarotonga, and they blended European and vernacular texts with local oral histories in an attempt to produce a more objective account "than either of us could have achieved alone" (xxii).

Historiographically, the core contribution of the book comprises the remaining three chapters: one on beachcombers and two case studies of Pacific Islands trades. "Beachcombers and Castaways" is a radical reinterpretation of beachcombers—a previously neglected or demonized category of Europeans in the Islands—as social conformists and cultural mediators whose survival depended on being useful to their island hosts and who were at least partly assimilated into local milieus. It is a universal favorite among Maude's essays, presumably because it appeals to the romantic escapism that the idea of the Pacific arouses in both popular and scholarly imaginations. It has inspired numerous subsequent studies.[5] Beachcombers occupied a twilight zone between the barter practiced by Islanders with passing European vessels and the establishment of routinized trading relations. While an outline of European trade in the Pacific Islands had been sketched in Douglas Oliver's 1951 general text,[6] detailed studies of particular episodes were lacking. Here, Maude was the pioneer with substantial essays on "The Tahitian Pork Trade: 1800–1830" and "The Coconut Oil Trade of the Gilbert Islands."

Both essays were ground-breaking. Although firmly based on contemporary European texts, they opened new possibilities by replacing the usual easy generalizations and stereotypes with precise details on actual trading procedures, cargoes, profits, and losses—matters that had never been seriously considered or adequately researched in Pacific historiography, except in Davidson's unpublished Ph.D. thesis.[7] In "The Tahitian Pork Trade," Maude's innovative use of shipping lists in Sydney newspapers demonstrated how much could be retrieved from an unlikely resource and how this information elucidated the overall pattern of the enterprise. But he overstated the consequences of the pork trade on local politics (208–13, 222). Rather than being the sole cause of the rise of the Pomare dynasty, the pork trade has to be placed alongside missionary support and the exploitation of kinship ties and tribal alliances.[8]

The high point of the collection is "The Coconut Oil Trade of the Gilbert Islands." This episode was even more difficult to research than the Tahitian pork trade, which had at least left a clear paper trail because it was conducted largely under the aegis of the New South Wales authorities, if only as buyer. But since few private traders left papers, Maude's essay on the coconut oil trade in the Gilberts (now Kiribati) was "in the nature of a case study aimed at discovering whether the source materials for trading history in fact exist and can be recovered" (234). With the long-term assistance of Ida Leeson (1885–1964),[9] acknowledged as coauthor, Maude assembled a fragmented assortment of "snippets" (233) —dredged from a remarkable range of texts, including one by a Gilbertese author—into a "detailed microcosmic study" of a particular Pacific Islands trade from start to finish. In the process, he traced "a progression of trading procedures, from the first barter of the explorer" through several stages, culminating in the "island trade" (282–83). The essay described the various trading methods employed; the inception, organization, vicissitudes, and demise of the trade; its financing and profitability; traders' relations with missionaries; Gilbertese participation in the trade and its local effects. Moreover, some of the traders were no longer anonymous figures but were evoked as individual personalities whose reciprocal engagements with Islanders had an undoubted impact. It was a masterly effort.

Of Islands and Men is striking for its sheer variety of subject matter

which, if it detracts from the overall coherence of the volume, attests to
the author's astonishing versatility and grasp of his material. All but one
reviewer enthused, not least about Maude's infectious enthusiasm for
his subject, the depth of his documentary research, the appealing "combination of scholarship and romanticism," and his felicitous prose.[10] The
gainsayer was Gordon Parsonson, who considered the book as a whole
to be "thoroughly Eurocentric."[11] While appropriate enough to the
chapters on exploration, the charge of Eurocentrism cannot otherwise
be sustained. Rather, *Of Islands and Men*, even though based heavily on
European documentation and largely about European activities, shows
how the Europeans in question were channeled and constrained by
Islanders' actions, desires, and agendas. Moreover, two of the essays
point to the historical value of indigenous accounts, both written and
oral, a theme that loomed large in Maude's subsequent historical thinking and practice.[12] Another reviewer remarked that Maude's meticulous
researches, evidenced in a 494-item bibliography, would help put an end
to anthropologists' indifference to documents because "we have been
shown where to look."[13] The tribute hinted at Maude's central part in
establishing the nuts and bolts of the emerging subdiscipline of Pacific
history: a professional journal of bibliographic bent, a publication series,
and a document copying project. Fellow historians warmly acknowledged Maude's inspiration, notably Greg Dening, for whom he was a
mentor whose "particular genius has been to show how much of . . .
native history can be retrieved if one sifts the records wherever they are
to be found."[14] Arguably, though, Maude's single greatest influence was
his encouragement of Dorothy Shineberg's seminal research on the
Melanesian sandalwood trade.

Dorothy Shineberg's (1927–2004) involvement in Pacific history began
with an appointment, as a twenty-one-year-old recent Melbourne honors graduate, to teach colonial history at the Australian School of Pacific
Administration in Sydney, which trained patrol officers for service in
the territories of Papua and New Guinea.[15] From 1953 to 1955, after
postgraduate study in the United States, she taught an honors course on
Pacific history at the University of Melbourne, probably the first of its
kind. In the early 1960s, she embarked on a Ph.D. thesis on initial cul-

ture contact in the New Hebrides (now Vanuatu), at first focusing on missionaries whom she imagined to have been the pioneer Europeans in the region. She quickly realized, however, that almost everywhere missionaries had been preceded by their bitter rivals, the sandalwood traders. Inspired by Maude's 1959 article on the Tahitian pork trade and tutored by him in techniques of mining shipping lists and reports in Sydney newspapers for information about traders, their cargoes, and their activities, she switched her inquiry to the sandalwood trade in the wider southwest Pacific and gained her doctorate in 1965.[16] Appointed as a research fellow to the Department of Pacific History at the ANU, Shineberg revised the thesis for publication as *They Came for Sandalwood*—in historiographic terms, perhaps the most important and influential book produced by an island-oriented Pacific historian.

Like Maude in "The Coconut Oil Trade of the Gilbert Islands," first published in 1965, Shineberg told a multifaceted story of an entire trading episode, from inception to demise. Both works are divided into narrative, biographical, and thematic sections, concluding with an evaluation of the local impact of the respective trades. As a book rather than an article, however, *Sandalwood* is far wider in geographical span, much richer in historical detail, and deeper in analysis—though it contains few comparisons with analogous episodes, within or beyond Oceania, a legacy perhaps of its genesis as a thesis. By contrast, the scope and variety of Maude's oeuvre gives it a built-in comparative dimension that he occasionally reinforced by acknowledging parallels elsewhere. *Sandalwood*'s major focus was a region that had largely been neglected by Pacific historians (though not by anthropologists). Maude, for example, wrote about Micronesians, Polynesians, and Fijians, particularly those he knew well from personal experience. In passing, he rehearsed invalid stereotypes of Melanesians as globally "inhospitable," unreceptive to strangers, and devoid of written vernacular material or oral traditions (*Of Islands and Men*, xx, 146, 149, 283). Shineberg exposed the inadequacy of such stereotypes. She showed that in Melanesia, as elsewhere in the Pacific Islands, reception or rejection of foreigners was always situational and strategic. Although she could not do the sustained fieldwork needed to tap the rich vernacular histories of Melanesian communities, her appointment to the ANU enabled her to travel widely in the region and enliven her narrative with stories told by descendants of some of her historical protagonists.

Unlike Maude, Shineberg did not explicitly reflect on her research

methods. Yet they were exemplary in one respect—historical detection
—and prescient in another—historical critique. *Sandalwood* is a remarkable work of historical investigation and recuperation. On the one hand,
it is based on an exhaustive process of creative trawling through scattered, disparate texts for information about traders and trading in the
Islands: shipping reports; the exiguous letters, logs, and journals left by
traders themselves; and the accounts of missionaries and naval officers.
On the other hand, it depends on a skeptical reading of the abundant but
hostile writings of socially or politically dominant observers about
(mostly) marginal men and their disapproved activities in indigenous
settings. In practice, if not in theory, Shineberg not only broke deci-
sively with the Eurocentrism of imperial history, but anticipated several
key strands in more recent critical and postcolonial approaches:[17] the
technique of reading against the grain of dominant texts; a stress on the
ambiguities, tensions, and fissures in European authority; a concern to
de-essentialize and complicate the binary ethnic categories *white* and
black; and an acute awareness of the contingency and messiness of actual
cross-cultural encounters.

   While Davidson and others had conscientiously adhered to the dic-
tum that Islanders and their cultures should be kept central in studies of
culture contact and its effects, they did not seriously challenge the
assumed dominance and overwhelming linear impact on Islands communities of the exploring, missionizing, or colonizing Europeans on whose
writings they relied. Maude did do so in "Beachcombers and Castaways," first published in 1964, arguing generally, within the limitations
of an overview article, that such men exercised little control in local situations and demonstrating that cross-cultural impact was never a one-
way street. *Sandalwood* was also a "broad sweep,"[18] synoptic rather than
particularistic, but its book format allowed greater scope for detailed
historical reconstruction and thematic development. Shineberg crafted
a vivid picture of "the meeting of very different peoples on a relatively
equal basis." Contesting the still current humanitarian stereotype of
traders as "swashbuckling pirates who always got their way," she argued
convincingly that they were "quite often on the wrong side of the power
equation."[19]

   This interpretive core of the book is in the final five chapters, which
comprise a sustained refutation of the hoary, "entirely European-ori-
ented" assumption of "the passive role of the Melanesian in culture con-

tact"—that Islanders were "simply the passive objects of European exploitation" in trading relations and that, when violence occurred, "there must be a white man behind every brown" (15, 214–15). Shineberg argued, in contrast, for what would now be termed Islander agency: she repeatedly demonstrated "their use of their bargaining power to excellent effect" in trading situations (145–60) and specifically addressed the "problem of interpretation" that typically explains Islanders' violence toward Europeans in moralistic "retaliation-only" terms, as "blind revenge for the atrocities committed by the white man" (199–214). In the process, she cogently rebutted the standard belief that traders owed their (alleged) dominance to the inevitable superiority of firearms over local weapons:[20] in practice, under Islands conditions, the quality and performance of the single-shot firearms generally available to traders accorded them no great advantage, given their usual great numerical inferiority. The one new condition not easily explained or controlled by Islanders was the epidemics of previously unknown diseases that accompanied the arrival of foreigners (169–76). Shineberg concluded that "the islanders played a very lively part in their relations with the Europeans and that they endeavoured to turn the coming of the white men to their best possible advantage" (216), if necessary by force.

There is nothing a priori about this radical rethinking of early culture contacts. Rather, it emerged inductively from imaginative attention to the recorded details of particular situations of encounter, including traders' accounts of their efforts to anticipate "the tastes of Melanesian buyers" (149). Nor, moreover, did Shineberg romanticize Islanders, stressing instead the flawed humanity they shared with traders and other Europeans. Indeed, the other side of this admirable humanist coin, especially in her analysis of the economics of the trade, is an ethnocentric secular rationalism that largely neglected the particularities of Melanesian cultures, especially their exchange systems and pragmatic religiosity: normal market conditions (157), the laws of supply and demand, ordinary processes of bargaining (158), power, the laws of self-preservation and the dictates of self-interest (164), business (192), reason (202), and logic (203) are global reifications that in local cultural practice take widely varied, historically contingent shapes. Yet, notwithstanding her expressed commitment to liberal universalist values,[21] Shineberg was not so much insensitive to Melanesian cultural specificities as forced by the wide-ranging scope of her study to engage in a degree of strategic ethnocentrism. Ethnographic precision was a luxury she simply could not afford.

Both Maude and Shineberg saw the influx of European goods, especially metal tools, as initiating a technological revolution that propelled Pacific Islanders precipitately into the industrial age and jeopardized their independence as subsistence producers. A residual romantic attachment to the idea of pre-European culture fed Maude's ambivalence about "acculturation," which he attributed unproblematically to linear European influence (while acknowledging that indigenous Gilbertese culture was not static) and linked to "a decline in morals, political stability and health" (168–69, 222, 275–79). Although Shineberg's word choices at times imply a conventional nostalgic identification of social and cultural change with loss, "decay," and "dislocation," she also acknowledged positive aspects, local agency, and an internal dynamic: there was a marked "lightening of labour in subsistence agriculture," at least for men; in the main, Islanders demanded trade goods that "served the ends of indigenous activities more effectively"; but technological change itself "slowly undermined" their social structure "from within." In this process, European goods were "the thin edge of the wedge" since they soon became "necessities instead of luxuries" (158–62).

Somewhat at odds with the overall tenor of the book, there is a familiar elegiac ring to Shineberg's concluding aphorism that the "final preponderance of the white man" was "assured" by 1865, the end of her period of study (216). This rhetorical presumption—which many modern colonial historians would qualify as premature and not always appropriate to the vagaries and ambiguities of colonial situations in the Pacific[22]—rested in part on her just assessment that a late structural shift in the sandalwood trade, from itinerant vessels to permanent shore stations employing labor gangs imported from other islands, had brought about a transformation of "the Melanesian" from "an independent trader among his own people" into "a migrant wage-labourer, dependent on his employer" (190–98). In such circumstances, the agency of indigenous people was undoubtedly circumscribed, though not, it must be stressed, eliminated. A brief chapter (190–98) positioning "Migrant Labour" within Melanesia as a precursor to the wider Pacific Islands labor trade anticipated Shineberg's recent important study of New Hebridean laborers in New Caledonia.[23]

Shineberg's rejection of the trope of Islander passivity in cross-cultural encounters is now a convention in professional Pacific historiography.[24] However, like the island-oriented approach generally, it has made little impression on popular imagery, which maintains the venerable elegiac objectification of noble savages in paradise supinely undergoing the Fatal Impact of European contact. Similarly, like Maude's article on the Tahitian pork trade, *Sandalwood* was an important contribution to the early commercial history of the Australian colonies. But whereas Maude's essay was rightly acknowledged by one reviewer as "a mine of data and ideas for Australian historians,"[25] they seem to have neglected *Sandalwood*, in part perhaps because of its exotic library subject classification under "sandalwood trade" and "Melanesia." The book had a large print run of nearly seven thousand copies and was very widely reviewed internationally but relatively sparsely in Australia, where it did not sell particularly well. The reviewers overall were almost uniformly favorable, though a couple queried Shineberg's analysis of the profitability of the trade, one had "reservations about her justification of the activities of the sandalwood traders," and another took issue with this otherwise "admirable study" for its relativistic "attempt to judge intercultural exchange by non-Western values," which would inevitably be obliterated by "Western civilization."[26] The single exception was again Parsonson, whose tendentious catalogue of alleged misinterpretations, omissions, and mistakes was itself so error-ridden that Shineberg felt constrained to publish a rebuttal.[27]

Despite their ongoing appeal and relevance, *Of Islands and Men* and *They Came for Sandalwood* were to some degree products of their time, notably with respect to the concepts of race and gender. Though their humanist credentials were undoubted, both authors took for granted the reality of distinct races and used the term conventionally. Maude, the former colonial administrator, did so quite unselfconsciously—"racial self-respect," "by race as well as calling," "the Gilbertese are one of the most highly-specialized races on earth" (xviii, xix, 320)—and was rebuked for it by the anthropologist Ian Hogbin, for whom the term was already problematic in the mid-1960s.[28] Shineberg had occasional rhetorical or ironic recourse to the word: "seamen, like most of the white race in this period, believed that the laws of human brotherhood simply did not extend to coloured people"; "a three-cornered luxury trade . . .

proving that human frailty knows no race" (91, 151). Both unthinkingly
gendered the world male and encompassed women within the masculine
generic, according to contemporary linguistic convention: Shineberg's
essential "Melanesian" was always "he," as was Maude's "native." Few
women feature in their writings: Maude made an occasional passing reference to a female chief or concubine; Shineberg acknowledged the negative impact on Islands women of the technological revolution brought
about by the sandalwood trade (160–62) and cited poignant passages
from the correspondence of the indomitable Elizabeth Henry, wife of the
always unlucky trader Andrew. That Shineberg subsequently admitted
Sandalwood's bias and omissions with respect to gender is clear from her
recent book *The People Trade,* which pays scrupulous attention to the
specifics of gender (and age) and includes powerful chapters on women
and children in the labor trade.[29] She also admits regret for having
ignored the deleterious ecological impact of the ruthless exploitation of
sandalwood on Islands environments, but again the issue did not seem
pertinent at the time.[30]

Minor caveats notwithstanding, *Of Islands and Men* and *They Came
for Sandalwood* remain superb exemplars of the threatened art, craft, and
calling of the historian. Beyond their publications, Maude and Shineberg
both made outstanding personal contributions to the discipline. Maude
was a meticulous supervisor who freely shared with his students a lifetime of experience and learning. He commented in detail on their drafts,
gladly loaned them books from his vast library, and supported them
totally. It was impossible not to be moved by his enthusiasm and erudition, his love for the subject, and his generosity. Shineberg had similar
qualities. During four decades as teacher and supervisor, she excited,
challenged, inspired, and trained several generations of undergraduate
and graduate students. She gave them their heads, but the high degree
of rigor in reading, research, and presentation that she demanded (and
often got) in return has now, perhaps, itself largely become history.

Notes

1. For biographical details, see Susan Woodburn, *Where Our Hearts Still Lie: A
Life of Harry and Honor Maude in the Pacific Islands* (Adelaide, 2003); Robert Lang-
don, "Harry Maude: Shy Proconsul, Dedicated Pacific Historian," in *The Changing
Pacific: Essays in Honour of H. E. Maude,* ed. Niel Gunson (Melbourne, 1978), 1–21.

2. Niel Gunson, "An Introduction to Pacific History," in *Pacific Islands History: Journeys and Transformations*, ed. Brij V. Lal (Canberra, 1992), 4–6.

3. Woodburn, *Where Our Hearts Still Lie*, 254n. 36.

4. Ibid., 70, 127, 131. See also M. Ruth Megaw, "The Scramble for the Pacific: Anglo-United States Rivalry in the 1930s," *Historical Studies* 17, no. 69 (1977): 458–73.

5. Most significantly, I. C. Campbell, *"Gone Native" in Polynesia: Captivity Narratives and Experiences from the South Pacific* (Westport, CT, 1998), 7n. 8.

6. Douglas L. Oliver, *The Pacific Islands* (Cambridge, MA, 1951), 77–86. Oliver encompassed traders along with whalers and missionaries in a short chapter that—perhaps inevitably, given the lack of empirical studies—propounded many of the stereotypes that Maude or Shineberg would later confront: "most of the Melanesian islands were avoided" because of the inhabitants' inhospitality and cannibalism; such trade as there was in Melanesia was dominated by "men of Salem"; traders "chalked up a record of chicanery, violence, and evil"; beachcombers were an "infestation"; and it was "good sense . . . to attribute ferocity among the natives to revenge for misdeeds of alien white men."

7. J. W. Davidson, "European Penetration in the South Pacific, 1779–1842" (Ph.D. thesis, Cambridge University, 1942).

8. For example, Douglas L. Oliver, *Ancient Tahitian Society*, vol. 3: *Rise of the Pomares* (Honolulu, 1974), passim; Colin Newbury, *Tahiti Nui: Change and Survival in French Polynesia, 1767–1942* (Honolulu, 1980), 1–33; K. R. Howe, *Where the Waves Fall: A New South Sea Islands History from First Settlement to Colonial Rule* (Sydney, 1984), 125–51. D. R. Hainsworth, after reworking Maude's economic data and considering "certain supplementary data," suggested that he had underestimated the profitability of the Tahitian pork trade. *The Sydney Traders: Simeon Lord and his Contemporaries, 1788–1821* (Melbourne, 1972), 158–64. Nevertheless, as an innovative and painstakingly researched pioneering study, there is no taking away Maude's achievement.

9. *Australian Dictionary of Biography*, vol. 10: *1891–1939* (Melbourne, 1986), 58–59.

10. For example, O.H.K. Spate, *Journal of Pacific History* 3 (1968): 219; G. B. Milner, *Australian Journal of Politics and History* 16, no. 2 (1969): 139–40; John Young, *Australian Economic History Review* 11, no. 1 (1971): 72.

11. G. S. Parsonson, *New Zealand Journal of History* 5, no. 2 (1971): 204.

12. H. E. Maude, "Pacific History: Past, Present and Future," *Journal of Pacific History* 6 (1971): 3–24; Woodburn, *Where our Hearts Still Lie*, 242–68 passim.

13. Antony Hooper, *Journal of the Polynesian Society* 80, no. 4 (1971): 526. Hooper took his own injunction to heart, in Judith A. Huntsman and Antony Hooper, *Tokelau: A Historical Ethnography* (Auckland, 1996).

14. Greg Dening, *The Bounty: An Ethnographic History* (Melbourne, 1988), 95; see also the numerous tributes in Maude's *Festschrift*, *The Changing Pacific*, ed. Gunson.

15. For biographical details, see Dorothy Shineberg, "The Early Years of Pacific History," *Journal of Pacific Studies* 20 (1996): 1–16.

16. Dorothy Shineberg, "The Sandalwood Trade in the South-west Pacific, 1830–1865: with Special Reference to the Problems and Effects of Early Contact between Europeans and Melanesians" (Ph.D. thesis, University of Melbourne, 1965).

17. For a historiographical overview that positions "island-oriented" history in relation to "imperial" and "postcolonial," see Bronwen Douglas, "Imperial Flotsam? The British in the Pacific Islands," in *Oxford History of the British Empire,* vol. 5: *Historiography,* ed. Robin W. Winks (Oxford, 1999), 366–78.

18. The phrase was Maude's, describing "Beachcombers and Castaways," and quoted in Woodburn, *Where our Hearts Still Lie,* 254n. 27.

19. Shineberg, "The Early Years," 9.

20. Maude, for instance, had taken for granted that firearms constituted "a new offensive weapon against which there was no adequate local defence" (*Of Islands and Men,* 156). For an extended reinterpretation, see Dorothy Shineberg, "Guns and Men in Melanesia," *Journal of Pacific History* 6 (1971): 61–82.

21. Shineberg, "The Early Years," 5–6.

22. See, for example, James Belich, *The New Zealand Wars and the Victorian Interpretation of Racial Conflict* (Auckland, 1986); Bronwen Douglas, *Across the Great Divide: Journeys in History and Anthropology* (Amsterdam, 1998).

23. Dorothy Shineberg, *The People Trade: Pacific Island Laborers and New Caledonia, 1865–1930* (Honolulu, 1999). Maude, too, crowned his academic career with a book on the labor trade, his much-admired *Slavers in Paradise: The Peruvian Labour Trade in Polynesia, 1862–1864* (Canberra, 1981).

24. For example, Jane Samson retrod similar ground, including mislabeling the "retaliation only" interpretation, but failed adequately to acknowledge Shineberg's pioneer contribution. *Imperial Benevolence: Making British Authority in the Pacific Islands* (Honolulu, 1998), 81–97.

25. D. R. Hainsworth, *Australian Book Review* 8, no. 4 (1969): 72.

26. Geoffrey Blainey, *Historical Studies* 13, no. 52 (1969): 573–75; Robert Craig, *Mariner's Mirror* 55, no. 2 (1969): 216; Jacques M. Downs, *Business History Review* 47, no. 3 (1973): 407. Shineberg had stressed that popular perceptions of the huge profitability of the sandalwood trade were largely illusory. In a generally very positive review, Blainey remarked that Shineberg's downward revision of sandalwood profits was still an overestimation and that her figures were "not very revealing, because they concentrate on aggregate profits and tend to ignore the rate of return on the investment and also the sharply changing value of money" (575). Shineberg later commented that prior access to Blainey's expertise would have enabled her to puncture the myth of fabulous profits even more effectively.

27. G. S. Parsonson, *Australian Journal of Politics and History* 14, no. 2 (1968): 287–89; Dorothy Shineberg, *Australian Journal of Politics and History* 14, no. 3 (1968): 453.

28. Ian Hogbin, *Oceania* 34, no. 3 (1964): 238, quoted in Woodburn, *Where our Hearts Still Lie*, 243.

29. Shineberg, *The People Trade*, 90–122.

30. In contrast, Gerard Ward, who as a geographer was already more sensitive to environmental considerations, stressed the lasting consequences of the deforestation occasioned by the bêche-de-mer trade in Fiji. "The Pacific *Bêche-de-mer* Trade with Special Reference to Fiji," in *Man in the Pacific Islands: Essays on Geographical Change in the Pacific Islands*, ed. R. Gerard Ward (Oxford, 1972), 117–18.

CHAPTER 12

Unsettling New Zealand History:
The Revisionism of Sinclair and Ward

Vincent O'Malley

The Origins of the Maori Wars, by Keith Sinclair.
Wellington: New Zealand University Press, 1957; 2nd ed., Auckland:
Auckland University Press, 1961.

*A Show of Justice: Racial "Amalgamation" in Nineteenth Century
New Zealand*, by Alan Ward.
Canberra: Australian National University Press, 1974. 2nd ed., Auckland:
University of Auckland Press, 1995.

IN 1950, in a line destined to be quoted in several later surveys of historical writing in New Zealand, the young historian Keith Sinclair called for a "generation of pedants" to examine the nation's past.[1] Sinclair's comment was part challenge to the then existing historiography—heavy on general histories but light on detailed monographs of important subjects[2]—and part manifesto. His first major publication, *Origins of the Maori Wars*, published in 1957, was the fruit of nearly a decade's painstaking archival research into the subject, and tapped into a hitherto neglected range of sources that would help to forever change the way Pakeha scholars and general society viewed the origins of these conflicts, at the same time legitimizing many aspects of the nearly century-long grievances Maori had passed down to each generation in relation to what they referred to as *Te Riri Pakeha*, the white man's anger. Sinclair's call to arms would be taken up by a further generation of historians in the 1960s and 1970s, part of the rapid growth of New Zealand historical writing that Sinclair himself had done so much to foster and encourage. No history publication from this later period stood out more as toiling at the minutiae of evidence that Sinclair had called for than Alan Ward's astonishingly detailed study of nineteenth-century native policy in New Zealand, *A Show of Justice*, published in 1974. Along with Sinclair's

Origins, it continues to rank among a small handful of really important works of history to be published about New Zealand.

Sinclair (1922–93), the wharfie's son from Point Chevalier, Auckland, and Ward (born 1935), who grew up on a marginal farm at Waipaoa, Poverty Bay, represented urban and rural success stories of a more accessible university education system in the "cradle to grave" welfare state era. Both followed the new path of upward social mobility, teachers' training college, in Ward's case followed by a stint school teaching and in Sinclair's by "rehab" bursary-funded study after an uneventful period of service in World War II.[3] Ward grew up in a district with one of the highest proportions of Maori in the country and studied the convoluted history of local land dealings for his master's thesis—the findings of which made him "angry and ashamed" at the manipulative tactics used against Maori to acquire their lands.[4] Sinclair consciously broke the law in offering financial support to his locked-out father during the 1951 confrontation between the watersiders and the government of Sidney Holland and was proud in later life to discover his own Maori ancestry.[5] Both historians, like many of their generation, brought an angry and at times radical new edge to previously stultified New Zealand universities.

With the benefit of hindsight, a focus on New Zealand history appears inevitable for one of the country's great nationalist historians. Yet as Sinclair later recalled in his autobiography, his intention had originally been to study Pacific, rather than specifically New Zealand, history. It was a lunch at the British Museum with the New Zealand–born historian W. P. Morrell, shortly after the war's end in 1945, that turned Sinclair's mind to the history of his own country and led to his 1946 master's thesis on the Aborigines Protection Society in New Zealand.[6] A lectureship in the Auckland History Department followed soon after and in 1950 a short publication on an aspect of the Taranaki Wars was produced.[7] It met with a mixed response. Sinclair was awarded the Walter Lewen Lord Prize of the Royal Colonial Society,[8] but one reviewer described *The Maori Land League* as difficult to follow without a fuller exposition of the general situation applying in Taranaki at the time.[9] It is chiefly remembered today for the expression "generation of pedants."

Nevertheless, Sinclair's interest in what were at the time referred to as the Maori Wars was suitably stoked. In 1953, following further research at the Public Record Office in London, the Dominion Archives and Alexander Turnbull Library in Wellington, and a fair amount of

detective work in tracking down privately held manuscripts in the possession of descendants of many of the leading European figures
involved, Sinclair submitted his manuscript on the origins of the wars
to Oxford University Press. It was rejected, but after sharpening up the
prose—and at the suggestion of James Rutherford—in 1954 Sinclair
was awarded a Ph.D. for a revised version of this, which was published
by the New Zealand University Press in 1957.[10]

One reviewer wrote at the time that following Sinclair's book there
could no longer be any reasonable doubt that the government, with the
solid backing of the settlers, had been the aggressor in the wars of the
1860s.[11] As a more recent commentator put it, Sinclair's work "transformed the wars and helped to free the tangata whenua from an oppres-
sive Pakeha stereotype."[12] A Royal Commission in the 1920s, and a
number of contemporary humanitarian critics such as Sir William Martin, had previously concluded that the first Taranaki War of 1860–61, in
particular, had been unjust, but none had done so with such panache or
with such an impressive array of supporting documentation as Sinclair
had managed to marshal in support of his argument. Sinclair's often
witty, and always lively, prose lifted his work from the realm of dry history, while (as Ian Wards wrote) his careful and diligent use of sources
placed Sinclair in the vanguard of those who helped to transform the
writing of New Zealand history from the amateurism of earlier writers
such as William Pember Reeves (the subject of a later laudatory Sinclair
biography) to a truly professional and legitimate vocation.[13]

Denying any intention to write a general history of New Zealand
"from Cook to Te Kooti," Sinclair nevertheless devoted the first seven
chapters of the book to considering the general factors making war likely
in the period after 1840, followed by the heart of the work—a detailed
examination of the immediate casus belli of the first Taranaki War, the
infamous government purchase of the Waitara block, and its aftermath
—before ending with a brief and cursory examination of the origins of
the later and more significant Waikato War of 1863–64, a mere six-page
afterthought to a 272-page book.[14] In Sinclair's view, the war "began in
the minds of many men of both races long before it occurred in the
fields and bush" (6). Settler prejudice, along with the waning influence
of the humanitarian lobby, led by the missionaries, tended toward a war
that "native" policy could not reverse. Yet beyond all else, in Sinclair's
estimation, was the conflict over land. In short, Maori had it, and the

settlers coveted their territory, particularly after the collapse in agricultural prices in the mid-1850s, prompting a shift in emphasis over to pastoralism, which required even more extensive tracts on which sheep could graze. Increasing Maori mistrust and suspicion of settler motives, giving rise to a new Maori nationalism as embodied in the King movement, saw land sales in the 1850s fail to satisfy settler demand. Something had to give or the two worlds were headed for what, Sinclair implied, was a near inevitable collision (193).

In these circumstances the immediate facts behind the 1860–61 conflict seem less significant, although Sinclair demonstrated why Taranaki was always likely to be a prime candidate for war and how, in a context in which fighting was "probable," certain historical actors "played a part in bringing it about in the particular way in which it occurred" (205). Governor Thomas Gore Browne, whose acceptance of an offer of land at Waitara from the Te Atiawa chief Teira, against the wishes of Wiremu Kingi and other owners, in March 1859 gave rise to the subsequent conflict, emerges from Sinclair's study as incompetent rather than malevolent. As Sinclair brutally wrote, "the Governor was a simple man, often confused, but incapable of playing the colonial Machiavelli" (142). Such a role is instead reserved for Donald McLean, who Sinclair suggests, ought to have, and probably did, know that Teira had no right to sell the Pekapeka block without the consent of Kingi and other owner-occupiers of the land.

Yet in Sinclair's analysis, dissecting the fatal decisions or actions taken by Gore Browne, McLean, C. W. Richmond, and others in relation to Waitara served only to demonstrate "how war might have been prevented on that occasion, not how it could have been avoided altogether" (206). The war arose not from the actions of a few men over a few years, but "the acts of thousands of men over nearly a hundred years," from the time of Captain Cook's first visit to the country. If the basic conflict over land was not settled at Taranaki in 1860, it would almost certainly have to be resolved at another time. This was, in Sinclair's conception, a natural concomitant of the colonization process itself (205).

Looking back on his lifetime works, such a gloomy conclusion appears at first view out of character for someone who would later carve out a reputation as a remarkably upbeat and Whiggish historian.[15] From Sinclair's perspective, it was entirely consistent with an optimistic and progressive view of the nation's past. Land was the great impediment to cordial relations between Maori and Pakeha. Once the settlers had it, through confiscation and the Native Land Court, Sinclair argued, Pakeha "willingly changed their minds and adopted a superficially sentimental attitude towards the Maoris, so that by the twentieth century large numbers of European New Zealanders were humanitarian in their views on native questions" (225). Such a perspective, which entirely ignored lingering Maori resentment and barely concealed bitterness over the unfair expropriation of their resources, would later be taken to extremes by Sinclair in one of his most notorious articles—to the extent that he deemed it unnecessary to prove that New Zealand had better race relations than similar settler colonies, but simply considered this axiomatic.[16]

The problem, as later historians recognized, was that in focusing almost entirely on the origins of the Taranaki conflict, Sinclair had fixed on a province with acute, and in some respects quite exceptional, difficulties over the land question. In 1967 Brian Dalton unsuccessfully sought to overturn Sinclair's findings with respect to the Waitara dispute, and argued instead that Wiremu Kingi had no valid claim to the land as a consequence of which no injustice had been committed in ignoring his protests regarding the transaction.[17] He did, however, in conjunction with Alan Ward, succeed in shifting the focus of attention to the origins of the Waikato War of 1863–64, which Sinclair had previously regarded as little more than an extension of the Taranaki conflict. Ward, writing in the first volume of the *New Zealand Journal of History* (a journal Sinclair had almost single-handedly founded), pointed to the involvement of Kingitanga Maori from Waikato in the Taranaki conflict as highlighting issues beyond simply settler hunger for Maori lands, "that were resolved, after a fashion, by Grey's ordering the invasion of the Waikato in July 1863."[18] In Ward's view "the ultimate question of which race and which society was going to prevail and admit the other on sufferance" was one "that had to be resolved in any colonial situation, whether or not the centre of resistance of the indigenous people was itself coveted for purposes of exploitation." It was this that made the Waikato conflict, not Taranaki, "the climactic event in New Zealand race relations."[19]

Ward's focus was thus not simply the expropriation of land, but also the imposition of British law. His doctoral dissertation, completed at the

Australian National University (ANU) under the supervision of J. W. Davidson in 1967[20] reflected this interest, which had been triggered by Maori reactions to the 1961 publication of the Hunn Report, seen by many as simply a continuation of long-pursued assimilationist policies under the new garb of integration. Published in 1974 as *A Show of Justice,* Ward's magisterial study of nineteenth-century native policy remains, more than a quarter of a century later, the standard reference work on the subject. Granted unrestricted access to the archives of the former Native Department, Ward took full advantage to produce a richly detailed and superbly researched work of history, approached with a certain awe and trepidation by many an undergraduate student ever since it first appeared.

Yet for all its dense detail, *A Show of Justice* was more than simply an encyclopedic-style administrative history (though many a scholar has subsequently relied on the book for precisely such purposes). As Judith Binney wrote in a 1975 review, while undoubtedly the best study of nineteenth-century racial policies in New Zealand, it was also "probably the angriest."[21] Ward demonstrated how policies purportedly aimed at the amalgamation of Maori into the mainstream of colonial settler society were never pursued honestly enough to allow Maori genuine entry into this new order on terms other than those of subservience. Amalgamation, in itself a relatively enlightened concept by comparison with alternative nineteenth-century models of native policy, was blighted in its implementation by ethnocentrism and instead became an instrument of imperial subjugation, for the benefit of the conquering race. As one astute settler commented in the early 1860s, nominal legal equality, without genuine economic and social equality, could only operate to "destroy the weaker [party] under a show of justice."[22] The injustice, Ward suggested, lay less in the policy prescription than in the failure to stick to it.

This was, in Ward's view, all the more unfortunate, since nineteenth-century Maori society responded to colonization in "highly intellectual, flexible and progressive" ways, demonstrating along the way a willingness, and even eagerness, to engage with the new colonial order on terms of mutual partnership and mutual benefit (viii). In short, Maori were committed biculturalists over 130 years before the concept would (briefly) become fashionable among a minority of middle-class, liberal Pakeha. And the real problems began not because Maori proved incapable of being admitted to colonial society on terms of genuine equality, but precisely when they began to look like becoming "*too* effective in their mastery of the techniques of government and administration and would use their skills to close the land to settlement." As Ward wrote in the preface to a later edition of the book, consequently "that most precious institution of British culture, the rule of law, was prostituted to the land grab, and brought into the contempt in which many Maori today regrettably still hold it" (preface to 1995 edition, ix). It was, Ward argued, the Native Land Court, introduced in 1864 and associated with the "sordid, demoralising system of land-purchasing, not war and confiscation, which really brought the Maori people low." With communal titles to land ignored in favor of the kind of individual right to alienate bits of the tribal patrimony that the Crown had sought to recognize at Waitara in 1860, "chiefs betrayed their people and commoners betrayed chiefs." Nothing, Ward suggested, "save perhaps epidemic disease, was so disruptive of Maori life as this" (267).

There was, however, no room for sullen Maori demoralization and withdrawal in Ward's work. Even after defeat in the wars of the 1860s, and during the first few decades when the impact of the Land Court was felt most acutely, Ward demonstrated that Maori continued to actively embrace the possibilities evidently held out by government rhetoric of equality, even while continually (and increasingly) encountering the reality of their own state-directed dispossession and disempowerment. Maori communities around the country over and over again took the initiative in (selectively) reviewing and reforming their own customs and institutions in the hope of making these both more effective and more palatable to the settlers, and in expectation of extracting some corresponding concessions from the government to mitigate the worst excesses of the colonial order, but to little avail.

Ward's study was ultimately, therefore, a story of lost opportunities and "of a history that might have been," if only nineteenth-century officials had followed through on their rhetoric and allowed Maori a genuine share in the administration of their own (and the colony's) affairs.[23] In the Resident Magistrate system, introduced in 1846, for example, Ward saw enormous potential for success, through the cautious application of Pakeha law, with appropriate Maori involvement through the appointment of assessors, which was stifled through the retrenchment of Native Department machinery from the late 1870s onward. Governor George Grey's "New Institutions" scheme of 1861–62, premised on the recognition of Maori runanga (tribal councils), was similarly seen by Ward as promising enough to have potentially defused tension with the King movement, and possibly to have avoided the impending war in the Waikato, if only it had not been tainted through ulterior motives based on undermining the Maori king.

As one recent commentator has noted, *Show of Justice* "constituted the first major breach in the historiographical climate."[24] It has not, however, been without its critics. Mark Francis has labeled its approach "hindsight historiography" and described the work as "encumbered with moralism."[25] Richard Hill, writing from an altogether different perspective, and critiquing what he describes as the "lost opportunity" school of New Zealand race relations historiography and its liberal paradigm, considers such an approach as ignoring the coercive and hegemonic function of the state as an instrument for enforcing "peace and good order."[26] In Hill's view, the state has "never once," from 1840 onward, been interested in supporting Maori self-determination but had only ever taken steps to co-opt and appropriate perceived threats to the body politic. It was this imperative, Hill argues, not humanitarianism, that had underlain all Crown policy with respect to Maori in the nineteenth century.[27]

However one views such a critique, there can be little doubt that Ward's work captured perfectly the charged political atmosphere around Maori-Pakeha relations that had emerged by the early 1970s. A year after its publication, Whina Cooper led a Maori land march involving more than thirty thousand people along the way from Te Hapua, in the Far North, to the steps of Parliament in Wellington, to demand that "not one more acre of Maori land" be alienated. Thanks to Ward's book, ignorance as to the unfair methods used to expropriate the bulk of Maori lands in the nineteenth century, and the denigration and disempowerment of Maori leaders, could no longer be a valid excuse. As Eddie Durie, later chairperson of the Waitangi Tribunal (established in 1975 and empowered ten years later to investigate historical Maori grievances dating back to 1840), later wrote,

> What heart it gave to young Maori, when *Show of Justice* emerged during the Maori protest days, that scholarship could establish so amply what Maori were on about. This is not just a story of the past but an explanation of the present and a guide to mediating future race relations. Nor did

it prove to be just a history book. It became a historical landmark in its own right, providing an academic base for much of the formal claims process that began the following year.[28]

That Ward's work could be republished more than twenty years later (in 1995) due to popular demand, with all but a few corrections and to an overwhelmingly positive response,[29] was ample testament to its ongoing relevance. Yet as Lorenzo Veracini comments, between the two editions of *Show of Justice* "rested a comprehensive and radical process of historical reappraisal" both within academic history and in the context of the new Treaty claims-driven process of historical research in which Ward himself would become deeply engaged.[30] Ward's book may not have been responsible for this process of historical reappraisal, but it was certainly at the forefront of it.

The historiography associated with the Waitangi Tribunal process is frequently criticized for its alleged emphasis on Maori grievances, at the expense of other, more positive aspects of Maori-Pakeha history in New Zealand. Yet there is little doubt that Ward's history, like that of Sinclair before him, has a fundamentally positive vein to it. New Zealand may not, as many generations of schoolchildren were confidently informed, have had the best race relations in the world. The official ideology of racial amalgamation did, however, at least ensure Maori nominal equality before the law, most of the time, while also frowning on blatant racism against Maori, some of the time. It made multiracial schools and rugby teams possible, and sanctioned interracial marriage. And at a political level it ensured just enough amelioration of adverse Maori circumstances to avert complete despair of the system. All this may not have been cause for self-congratulatory and patronizing remarks concerning how well "our Maoris" were treated, but it provided (and continues to provide) just enough basis, along with ongoing Maori commitment to a racially inclusive future, for a "genuine unity of races, based on mutual respect" (315).

If all history is a product of its time, then Sinclair's *Origins* reflected an essentially optimistic, postwar generation, intent on building a better world for themselves and their children. Ward's *Show of Justice* emerged at a less certain time and played its own part in shaking off a few of the old certainties, while at the same time clinging to some cherished notions concerning the fundamental decency and fair-mindedness of the average New Zealander, be they Maori or Pakeha.[31] Sinclair's work is now dated, Ward's remains relevant. Yet in large measure, it was Sinclair's pioneering study that made Ward's later work possible. Together the works of these two great pedants played a significant part in helping to change the way New Zealanders viewed the history of their country. Later generations of historians ought to be eternally grateful.

Notes

1. Keith Sinclair, *The Maori Land League: An Examination into the Source of a New Zealand Myth* (Auckland, 1950), 3.

2. Useful historiographical reviews include James Belich, "Colonization and History in New Zealand," in *The Oxford History of the British Empire*, vol. 5: *Historiography*, ed. Robin W. Winks (Oxford, 1999), 182–93; Jock Phillips, "Of Verandahs and Fish and Chips and Footie on Saturday Afternoon: Reflections on 100 Years of New Zealand Historiography," *New Zealand Journal of History* (hereafter *NZJH*) 24, no. 2 (1990): 118–34; Erik Olssen, "Where to From Here?: Reflections on the Twentieth-Century Historiography of Nineteenth-Century New Zealand," *NZJH* 26, no. 1 (1992): 54–77. See also Grant Young, "The War of Intellectual Independence: New Zealand Historians and Their History, 1945–72" (master's thesis, University of Auckland, 1998).

3. Keith Sinclair, *Halfway Round the Harbour: An Autobiography* (Auckland, 1993), 55, 111ff. Ward's youth is movingly recalled in Lloyd Ashton, "A Sense of Anger," *Mana* 28 (June–July 1999): 35–38. A sickly child, brought up in damp and miserable housing conditions, Ward here attributes his survival to the district nurse and declares that "I owe both my life and my education to the state." Like Sinclair, he would later become unwaveringly committed to social democratic principles (and a firm supporter of the Labour Party) as a consequence.

4. Trevor Burnard, "The Continuing Relevance of the Treaty of Waitangi: An Interview with Alan Ward," *History Now* 5, no. 2 (1999): 7; Ward, "Comfortable Voyagers? Some Reflections on the Pacific and Its Historians," *Journal of Pacific History* 31, no. 2 (1996): 236–37; idem, "The History of the East Coast Maori Trust" (master's thesis, Victoria University College, 1958).

5. Sinclair, *Halfway Round the Harbour*, 129, 160–61.

6. Ibid., 103; idem, "The Aborigines Protection Society and New Zealand: A Study in Nineteenth Century Opinion" (master's thesis, Auckland University College, 1946).

7. Sinclair, *The Maori Land League*.

8. Sinclair, *Halfway Round the Harbour*, 126.; Donald H. Simpson, ed., *The Manuscript Catalogue of the Library of the Royal Commonwealth Society* (London, 1975), 23.

9. Harold Miller, *Landfall* 5, no. 2 (1951): 152.

10. Sinclair, *Halfway Round the Harbour*, 129.

11. M.P.K. Sorrenson, *Journal of the Polynesian Society* 66, no. 4 (1957): 438.

12. Erik Olssen, "Keith Sinclair, 1922–1993 (Obituary)," *NZJH* 27, no. 2 (1993): 219.

13. Ian Wards, Review *(Halfway Round the Harbour)*, *Archifacts* (October 1993): 81.

14. As Gerald Hensley noted in an otherwise positive review, this gave the work an "inconclusive and somewhat anti-climactic" ending. *Landfall* 12, no. 3 (1958): 289. Somewhat similar view were expressed by W. H. Oliver, *Historical Studies, Australia and New Zealand* 8, no. 32 (1959): 441; J. W. Davidson, *Australian Journal of Politics and History* 5, no. 2 (1959): 257.

15. See, for example, W. J. Gardner, "A Destiny in Auckland: The Contribution of Sir Keith Sinclair to N.Z. History," *Historical News* (Christchurch) 56 (1988): 2.

16. Keith Sinclair, "Why Are Race Relations in New Zealand Better than in South Africa, South Australia or South Dakota?" *NZJH* 5, no. 2 (1971): 121–27.

17. B. J. Dalton, *War and Politics in New Zealand, 1855–1870* (Sydney, 1967). Sinclair's review of this book pointed out that Dalton had ignored considerable evidence that established Kingi's claim to the land and had misinterpreted other crucial documents on this point. *New Zealand Listener*, 21 July 1967, 20. M.P.K. Sorrenson accused Dalton of "over-playing his hand." *NZJH* 2, no. 1 (1968): 94–97.

18. Alan Ward, "The Origins of the Anglo-Maori Wars: A Reconsideration," *NZJH* 1, no. 2 (1967): 149.

19. Ibid., 165. As W. H. Oliver wrote, Sinclair went on to purposefully study the major divisions of New Zealand history—"A Destiny at Home," in *Essays in Honour of Sir Keith Sinclair*, special issue of *NZJH* 21, no. 1 (1987): 10. A bibliography of Sinclair's massive scholarly (and smaller literary) output can be found in the same issue of *NZJH* on pages 189–93. His significant subsequent publications include *Kinds of Peace: Maori People after the Wars, 1870–1885*, published in 1991, and an autobiography *(Halfway Round the Harbour)* that appeared shortly before Sinclair's death in 1993.

20. Ward's high praise for Davidson's qualities as a Ph.D. supervisor is expressed in George Shepperson, P.E.H. Hair, and Doug Munro, "J. W. Davidson at Cambridge University: Some Student Evaluations," *History in Africa: A Journal of Method* 27 (2000): 226n. It is not generally known that Ward's original Ph.D. topic in 1962 was a history of the Melanesian Mission.

21. Judith Binney, *NZJH* 9, no. 2 (1975): 194.

22. Quoted in Alan Ward, *A Show of Justice: Racial "Amalgamation" in Nineteenth Century New Zealand* (Canberra, 1974), 34. All subsequent references to this work are to the 1974 edition, unless otherwise stated.

23. Jenny Murray, Review (1995 edition), *The Press* (Christchurch), 10 June 1995.

24. Lorenzo Veracini, "Negotiating Indigenous Resistance in the South Pacific:

Australia, Aotearoa / New Zealand and Kanaky-New Caledonia. Three Cases in Historical Redescription" (Ph.D. thesis, Griffith University, 2001), 149.

25. Mark Francis, "Settler Historiography in New Zealand: Politics and Biography in the Early Colonial Period," *Political Science* 52, no. 2 (2000): 159, 165.

26. Richard S. Hill, "Autonomy and Authority: Rangatiratanga and the Crown in Twentieth Century New Zealand: An Overview" (unpublished research report), (Wellington, 2000), 9–10. Hill's perspectives are discussed in Doug Munro, "At the Interface of History and Action: An Interview with Richard Hill," *History Now* 7, no. 2 (2001): 2–4.

27. Hill, "Autonomy and Authority," 10, 17; idem, *State Authority, Indigenous Autonomy: Crown-Maori Relations in New Zealand/Aotearoa, 1900–1950* (Wellington, 2004), passim.

28. Eddie Durie, back cover of *Show of Justice* (1995 edition).

29. Jenny Murray, *The Press*, 10 June 1995; Ralph Johnson, *New Zealand Herald*, 1 July 1995; Kerry Howe, *New Zealand Listener*, 27 May 1995.

30. Veracini, "Negotiating Indigenous Resistance," 150. See Alan Ward, *National Overview*, 3 vols. (Wellington, 1997); idem, *An Unsettled History: Treaty Claims in New Zealand Today* (Wellington, 1999). Also Ward's 1999 Stout Annual Lecture, "An Unsettled History," *New Zealand Studies* 9, no. 2 (1999): 30–37. Ward is one of several former members of Jim Davidson's department at ANU to perpetuate his tradition of "participant historian." In 1988 Ward became a historian with the Waitangi Tribunal on a part-time basis, and 1996 he resigned from the chair of History at the University of Newcastle (NSW) to engage in full-time research for the Tribunal. Before that, Ward was an adviser and consultant on land issues in Papua New Guinea and Vanuatu. He has also published on the more recent history of New Caledonia, including *Land and Politics in New Caledonia* (Canberra, 1982); and Michael Spencer, Alan Ward, and John Connell, eds., *New Caledonia: Essays in Nationalism and Dependency* (Brisbane, 1988).

31. As even more recent historical works have done. See, for example, Michael King, *The Penguin History of New Zealand* (Auckland, 2003), 518. See King's sympathetic profile of Sinclair in *Hidden Places: A Memoir in Journalism* (Auckland, 1992), 58–62. See also Nicholas Tarling, "Sir Keith Sinclair," in *Auckland Minds, Auckland Matters*, ed. Nicholas Tarling (Auckland, 2003), 155–65.

CHAPTER 13

Passage across the Sea: Indentured Labor to Fiji and from the Solomons

Brij V. Lal

Fiji's Indian Migrants: A History to the End of Indenture in 1920, by K. L. Gillion.
Melbourne: Oxford University Press, 1962. Reprinted 1973.

Passage, Port and Plantation: A History of Solomon Islands Labour Migration, 1870–1914, by Peter Corris.
Melbourne: Melbourne University Press, 1973.

SYSTEMATIC LARGE-SCALE labor recruitment in the Pacific Islands was a phenomenon of the nineteenth century. At the beginning of the twentieth century, around 500,000 people were involved in the Pacific labor trade under various forms of indenture. Among them were 60,965 Indian indentured laborers and about 30,000 Solomon Islanders. The Indian indentured workers were confined to Fiji, mostly to the plantations owned by the Colonial Sugar Refining Company, while the Solomon Islanders worked predominantly in Queensland and Fiji, as well as New Caledonia and Samoa.[1]

The two foundational texts on indentured servitude in the Pacific Islands are K. L. (Ken) Gillion's *Fiji's Indian Migrants* (1962) and Peter Corris's *Passage, Port and Plantation* (1973), which represented a decisive shift in approach and methodology from their respective historiographies. Despite their disparate subject matter, both books have much in common. Both emerged from doctoral dissertations written in the (then) Department of Pacific History in the Research School of Pacific Studies at the Australian National University (ANU). Both combine solid archival research and more limited oral evidence and are written in an accessible narrative style characteristic of the postwar historical scholarship in English. Both are pioneering works that attempt to offer a "total explanation" of the subject under study, not a specialized account of only selected segments. Neither is overtly comparative, especially Gillion. Solidly empirical, both are untouched by theory, untroubled by introspection about the construction of cross-cultural knowledge, about the difficulty of ascribing motives, of discerning the patterns of behavior of actors on the other side of the "beach." And finally, while the central arguments of both the books have been revised or refined, the original achievements substantially remain.

Gillion and Corris came to their respective topics via unusual routes —Gillion at a time when Pacific historiography was still in its infancy, Corris when the subdiscipline was reaching maturity. Ken Gillion (1929–92), a New Zealander, did a master's thesis on "The Indian Political Problem in Fiji" in 1955. After a spell in the New Zealand foreign service, he joined Davidson's department, sure of what he wanted to accomplish. In Davidson's opinion, Gillion required the least supervision of all the students he had.[2] But Gillion's Fiji work was both more and less than Pacific history; it was as much an exercise in overseas Indian historiography, an extension of his interest in India, to which he returned to write what he himself considered his best book, an urban history of the Gujarat textile city of Ahemadabad.[3] His final book was on the Fiji Indians in the interwar years, but that too is situated within the context of overseas Indians—their struggle for political equality.[4] Gillion spent much of his professional career teaching Indian history until he retired in 1978 after a five-year appointment as senior research fellow in the (renamed) Department of Pacific and South East Asian History at the ANU.

Peter Corris (born 1941), an Australian, came to Davidson's department in 1967 via undergraduate history at the University of Melbourne and a master's thesis on Aboriginal encounters with European settlers in western Victoria in the late nineteenth century at Monash University.[5] From that work emerged his interest in race relations between whites and nonwhites. He proposed the subject of "race relations in Queensland in the late nineteenth and early twentieth centuries as a possible PhD topic," examining the "background of the Pacific Islanders who came to Australia, their treatment when here, their activities, local reaction to them, etc."[6] Corris's proposal interested the members of the Pacific History Department and he was admitted as a research scholar. He was successively appointed postdoctoral fellow (to edit the journals of W. T. Wawn[7]) and research fellow (to revise his thesis for publication). Subsequently he taught history to undergraduates, hoping to become a full professor at an early age. But soon his enthusiasm wavered. As he said, "I looked around for another research subject and couldn't really find one, and by then the universities had changed. I was an old style performance-oriented-performance kind of student. And it had got to progressive assessment and all kinds of changes in the whole way in which university teaching operated. I lost interest, and didn't like it any more."[8] At the end of 1975, he became a freelance journalist, although he continued with academic work—namely, an edition of J. D. Melvin's newspaper articles on an 1892 recruiting voyage through the Solomons, collaborating with Roger Keesing to write an anthro-historical account of the Bell massacre of 1929 as well as a history of professional boxing in Australia.[9] About the same time he began a long and flourishing career as a writer of Cliff Hardy crime fiction based in and around Sydney, although he has returned sporadically to nonfiction and non-Pacific writing.[10]

Both *Fiji's Indian Migrants* and *Port, Passage and Plantation* were the first substantial pieces of modern scholarship on their respective subjects that broke the conventional mold. Let me take Indian indenture first. Although Indian indentured emigration started in 1834, scholarly accounts of that labor trade emerged only in the middle decades of the twentieth century. They were written not by professional historians but by public-spirited individuals, most engaged in some way with the Indian nationalist struggle. The political and imperial dimensions of the trade and its links to India's struggle for independence dominated the literature. Invariably this literature, designed to buttress a political agenda, exaggeratedly emphasized the iniquities in the system: the fraudulent recruitment of the laborers by unscrupulous recruiters (for no one in their right mind would ever enlist for indenture), the wholesale abuse of the system of administrative arrangements created to enforce the labor laws, the callous officials who oversaw it, the relentless pace of work on the plantations.[11] The indentured laborers themselves—"those floating caravan of barbarian tourists"[12]—are relegated to the margins, pawns in the game of chess played by the formulators of high imperial policy. In contrast to the Indian nationalist writers, the imperial historians tended to emphasize the beneficial, liberating aspects of migration and indenture.

The intraregional Pacific labor trade has also received its share of scholarly and not-so-scholarly attention. It is a huge literature comprising over 240 books, articles, and chapters on the Queensland segment alone.[13] Much of the revisionist thrust in modern historical scholarship on the Pacific Islands was inspired by work on the labor trade by members of Davidson's department, notably Corris and his supervisor Deryck Scarr. The earlier writing on the subject was of two kinds. There was the kidnapping/whips-and-chains school of thought, which sensationalized the labor trade, and which accorded Islanders no agency or individuality;[14] and there were the historians of empire who saw the trade as essentially a law and order problem, focusing upon the attempts by the British government to control it, to bring stability on a lawless imperial frontier. Both approaches crowded out the very people who were its principal subjects.[15]

Gillion's and Corris's singular achievement, then, was to move the indentured workers from the shadows more to the center stage, though never completely. The social and economic conditions that prompted their migration are assessed along with individual motivations. Sensitivity and sympathy are the hallmark of their scholarship. They note the inequities in the system of recruitment and the fraudulence of the recruiters but they are aware of the importance of other factors. They acknowledge official benevolence but recognize its limitations and failures. Corris in particular restores an element of agency and individual choice to the laborers. The impact of *Port, Passage and Plantation* has often been emphasized. It was regarded by Kerry Howe as a "revolutionary interpretation." More specifically, Doug Munro has described the book as "the great leap forward in labor trade studies," the text that "set a standard in approach and methodology by which subsequent studies on the subject would be judged," suggesting that many later studies failed to meet that standard.[16]

Both Gillion and Corris present new information about their subject. Gillion, however, is far less explicitly revisionist than Corris. He argues that emigration was not popular with the people of India for religious reasons, for crossing the *kala pani* (literally, dark waters, that is, to overseas destinations) caused ritual pollution and loss of caste. The Indian was inherently conservative, a landlubber, wedded to the joint-family system, showing "a spirit of acceptance of the lot one's karma had brought." Two things flow from this. One is that people migrated reluctantly and then only under the most extreme conditions, when they were faced with famine or some other natural calamity. And the second is the deceitful role that recruiters played in enticing people into migrating. Concerned to be balanced and reluctant to adjudicate, Gillion accepts the role that both economic necessity and false promise played in causing migration, but does not assign deception the importance the earlier writers did.

Corris's major revisionism concerns the active role of Islanders in the labor trade. He acknowledges that fraud and violence characterized the early stages of recruitment, but argues that they were overshadowed by voluntary cooperation as the benefits of the trade began to be understood and people appreciated the advantages that emigration brought to the individuals who enlisted and to their tribes and communities.[17] In support, Corris draws attention to the large number of returned hands who reenlisted, the role they played in facilitating recruitment, and their eventual awareness of the advantages and disadvantages of the different destinations. Perhaps the most important aspect of recruiting that Corris illuminates is the role of the "passage masters," indigenous men of ambition, skill, and power who acted as intermediaries between the recruiters and the recruits and generally used their position to further their own agendas.[18]

But how have these two revisionists themselves been revised, and where does this leave their books? Let us take Gillion first. It is true that emigration was not popular with the people of India, but what Gillion underemphasizes is the extent of internal mobility in late-nineteenth-century rural India. In large parts of eastern Uttar Pradesh from where the bulk of the migrants to Fiji came, the benefits of emigration were known to outweigh its disadvantages. For impoverished peasants and ejected tenants, migration had become an important strategy to cope with life's vagaries. In the Benares Division alone, the census commissioner wrote in 1911, there was hardly a family that did not have at least one member in some other province in search of employment.[19] It was from this uprooted mass of peasantry that the indentured laborers were recruited. Indeed, indentured emigration was an extension of the larger process of internal migration taking place within India itself. This puts the deception theory into its proper context.

Corris argues that what was once a one-sided trade, attended by violence, became a voluntary transaction in time as its benefits permeated society. Nonetheless, perhaps the nature and extent of *individual* voluntary participation is exaggerated. Clive Moore demonstrates that the decision to recruit was related to "existing exchange networks, political and social pressures present in Melanesian society, and to predictable stages in traditional life-cycles which coincided with the requirements of the labour trade."[20] He also disputes that the labor trade significantly disrupted the traditional lifestyle of the community.[21] Roger Keesing has also pointed out that "ex-recruits very often compartmentalised their plantation period away in memory (as many ex-servicemen compartmentalise their wartime experience) and carried on as pagan priests, warriors, and feast givers, outwardly unaffected by the experience in Queensland or Fiji: for many it seems to have been an extended kind of initiatory seclusion, a liminal state from which they returned to 'real life'—but as men, not boys."[22]

There have been cavils. Moore has introduced the idea of cultural kidnapping to modify the notion of voluntary transaction. By this he means an unequal knowledge of what the process entailed between the recruiters and the recruited. The recruiters knew exactly what the work on the plantations entailed, its risks and opportunities, but not the recruited. It was, in this sense, an unequal transaction. More recently, Doug Munro has questioned the extent to which the labor trade was a voluntary affair, and he proposes the term *voluntary compulsion*. Either the recruits were prepared to undergo the risks and hardships of plantation life because it was their only means to obtain desired items of European manufacture, or else they were pushed into this by community elders with an eye to obtaining the eventual bounty.[23]

The plantation experience of the indentured workers forms an important part of both the books. Gillion describes the lines, the living quarters of the indentured laborers, as places of filth and degradation. The squalor and moral poverty, the legacy of the relentless pace of work, emerge clearly. He also shows a sympathetic appreciation of the difficult position of the overseers. Gillion is keen to provide a balanced, "on the one hand, on the other," picture of a complex and troubling situation. A typical sentence goes like this: "Of course, all overseers were at times provoked by immigrants, but there were some who were habitually brutal" (112). There were overseers who perpetrated atrocities, "but these men were accidental misfits who were eventually detected and fined, imprisoned or dismissed, or fled the country" (104). In point of fact, the prosecution rate of the offending overseers was paltry. He describes the various mechanisms to enforce regulations relating to indenture, and shows an awareness of the disparity between intention and execution, but then says, contrary to all the evidence, that those "who pleaded sickness were sent for medical treatment" (103). Not always, but when they were, the days spent at hospital were added to the laborer's contract. "The size of the task depended on the nature of the soil and the state of the cane, and allowance was made for inexperienced immigrants," he says. But the reality on the ground was different.

There is a touch of austerity to Gillion's writing. Davidson's assessment that Gillion made "rather less of his material than he might have done," and that "in the interpretation of documents, his scrupulousness induces a degree of caution that often seems to me to be excessive" rings true to me.[24] Owen Parnaby went so far as to say that "Gillion's judgements on the motivation for emigration and on the character of the emigrants are given with such reservations that only by a careful reading can one be satisfied that they are not contradictory."[25] And Hugh Tinker, in his influential *A New System of Slavery*, chided Gillion for being "perhaps a little too concerned to be 'balanced,'" and for sometimes holding back "from the most searching probe into the sordid."[26] The latter claim can be dismissed given Gillion's emphasis on the unpleasant and iniquitous features of plantation life. Gillion for his part accused Tinker of writing a book that was "deliberately moralistic in tone,"[27] sublimely unaware that the same comment applies to his own assessment of the human costs of plantation life. Gillion not only endorsed the contemporary critics of Indian indenture but appropriated their moralistic vocabulary, which strangely contrasts with his normally austere and balanced style of exposition.

Corris's account of the life on the plantation concentrates on Queensland and draws in the other areas of employment where Solomon Islanders served, especially Fiji, for purposes of comparison. He demonstrates the variability of the conditions on plantations, and mortality rates, not only over time but between districts and even between plantations in the same district. Corris claims that the extent of violence on the plantations has been exaggerated. In Queensland, physical abuse rather than excessive violence was the norm (82), while in Fiji the fear of losing laborers kept things in check (83). Some of Corris's mellower conclusions about plantation life and labor (e.g., "The illness and death rates seemed to have concerned masters and officials more than the men" [78]) have been disputed by other scholars. Kay Saunders and Adrian Graves, for example, argue that coercion and brutality toward laborers was the norm.[28] One does not have to accept the totality of their argument to register a point of debate with Corris. And Ralph Shlomowitz's painstakingly detailed statistical analysis of the mortality rates of the workers points to epidemiological reasons for high mortality rates rather than necessarily to the conditions on the plantations.[29]

Both Gillion and Corris tell a human story unencumbered by theoretical insight or comparative perspective. Gillion discusses the rigors and the sheer drudgery of plantation life but there is little consideration of the structure of the plantation system itself, which regulated every feature of the worker's life. He focuses on the actions of individual overseers, for instance, but does not grasp the fact that the individual overseer's humanity (or lack of it) was compromised by the demands made upon him by the production quotas.[30] It is the same with Corris, although in his case there is a keen recognition that the temperament of the overseers greatly varied and that this had a large bearing on the quality of a laborer's plantation experience (80–81).

The focus on the experience of individual workers says little about the way in which they collectively resisted the demands made upon them. Clive Moore discusses the resistance strategies Solomon Islanders adopted in Queensland, which usually stopped far short of outright defiance. Borrowing insights from Eugene D. Genovese and James C. Scott, he argues that the laborers' "lack of obvious active resistance or protest relates not only to the authoritarian character of the plantation system but also to their deliberate choice of methods of response . . . Their response was to mediate their working and private lives through their own beliefs, institutions, and forms of behavior, which were in partial operation in the colony."[31] And for Fiji—and also taking a leaf from Genovese's work—I have discussed the impediments to organized worker protest and the strategies they adopted to cope with their situation: "Some vented their rage on the crops and tools of the employers, feigned illness, and absented themselves from work in protest against the system. Others, fed up with the constant drudgery of work and the hopelessness of their situation, took their own lives through suicides, while a few avenged acts of injustices against them by murdering their overseers and sirdars."[32] In the end, though, the majority chose nonresistance as the most logical way to deal with the demands made on them.

Another subject largely ignored in Pacific labor studies until recently was gender. Corris notes the small number of Solomon Island women who migrated. There was no stipulated quota to fill, and cultural and social constraints prevented female mobility in the islands. Women constituted less than 10 percent of all the recruits (46). Despite Corris's best efforts, the women recruits (about 8 percent of the total) remain hidden in the shadow of statistics, nameless and faceless, their identity and individuality lost. Even the archival record is largely silent. With little exception, not much advance has been made on Corris.[33] For Fiji, by contrast, John Kelly has provided a theoretically sophisticated, anthropologically based account of gender issues on plantations.[34]

Indian indenture is different. From the very beginning, the government of India insisted that forty women accompany a hundred men on each shipment. The recruiters made much of the difficulty in recruiting women, but the quota was always met. Gillion has better sources and makes most of the opportunity. But my own work has extended knowledge of the work experience of women on the plantations by drawing attention to the disparity in the attendance, absence, and wage levels between men and women, the amount of task work they were able to accomplish, the different degrees to which men and women were struck down by disease and ill health. And I attempted to rescue the indentured women from the "veil of dishonor" by demonstrating that women's alleged infidelity and mercenary spirit as the main cause of Fiji's high suicide rate was a gross exaggeration about a deeply complex situation.[35] Not women but the conditions of work on the plantations produced the calamity. The indentured women bore the brunt of both sexism and racism. Gillion writes about the difficulty of recruiting women, and says that few families were recruited (55). He is wrong. Altogether 4,627 families migrated from North India as families from their districts of origin. They were not unions of convenience, as Gillion and others suggest, formed at the behest of the recruiters to facilitate enlistment.

Both Gillion and Corris were able to interview surviving indentured laborers in the course of their research. But in keeping with the scholarly traditions of the time, the voice of the workers is subdued in the text, playing a distant second fiddle to the archival record. Oral testimony is used sparingly and then only to bolster a point already established in the written sources. This is a pity, for the voice of those who survived the initial crossing is now lost forever, although less so in the case of Corris than in the case of Gillion. Also lacking in the Gillion and Corris texts is the attention we now pay to culture and religion as tools of survival as well as instruments of resistance. Corris is aware of the cultural and social contexts from which the recruits come, but does not remark on the way in which they used their cultural heritage to cope in their new environment.[36] Indeed, he thinks that the Solomon Islanders suspended the observance of customary practices in Queensland (96). But the detailed researches of Patricia Mercer and Clive Moore show that these figured prominently in the life of the community.[37] Gillion writes about the festivals and rituals that laborers observed, but does not use the material to provide deeper insights into the community. This is a mystery. He had with him an unpublished manuscript by Totaram Sanadhya, but unfortunately only snippets feature in his work, without assessment or commentary.[38] It is in the area of the cultural analysis of the plantation experience that much new work has been done in the last decade or so.

Both Ken Gillion and Peter Corris enlarged our knowledge and understanding of Pacific Islands labor trade. They brought out the human dimension of their respective subjects in ways that previous historians had not. They broke from the confines of conventional historiography. Since the publication of their works more than three decades ago, the field has inevitably moved on, influenced by new developments and new intellectual concerns. Different questions and alternative lines of thinking have yielded new answers. Gillion and Corris opened up new windows through which those who followed them saw different vistas and drew different sketches. That is all that one can ask of any good scholarship.

Notes

1. See Doug Munro, "The Origins of Labourers in the South Pacific: Commentary and Statistics," in *Labour in the South Pacific*, ed. Clive Moore, Jacqueline Leckie, and Doug Munro (Townsville, 1990), xxxix–li. The recruitment of Solomon Islanders on contracts of indenture for destinations outside their own island group lasted from 1870 to 1911. The export of indentured laborers from India to Fiji occurred between 1879 and 1916.

2. This is based on Gillion's confidential file, held by the Division of Pacific and Asian History, Australian National University. For a more detailed account of Gillion's career, see my obituary to him in *Journal of Pacific History* 28, no. 1 (1993): 93–96.

3. Gillion, *Ahemadabad: A Study in Indian Urban History* (Berkeley/Los Angeles, 1968).

4. Gillion, *The Fiji Indians: Challenge to European Dominance, 1920–1946* (Canberra, 1977).

5. Published as *Aborigines and Europeans in Western Victoria* (Canberra, 1968).

6. Peter Corris to Diane Barwick, 18 July 1966, Corris's confidential file, Division of Pacific and Asian History, ANU.

7. W. T. Wawn, *The South Sea Islanders and the Queensland Labour Trade*, ed. Peter Corris (Canberra, 1973).

8. Clive Moore, "Writing for Fun: Interview with Peter Corris, Author of the Cliff Hardy Detective Novels," *Clues: A Journal of Detection* 21, no. 2 (2000): 58.

9. J. D. Melvin, *The Cruise of the Helena*, ed. Peter Corris (Melbourne, 1977); Roger M. Keesing and Peter Corris, *Lightning Meets the West Wind: The Malaita Massacre* (Melbourne, 1980); Corris, *Lords of the Ring: A History of Prize-fighting in Australia* (Melbourne, 1980).

10. Peter Cotton, "Peter Corris on his Craft, and Cliff Hardy," *National Graduate* (Canberra) 2, no. 3 (1991): 7–9. Corris provides some information on his time at the ANU in his autobiography, *Sweet and Sour: A Diabetic Life* (Lismore, 2000), 74–103.

11. For a discussion, see my "Leaves of the Banyan Tree: Origins and Background of Fiji's North Indian Indentured Migrants, 1879–1916" (Ph.D. dissertation, Australian National University, 1980), chap. 1.

12. Quoted in I. M. Cumpston, *Indians Overseas in British Territories, 1834–1854* (London, 1953), 174.

13. Clive Moore, "Revising the Revisionists: The Historiography of Immigrant Melanesians in Australia," *Pacific Studies* 15, no. 2 (1992): 61.

14. Originating with Thomas Dunbabin, *Slavers of the South Seas* (Sydney, 1935) and including Edward Wybergh Docker, *The Blackbirders: The Recruitment of South Seas Labour for Queensland, 1863–1907* (Sydney, 1970).

15. For example, O. W. Parnaby, *Britain and the Labor Trade in the Southwest Pacific* (Durham, NC, 1964).

16. K. R. Howe, "The Fate of the 'Savage' in Pacific Historiography," *New Zealand Journal of History* 11, no. 2 (1977): 150; Doug Munro, "The Labor Trade in Melanesians to Queensland: An Historiographic Essay," *Journal of Social History* 28, no. 3 (1995): 611, 612.

17. The point about benefits and voluntary participation was initially sketched out by Deryck Scarr, "Recruits and Recruiters: A Portrait of the Pacific Islands Labour Trade," *Journal of Pacific History* 2 (1967): 5–24.

18. A fuller treatment of this is in Corris, "Kwaisulia of Ada Gege: A Strongman in the Solomon Islands," in *Pacific Islands Portrait*, ed. J. W. Davidson and Deryck Scarr (Canberra, 1970), 253–66.

19. See generally my *Girmitiyas: The Origins of the Fiji Indians* (Canberra, 1983), and *Chalo Jahaji: On a Journey through Indenture in Fiji* (Suva, 2000).

20. Clive Moore, *Kanaka: A History of Melanesian Mackay* (Port Moresby, 1985), 47.

21. Ibid., 48.

22. Review (of *Passage, Port and Plantation*), in *Journal of Pacific History* 9 (1974): 216.

23. Moore, *Kanaka*, xi, 47–48; Doug Munro, "The Pacific Islands Labour Trade: Approaches, Methodologies, Debates," *Slavery & Abolition* 14, no. 2 (1993): 94–95.

24. Davidson's assessment is from Gillion's confidential file.

25. Owen Parnaby, *Journal of the Polynesian Society* 74, no. 2 (1965): 244.

26. Hugh Tinker, *A New System of Slavery: The Export of Indian Labour Overseas 1830–1920* (London, 1974), 407. An assiduous application of the Tinker thesis for Fiji is Ahmed Ali, ed., *The Indenture Experience in Fiji, 1879–1979* (Suva, 1979).

27. *Journal of Pacific History* 10, no. 4 (1974): 140.

28. Kay Saunders, *Workers in Bondage: The Origins and Bases of Unfree Labour in Queensland, 1824–1916* (Brisbane, 1982), chap. 4; Adrian Graves, *Cane and Labour: The Political Economy of the Queensland Sugar Industry, 1862–1906* (Edinburgh, 1993), chaps. 4–5.

29. See Shlomowitz's collected essays, *Migration and Mortality in the Modern World* (Aldershot, 1996).

30. A revealing overseer's account is Walter Gill, *Turn North-East at the Tombstone* (Adelaide, 1970).

31. Clive Moore, "The Counterculture of Survival: Melanesians in the Mackay District of Queensland, 1865–1906," in *Plantation Workers: Resistance and Accommodation*, ed. Brij V. Lal, Doug Munro, and Edward D. Beechert (Honolulu, 1993), 71.

32. Lal, *Chalo Jahaji*, 167–93 (quotation, 189).

33. Kay Saunders, "Melanesian Women in Queensland, 1863–1906: Some Methodological Problems involving Racism and Sexism," *Pacific Studies* 4, no. 1 (1980): 26–44; Margaret Jolly, "The Forgotten Women: A History of Migrant Labour and Gender Relations in Vanuatu," *Oceania* 58, no. 2 (1987): 119–39; Clive Moore, "A Precious Few: Melanesian and Asian Women in Northern Australia," in *Gender Relations in Australia: Domination and Negotiation*, ed. Kay Saunders and Raymond Evans (Sydney, 1992), 59–81.

34. John D. Kelly, *A Politic of Virtue: Hinduism, Sexuality and Countercolonial Discourse in Fiji* (Chicago, 1991). See also his "Discourse About Sexuality and the End of Indenture in Fiji: The Making of Counter-hegemonic Discourse," *History and Anthropology* 5 (1990): 19–61, and "Fear of Culture: British Regulation of Indian Marriage in Post-indenture Fiji," *Ethnohistory* 36 (1989): 372–91.

35. Lal, *Chalo Jahaji*, 195–238.

36. Roger Keesing uses oral testimony effectively in his *Custom and Confrontation: The Kwaio Struggle for Cultural Autonomy* (Chicago, 1992), 32–48.

37. P. M. Mercer and C. R. Moore, "Melanesians in North Queensland: The Retention of Indigenous Religious and Magical Practices," *Journal of Pacific History* 11, nos. 1/2 (1978): 66–88 (esp. 76).

38. A translated version of the unpublished manuscript, with editorial commentary, is in *Chalo Jahaji*, 239–60.

CHAPTER 14

Trumpet and *Road:* Two Classic Cargo Texts

Lamont Lindstrom

The Trumpet Shall Sound: A Study of "Cargo" Cults in Melanesia,
by Peter Worsley.
London: MacGibbon & Kee, 1957. 2nd ed., New York: Schocken Books, 1968.

*Road Belong Cargo: A Study of the Cargo Movement in the Southern
Madang District, New Guinea,* by Peter Lawrence.
Manchester: Manchester University Press, 1964. Co-published, Melbourne:
Melbourne University Press, 1964, and reprinted 1967.

CARGO CULTS, so they were called, boomed in the 1950s. Cargo
culting flourished both on the ground and in the library. The Melanesian
islands seemed then to be crawling with cultists. And soon the cargo cult
surfaced as an arresting topic of debate within Pacific Studies. Although
anthropologists and other observers had, during the first half of the
twentieth century, noted and occasionally poked into a range of island
movements, frenzies, and miscellaneous social disturbances, it was not
until after the Pacific War that these all would come to be bundled
together under the new rubric of cargo cult, F. E. Williams's accounts of
the Vailala Madness being the best known of these.[1] Peter Worsley initially defined the term, in *Trumpet,* as

> the rise of a large number of strange religious movements in the South
> Pacific during the last few decades. In these movements, a prophet
> announces the imminence of the end of the world in a cataclysm which
> will destroy everything. Then the ancestors will return, or God, or some
> other liberating power, will appear, bringing all the goods the people
> desire, and ushering in a reign of eternal bliss. (11)

The term *cargo cult* itself first appeared, at least in print, in the
November 1945 issue of the colonial news magazine *Pacific Islands*

Monthly (PIM). That month, Mr. Norris Mervyn Bird, whom *PIM* identified as "an old Territories resident," wrote to warn of postwar "flare-ups" among Islanders crazed by ill-digested Christian teaching and an increasingly liberal and dangerous colonial policy. Within just a few years, Australian-based anthropologists, including Lucy Mair (who, in late 1945 was lecturing at the Army School of Civil Affairs in Canberra), had smartly embraced *cargo cult*, which, as a term, possessed a catchy alliterative symmetry.[2] D'Arcy Ryan used *cargo cult* in his bachelor's honors thesis, the first of a number of student treatments of cargo cults at Sydney University.[3] And soon afterward, scholars moved into the field to inspect cultists face to face. Peter Lawrence, among the first to investigate cargo culting in situ, arrived in Papua New Guinea's Madang District—then a pressure cooker of cargoism—in April 1949.

The first academic accounts of cargo cults began to sprinkle into journals by the early 1950s.[4] The first monographs appeared in 1956. The period between 1956 and 1964, in fact, was cargo's golden age. During these years, six important analyses were published. Five of these dealt with particular cargo movements: Jean Guiart on the John Frum Movement; Margaret Mead and Theodore Schwartz on the Admiralty Islands; Kenelm Burridge on northern Madang; and, not too far away, Peter Lawrence's *Road Belong Cargo*. The sixth volume was Peter Worsley's compendium of cargo cults, *The Trumpet Shall Sound*.[5] Of these classics, Worsley's *Trumpet* and Lawrence's *Road* have been the most enduring, coming and going in and out of print, in several editions, over the past fifty years. *Road* appeared in French in 1974, and *Trumpet* in Russian in 1963, French in 1977, and Japanese in 1981.[6]

The Two Peters

Peter Worsley (born 1924) studied anthropology at the Australian National University (ANU) for a Ph.D. on the Wanindiljaugwa of Groote Eylandt, northern Australia.[7] In 1954, he rejoined the Department of Social Anthropology at Manchester University, then a hothouse of revolutionary study, cultic and otherwise. Mancunian scholars including Max Gluckman and Norman Cohn were busy tracking down social rebellion through time and place. Eric Hobsbawm joined them in 1956 to deliver the Simon Lectures, subsequently expanded into his influential *Primitive Rebels* (1959). Joining in, Worsley turned back to the Pacific and its resident brand of millenarianism—the cargo cult. His seminal *The Trumpet Shall Sound* mapped out the field for a growing crowd of anthropological cargo investigators, hard at his heels. Worsley framed many of the problems that have swirled persistently through cargo studies: prophets and charisma, rationality and madness, social change and nationalism, and the causes and cures of culting.

Based on Worsley's review of "English, French, German, and Dutch" (257) archival sources, *Trumpet* surveyed seventy-five years of culting stretching from Fiji to Papua (Netherlands New Guinea, in those days). Worsley began his banquet with a cultic hors d'oeuvre—the Tuka Movement of 1880s Fiji—and then sketched the material conditions of colonialism that were inducing Melanesians to embrace cults. Next, he followed cargo through space and time, marching mostly across New Guinea but also taking in cults of the New Hebrides (Vanuatu, nowadays) and the Solomon Islands. He argued, in a conclusion, that subjugated people have turned to cults, in many places including Europe, "as an expression of reaction against what is felt as oppression by another class or nationality" (227), and that cults function to integrate people into larger political unities—this particularly significant in societies, as in Melanesia, that mostly comprise autonomous clans and villages. Worsley proposed that cargo cults were "the first stirrings of nationalism" (254) but predicted that "more advanced, secular political movements" would eventually displace these.[8] The book concluded with an appendix in which Worsley criticized Max Weber's theory of charisma and Ralph Linton's attempts to tag a mess of movements, including cargo cults, as characteristically "nativistic." In 1968, Schocken Books in New York published a second, augmented edition of *Trumpet,* the augmentation being a lengthy new introduction in which he much elaborated his comments on charisma, religion, and millenarian politics.

Peter Lawrence (1921–87), studying anthropology at Cambridge University, began his Ph.D. fieldwork in 1949 among the Garia near Madang on the northern coast of New Guinea.[9] His "chief interest at the time was traditional socio-political structure" but he soon—despite his intentions and also those of local colonial administrators—found himself seduced by cargo cult. Years later, Lawrence would at last publish a monograph on the Garia.[10] But the book project he tackled first, after completing his Ph.D. thesis, was cargo cult.

Like *Trumpet,* Lawrence's *Road* is also subtitled a "study" of a cargo movement, but where Worsley provided a comparative overview of Melanesian culting (including its connections to millenarian movements everywhere), Lawrence focused on cults within a single region of coastal New Guinea. His case study followed the history of Madang cargoism through five phases, between 1871 and 1950. Where Worsley mined the literature and archives, Lawrence camped three years in the field (off and on, between 1949 and 1958). *Road*, like *Trumpet*, has also appeared in several editions (1989 the date of the most recent imprint) and a translation into the French language.[11] In 1986, Bill Tomasetti, a former administrative officer in Papua New Guinea, translated *Road* into Papua New Guinea's lingua franca Tok Pisin, a tricky, perhaps even Herculean, task.[12] This remains a major contribution to Pidgin literature.

Road's opening chapter on the native cosmic order is a magisterial summary of the cultural context of culting. This managed to nativize both cargo desire and cultic organization as intrinsically Melanesian. Several cultural elements predisposed Islanders to cargo culting, including the importance of wealth within traditional society, presumptions of active spiritual contributions to economic production, a disjunctive temporality, and customary polities wherein bigman leadership resembled that of cult prophets.[13] After this introductory cultural reading, Lawrence provided a detailed history of eighty years of Madang cargoism, culminating in the poignant story of Yali, its most recent and most celebrated prophet.

Where Worsley perceived at least some revolutionary potential within cargo culting, Lawrence took cults to be essentially conservative and, ultimately, a barrier to economic and political development (223). Lawrence was comfortable with the late colonial project of cultivating modernity, and he maintained close connections with local planters, selected missionaries, and administrators—one of which, J. K. McCarthy, of the Department of Native Affairs, provided the foreword to his book.[14] A particularly prickly issue of the day was who to blame for cargo cults.[15] Worsley argued that these were offspring of the invidious colonial system itself. They were a "religion of the lower orders" (225) that functioned to establish new unities so as to resist domination. Lawrence, conversely, stressed enduring continuities in Melanesian culture out of which cargo culting had sprung. The generative factor was deepseated Melanesian belief and practice, not colonialist oppression.

But even Lawrence, comfortable with his administrative associations, observed that "intensive contact brought very bad race relations" (57), and created the social context for cults. Moreover, despite his conservative and even reactionary politics, Lawrence echoed much of Worsley's materialism. Like Worsley, he subscribed to an economic cure (273). Simply educating Islanders would not cure their cargoism. Only economic development could ensure political and religious rationalization—or, as some Marxists were saying, infrastructure would determine superstructure. Lawrence accepted Worsley's argument that cults functioned to create wider polities and thus were a form of rudimentary nationalism (222).[16] He wrote with Worsley in mind, using his Madang data to qualify parts of Worsley's earlier comparative analysis (*Road*, 264–67).[17] Conversely, *Trumpet* drew on Lawrence's initial articles and Worsley, in his second edition, responded to Lawrence's comments in *Road* (*Trumpet*, augmented edition, lx–lxii).[18]

The Times They Were A-Changing

Why this efflorescence of cargo cult literature in the 1950s? The world was, of course, then deep into the Cold War. World War II had mortally wounded the colonial system, although the final effects of this would not play out in the Pacific until the 1970s. The pressing question was whether newly independent Third World states would go capitalist or communist. Both Worsley and Lawrence presented their analyses as likely to interest readers beyond academia. Worsley suggested that "the millenarian cult has become not merely a matter of theoretical importance to anthropologists, but also a matter of practical concern to governments" (11–12). Lawrence, too, interviewed by *Pacific Islands Monthly*, argued that "it is essential to understand how these people think of us and our way of life, because if you are going to change their ways of thinking and their way of living, you must know what you are up against" (*Pacific Islands Monthly*, February 1958, 59).

In the 1950s, people had social change—revolutions, even—on their minds. Two other celebrated accounts of protest and rebellion appeared alongside *Trumpet:* namely, Norman Cohn's *Pursuit of the Millennium* (1957) and Eric Hobsbawm's *Primitive Rebels* (1959). Issues of protest, insurrection, insurgence, and upheaval were then in the air. These percolated even in the far Melanesian fringes of the old colonial world. And, just over the horizon, were the 1960s. In much of the West, civil rights, women's rights, antiwar and antiauthoritarian movements would soon shake established powers and norms. Trance, dance, free love, drugs, cult communitarianism, the New Man, the New Age, living the myth-dream all would soon impugn corrupt and immoral political systems. Bizarre cargo cults, in obscure Melanesia, would echo within the rational capitalist mainland.[19] Worsley's second edition even made brief mention of the Black Power movements of 1960s America (lxiii).

The Cold War crept in between the books' covers. Worsley's analysis was perceived widely as Marxist, although Marx himself appeared only in a few scattered pages of the conclusion. (A decade later, Worsley in his second edition would "dissent" from his earlier Marxist orientation and its elements of determinism [lix].) His critics complained of his anticolonialist imputations of cargo cults, of his presumption that cults evolve from irrational religiosity to more reasoned politicking, and of his gentle critique that capitalism is also shot through with irrationality (35). Lucy Mair, for example, sniped that a reader of Worsley may well question "whether he is to be told that the cults dramatize the natives' intuitive recognition of the theory of surplus value."[20] Worsley, in return, protested that some "writers have a quarrel with Marx which they are conducting via my work" (lix). Since he mischievously borrowed the epigrams that head his chapters mostly from the Old and New Testaments, however, readers might well have presumed Worsley to imply that Christianity itself was a sort of aged cargo cult.

White fears of cargo cult and, moreover, of ethnographic studies thereof, impinged on Worsley and Lawrence alike. The Australian colonial government of Papua and New Guinea refused to let Worsley into the colony: "I was also banned by the Australian Government from conducting first-hand research in New Guinea itself" (196, lxi), which is why he ended up writing his Ph.D. thesis on Groote Eylandt.[21] Lawrence, similarly, despite his closer connections to Australian colonial power, also found himself prohibited to live where he first had planned: the administration "understandably refused me permission to go to the Rai Coast, the apparent centre of disturbance" (2).

Change, History, and Culture

Before 1956, no one had written a monograph on cargo cult although William's 1923 essay on Vailala Madness, and treatments of millenarian movements elsewhere, provided certain prototypes. Both Worsley and Lawrence needed to develop ways to write against the grain of structural-functionalist anthropology, the dominant British theoretical discourse in the 1950s. The most doctrinaire version of this held that anthropology, as a science, ought to focus on social relations and institutions, and that culture, psychology, and history were all of lesser importance. Borrowed from Durkheim's model of organic solidarity, the ideal primitive social structure was the segmentary lineage system. Lawrence later mocked this as "like the cross-section of an orange or the segments of cheese you buy in a box."[22]

No longer functionalist social coherence, the predicament of the postwar 1950s was social change. Functionalism, obviously, digested with great difficulty the mad frenzies of cargo culting wherein people were liable to dump traditional marriage custom in favor of free love, or resist economic modernity by discarding hard-earned shillings and pounds into the sea.[23] Worsley instead called for a new dynamic theory of change (266). And, in *Trumpet*'s appendix, he threatened to defect. If some might object that the basic approach of the work differs in important respects from that of much contemporary British anthropology (257), then Worsley was happy to consider himself engaged instead in a "general science of society" (260), especially in that the borders between anthropology and sociology seemed then to be appreciably dissolving. (This probably reflected as well Worsley's academic position within a joint department of social anthropology and sociology at the University of Manchester.)

An adequate understanding of cargo cults cried out for psychology (all those mad prophets and desperate followers), for culture (those peculiar beliefs and rituals), and especially for history.[24] Concerned with cult causes and futures, both Worsley and Lawrence mined the archives. Lawrence structured *Road* temporally, its chapters progressing through the several stages of Madang cargoism from 1871 to 1950. He wrote, notably, in the past tense rather than the standard "ethnographic present" that then dominated anthropological description. Lawrence also mapped history onto several tables that displayed progressions in cargo belief, prophets, and desires. Worsley, too, structured *Trumpet* temporally and geographically, the book leading off with cults of the 1880s and concluding in the 1950s. As several reviewers of the day noted, however, *Trumpet* conflated two sorts of history: the actual progression of events with this cult or that; and the materialist presumption that organizations founded in religion progressively evolve into more logical and political associations.[25] Worsley, forty years later, would continue to insist that "the time has come, then, to emphasize that every Cargo movement has an often complex *history*, and that the history of one community is likely to differ from that of others."[26]

And, finally, Lawrence and Worsley found themselves having to deal with culture, although neither much used the word. To explain Madang's cargoism, Lawrence began with a depiction of what he called "The Native Cosmic Order" (9, which in the Tok Pisin translation of his book became "Olgeta-olgeta-samting, olsem ol Madang Saut i tingim"). He referred to this as an "intellectualist" inquiry, or one concerned with native "epistemology" (*Garia*, 9; see also *Road*, 5). Lawrence, here, was grasping for terms to describe what elsewhere had long been tagged "culture." He had read his Margaret Mead but "culture," perhaps, was still too down-market to articulate. Nonetheless, in order to make sense of cargoism, Lawrence had to account for how Melanesians understood their world, call this cosmology, epistemology, or whathaveyou. Worsley, too, although only dipping into the "cultural goals" of movements in a few pages at the end of his book, admitted the necessity of plumbing the native point of view (251). He confessed, in the introduction to his augmented edition, that he "was in error to conceive of 'the situation' as something in which 'beliefs' exist, as if these latter floated around in some kind of container. The belief is itself *an element of* the situation, an important definitional component of what the situation is" (lxii). Cargo cults helped pull social change, history, culture, and psychology back into 1950s anthropology.

Blowing on Down the Road

Cargo cults today are scarce on the ground, Bougainville being an exception, but the literature marches on—particularly these two classic texts.[27] Worsley introduced *Trumpet* as "written in the firm belief that anthropology can be interesting to the non-specialist" (11) and his belief has proven true. Both *Trumpet* and *Road* continue to be read widely as important historical accounts of colonial-era Melanesia, and as contributions to the understanding of human religiosity and of political resistance. And they are read, at least occasionally, locally as well. J. K. McCarthy, who provided *Road*'s foreword, allowed himself to hope that the book, in the near future, "will be read by the New Guinea people . . . *Road Belong Cargo* would do much to teach them how the white man thinks" (ix). He might or might not have been pleased to learn that the book later came to serve as a sacred text, the Old Testament of the

Yali Movement.[28] Although not quite yet sacred texts in Pacific Studies, we can celebrate *Trumpet* and *Road* for renewing problems of history and culture, as Worsley and Lawrence sounded trumpets down along that cargo road.

Notes

I thank a seminar of colleagues and students at the Department of Anthropology, Research School of Pacific and Asian Studies, Australian National University, for their criticisms of an earlier version of this essay. Useful comments were also provided by Francis West.

1. F. E. Williams, *The Vailala Madness and the Destruction of Native Ceremonies in the Gulf Division* (Port Moresby[?], 1923); "The Vailala Madness in Retrospect," in *Essays Presented to C. G. Seligman*, ed. E. E. Evans-Pritchard et al. (London, 1934), 369–79.

2. Lucy Mair, *Australia in New Guinea* (London, 1948), 64.

3. Ryan D'Arcy, "The Influence of the Missions on Native Culture in Melanesia" (bachelor honors thesis, University of Sydney, 1947); Lamont Lindstrom, *Cargo Cult: Strange Stories of Desire from Melanesia and Beyond* (Honolulu, 1993), 37.

4. For example, Peter Lawrence, "Cargo Cult and Religious Beliefs among the Garia," *International Archives of Ethnography* 47 (1954): 1–20. A listing and categorization of the more prominent cargo cult researchers, to 1970, is provided by Friedrich Steinbauer, *Melanesian Cargo Cults: New Salvation Movements in the South Pacific* (Brisbane, 1971), 102–3.

5. Jean Guiart, *Un siècle et demi de contacts culturels à Tanna, Nouvelles-Hébrides* (Paris, 1956); Margaret Mead, *New Lives for Old: Cultural Transformation—Manus, 1928–1953* (New York, 1956); Theodore Schwartz, *The Paliau Movement of the Admiralty Islands, 1946–1954* (New York, 1962); Kenelm O. L. Burridge, *Mambu: A Melanesian Millennium* (London, 1962); Peter Lawrence, *Road Belong Cargo: A Study of the Cargo Movement in the Southern Madang District, New Guinea* (Manchester, 1964); Peter Worsley, *The Trumpet Shall Sound: A Study of "Cargo" Cults in Melanesia* (London, 1957). One might also include here Robert Maher's *New Men of Papua: A Study in Culture Change* (Madison, 1961), about the Tommy Kabu Movement of the Purari River delta area, only Maher does not use cargo cult idiom to frame his analysis. The term only appears as a bit of an afterthought on the book's final page when Maher warns that Purari people, although up to then pragmatic, might turn to cargo culting should their desire for social change be thwarted.

6. Burridge's *Mambu* has been equally influential and came back into print in the 1990s, as did Mead's *New Lives for Old*, republished partly in connection with her centennial birth year. One should also note Burridge's cargo overview, *New Heaven, New Earth: A Study of Millenarian Activities* (Oxford, 1969). The most

recent edition of *Trumpet,* issued by Waveland Press in 1991, had sold 1574 copies through 2002.

7. Peter Worsley, "The Changing Social Structure of the Wanindiljaugwa" (Ph.D. thesis, Australian National University, 1954).

8. See Jean Guiart, "Forerunners of Melanesian Nationalism," *Oceania* 22 (1951): 81–90.

9. Peter Lawrence, "Social Structure and the Process of Social Control among the Garia, Madang District, New Guinea" (Ph.D. thesis, Cambridge University, 1951).

10. Peter Lawrence, *The Garia: An Ethnography of a Traditional Cosmic System in Papua New Guinea* (Melbourne, 1988).

11. Peter Worsley, *Elle Sonnera la trompette: le culte du cargo en Mélanésie,* trans. Brigette Duval (Paris, 1977).

12. *Rot Bilong Kago* (Port Moresby, 1986).

13. Lindstrom, *Cargo Cult,* 53–62.

14. Lawrence dedicated his book to the *Tangalooma,* the cabin-cruiser of a Mr. and Mrs. Eric Snook of Madang, "on whose quarterdeck," he said, "I obtained one of my most important pieces of information" (xvii). What this was, exactly, remains a mystery. This dedicatory flourish recalls Lawrence's sense of humor apparent in his quirky poem, *Don Juan in Melanesia* (Brisbane, 1964), which first appeared the same year as *Road.* Some have suggested that the better sort of Australian colonial officer, in the 1960s, responded astutely to cargo cults, "knowing by heart entire chapters" of *Road.* Michel Panoff, "Peter Lawrence (1921–1987)," *Journal de la Société des Océanistes* Tome 85 (1987): 261 (my translation).

15. Lindstrom, *Cargo Cults,* 23–26. See also Peter Lawrence, "Statements About Religion: The Problem of Reliability," in *Anthropology in Oceania: Essays Presented to Ian Hogbin,* ed. L. R. Hiatt and C. Jayawardena (Sydney, 1971), 139–54.

16. See also Lawrence, "Cargo Cult and Religious Beliefs among the Garia," 20.

17. Since Worsley never made it to New Guinea, Lawrence and Kenelm Burridge lent a number of photographs of ritually inclined Islanders for the first edition of *Trumpet* (9). These, alas, did not make it into the book's second edition being, perhaps, too generic or too colonially tinged.

18. Worsley reviewed *Road* favorably as "an outstanding monograph . . . a major contribution to social science," pointing out that it was "neither orthodox structuralism nor 'ideographic' history" (*Sociological Review* 13 [1965]: 222–24). Many of the luminaries involved in the heyday of millenarian analysis weighed in on *Trumpet* and/or *Road.* Anthony Wallace, Lucy Mair, David Aberle, Kenneth Read, Cyril Belshaw, and Henry Riecken reviewed Worsley; and, in addition to Worsley, Anthony Wallace, Kenelm Burridge, and William Davenport reviewed Lawrence.

19. Lamont Lindstrom, "Mambu Phone Home," *Anthropological Forum* 9 (1999): 99–106.

20. "The Pursuit of the Millennium in Melanesia," *British Journal of Sociology* 9 (1958): 177–78.

21. *Trumpet* (augmented edition), lxi; S. G. Foster and Margaret M. Varghese, *The Making of the Australian National University, 1946–1996* (Sydney, 1996), 122.

22. See *Road*, 33, and *Trumpet*, 258–66, for their authors' comments on functionalism. Burridge, too, recalled that "history was tabooed" by ruling social anthropologists and that, furthermore, he was told "that cargo cults, mythology, and individuality were outside the purview of the subject!" "The Subject and the Profession," *Culture* 9 (1989): 90, 92.

23. I. C. Jarvie, in a celebrated critique, used cargo cultic disorder to skewer functionalism and its shortcomings, historical and otherwise, drawing partly on Worsley and Lawrence. *The Revolution in Anthropology* (London, 1964).

24. Lawrence made some fun of the functionalists' distrust of history in his poem *Don Juan in Melanesia:*

> . . . when incautious scholars sometimes spoke
> Of History—that is, the Time Perspective,
> The meresy mention of it would provoke
> A violent and merciless corrective.
> His dogma was the proposition that
> Pure scientistic thinking would be flat.

25. For example, Anthony F. C. Wallace (Review of *Trumpet*), in *American Anthropologist* 60 (1958): 775–76.

26. "'Cargo Cults' Forty Years On," in *Expecting the Day of Wrath: Versions of the Millennium in Papua New Guinea*, ed. Christin Kocher Schmid (Boroko, 1999), 147.

27. For cxample, several contributors to Holger Jebens, ed., *Cargo, Cult, and Culture Critique* (Honolulu, 2004) reflect their critique against Worsley's and Lawrence's foundational cargo cult accounts.

28. Garry W. Trompf, "What Has Happened to Melanesian 'Cargo Cults'?" in *Religious Movements in Melanesia Today (3)*, ed. Wendy Flannery (Goroka, 1984), 35.

PART IV

Island Groups

CHAPTER 15

Living in Archives and Dreams:
The Histories of Kuykendall and Daws

Jonathan K. Osorio

The Hawaiian Kingdom, by Ralph S. Kuykendall.
Honolulu: University of Hawai'i Press.

Vol. 1. *1778–1854: Foundation and Transformation*
(1938, reprinted 1957).

Vol. 2. *1854–1874: Twenty Critical Years*
(1953, reprinted 1966).

Vol. 3. *1874–1893: The Kalakua Dynasty*
(1967).

Shoal of Time: A History of the Hawaiian Islands, by Gavan Daws.
Honolulu: University of Hawai'i Press, 1968.

IT IS most fitting that Gavan Daws wrote the foreword to the fifth printing of Ralph Kuykendall's *Hawaiian Kingdom*. In 1978, Daws had spent seventeen of the previous twenty years in the Department of History at the University of Hawai'i, having virtually succeeded Kuykendall in the late 1950s as the department's "Hawaiian historian." Only in that way can these two men be said to have had something in common. But it is also characteristic of Daws that he could pay tribute to an author's work that was such an antithesis to his own. In a somewhat more substantial way, that is what I will be doing here.

In this essay I comment on the legacies of these two historians and contribute to an understanding of their value and their shortcomings from the perspective of a native historian. Obviously, this comes with certain (by now) well-established disparagements that apply equally to both scholars. They did not understand the indigenous language of this place; they were helpless to deal with the overwhelming abundance of native writings in the newspapers and various letters; they did not appear to think that this deficiency hampered their scholarship in any way; and they both accepted, though not in identical ways, the inevitability of colonialism and the helplessness of natives to challenge or defeat it.

I mention these disparagements in order to dismiss them. Not that I think that either writer needs my efforts to legitimize his work; their shortcomings as scholars, thinkers, writers, are largely irrelevant. They have had a serious influence on the development of Hawaiian historiography, in part because of their talents and in part because of their deficiencies. Both benefited by being pioneers of a sort—settler pioneers— who had little competition, and thus, few peers and colleagues for the kind of work they did. Both preceded the Hawaiian nationalist movement and the scholars that this movement produced. But their academic careers also bracketed the dawning of Pacific Islands historiography that was being pioneered at the Australian National University (ANU); the essays of H. E. Maude and J. W. Davidson should have had a very different look to someone who was nearing the end of a career, compared to one whose work and accomplishments were all still ahead of him.

The Hawaiian Kingdom

I don't know a single historian of the Hawaiian Islands who has not depended on the painstaking and detailed study of government documents, foreign exchanges, and letters that Kuykendall collected, organized, and incorporated into his massive three-volume chronicles between 1938 and 1967. I also cannot think of a single one of us who would depend on his histories as definitive nor as dependable interpretations of culture, or even believable explanations of change. Yet we should admire the task to which he committed himself.

In a 1976 seminar paper, Michiko Kodama, who would one day head the Oral History Project in Hawai'i, praised the late historian for having "helped to legitimise the writing of 'Pacific History.'"[1] Her paper summarizes Kuykendall's life in much the same way he would have approached biography. R. S. Kuykendall would have tried to evaluate what the individual had actually done, sparing little time or patience with theories about how the person's rearing or background might have influenced perspective, beliefs, or actions.

So there is little analysis of his Methodist family roots in California, almost nothing said about his personal life, except a revealing paragraph of how he tried to finish his third volume through illness and, perhaps, his own awareness of death approaching.[2] One is left with the impression of a man accustomed to gathering and sorting an enormous variety of data, compiling and ordering them into a sensible narrative that effaced his own intelligence and consciousness, and certainly his own personal situations, as much as he could manage it.

All things considered, it is hard to imagine a better strategy for someone who was summoned from doing research in Seville on early Spanish voyages to the West Coast of America to act as the executive secretary for the Hawaiian Historical Commission in 1922, and who arrived in Honolulu that June with no knowledge of Hawai'i, its history, or its people. Michiko Kodama reports that he entered upon his duties on the very day he arrived in Honolulu, visiting the Territorial Archives and the Library of Hawai'i. And of course he worked on the day, more than forty years later, that he left.

His contribution to Pacific Islands history needs to acknowledge several things. It is likely that he knew very little about Hawaiian or local culture, not just because he was a haole transplant, but because his life seems to have revolved solely around his work. When journalist Bob Krauss noted in his celebrated by-line column that the little-known Kuykendall had left the islands after forty years, he pointed out that "only a half-dozen of his close friends had come to see him off. Few know that he is gone."[3] He collected more than eight thousand pages of material from sources outside of Hawai'i and was probably more intimately familiar with the archives in Hawai'i than any other researcher, before or after, but one wonders how many Hawaiians he ever knew. He may well have kept every single jotted note, every letter received, every news article clipping. In the first of the fifteen file boxes of his notes that he left to the university is the cablegram sent him in Seville inviting him to work for the Hawaiian Historical Society at the salary of $3,500. He also kept a letter sent him in 1957 from a purported descendant of Kamehameha III, who wrote, "When the missionaries from Boston took the Islands away from us because our Queen was defenseless, some of us lost all of our lands and we were one of the losers."[4]

Clearly, he would have been familiar with the political tensions of his own age. While Hawaiian nationalism may have been muted by the overwhelming presence of American military and economic power in the 1920s and 1930s, a seasoned critique of the American takeover, as well as the treachery of the missionaries and the Hawaiians' loss of land, existed in his time and seems to have had relatively little impact on his historical perspective. It is not an exaggeration to say that *The Hawaiian Kingdom* is a "court history" to the glorification of the planter and merchant elite.

In fact, the highly favorable reviews of his first volume in 1938, including one by the noted American historian Richard Van Alstyne, reinforces what future Pacific Island historians would cite as a major problem of research and publication in the Pacific: that it was dominated by imperial history and told the story of Europeans and Americans and not the story of Islanders themselves.

> Few works on a subject as virgin as this can claim equal insight and finality... His work is more than an internal history of the islands. It is the study of the mid-Pacific rivalry of the three maritime Western powers ... and as such is an important addition to the literature on the expansion of the United States.[5]

In that sense, the first volume of *Hawaiian Kingdom* was the finest form of what Davidson would criticize and use as a call to a new field of inquiry.[6] Kuykendall would refine that form somewhat with the publication of volume 2 in 1953, but in his desire to avoid any kind of political bias, he would confine his narrative to describing the political and economic developments of the kingdom from the death of Kauikeaouli to the end of the Kamehameha ruling dynasty. The volume is almost entirely devoted to the development of the sugar industry and the people who are attended to are virtually only those who have some connection to sugar and its rising influence.

In the chapter entitled "The King and His People," there is a suggestion of a social history, though more by its title than contents. The chapter turns into a biography of Kamehameha IV, and the native people are described in only the most general terms, as victims of disease and demographic trends. Kuykendall appeared not to see the rich cultural analysis possible with the appearance of new Christian denominations such as the Anglicans and the Latter Day Saints, and he treats them primarily as political developments.

It is only in the final volume, the history of the rise and fall of Kalākaua, that the author Kuykendall actually narrates a story that presents native people with any sort of conscious opinions about Europeans and Americans and the strange society they were shaping in Hawai'i. It is the first time that he credits any kanaka outside of the king and a small number of Hawaiian intelligentsia for having a reasoned—though he believed misguided[7]—response to the growing haole influence. In fact he portrays the ordinary Hawaiian voter and politician as dimly perceptive of their weakened position, whose only recourse in the 1870s was racial politics.

It is certainly possible that Kuykendall began to feel the sway of opinions and analysis reaching from the western Pacific, but I also think that this historian could not have helped being affected by the ethnic tensions through which he and other residents in Hawai'i lived during the years of labor organization and confrontations, the celebrated Massie murder case (see *Shoal of Time*, 319–24), and martial law during World War II. One also wonders what this historian of the liberalization of Hawai'i made of the House Subcommittee on Un-American Activities and their prosecution of labor leaders in the 1950s. While these volumes are confined to the Kingdom era, it is simply unlikely that the perspective of this individual, even entranced by the myriad details of his research, would not be changed by living in a place where cultural and ethnic conflicts were common, and where Americans out of their own ethnic pride had committed such depredations of justice and fairness.

What distinguishes the third volume from its predecessors is the extent to which the author begins to deal with uncomfortable issues of ethics and democratic values in telling the story of the end of the Kingdom. And while he never clearly acknowledges a wrong done, the volume is still a far cry from the triumphal progressivism of the earlier volumes.

Indeed, Kuykendall's career provides us all with a remarkable insight into the changing nature of the historian's craft and the difficulties that face all of us as we begin our careers with certain kinds of expectations and end our careers as the scope, methodologies, and assumptions of our work are being seriously questioned. That his own contribution to an older, less intuitive, and certainly less introspective approach to history is not seriously criticized is much more a tribute to the quality of his work than its timing.

Shoal of Time

Shoal of Time is such a well-known and widely read history that some of Daws's other work, superior in my mind, goes unnoticed. His biography of Damien de Veuster *(Holy Man)*, his superb analysis of real estate development and politics in the early statehood years entitled *Land and Power in Hawaii*, and his magisterial work on prisoners of war,[8] together with *Shoal of Time* present a scholar with a wide range of abilities and a gift for historical writing. He was unusual in another respect. Usually thought of as an American, he is actually Australian by birth and upbringing, and he received his initial training at the University of Melbourne's then-renowned School of History.[9] Even at that stage he stood out for doing his own thing and being his own man. Notably, he admired the United States, and when that country fell out of favor with many of his fellow students, Daws made his statement by sporting a crew cut. He gravitated to the University of Hawai'i for his postgraduate training, and made Honolulu his hometown.

If *Shoal of Time* is the most widely read history of Hawai'i, it is also among the most criticized, and native scholars in particular find Daws's observations and piquant sense of humor and irony objectionable if not downright offensive. In many ways, Gavan Daws represents the irony of historiography itself: he was sympathetic to native culture in ways that Kuykendall would not permit himself to be, but lacking any way of understanding that culture, he chose to mock the institutions that he believed oppressed the poor and underclasses and spared no one, neither missionary nor native *ali'i*.

His writing, produced in the tumultuous American society of the mid-1960s, reflects the powerful ideological trends of the time. In the tradition of other scholars of colonialism who were breaking away from the modernists and developmental models of history, Daws focused on how foreign influences had conspired to enter and eventually control the Hawaiian Islands, damning the commercial influences as much as Kuykendall had extolled them. While still a teaching assistant he discussed his ideas for future research in a letter to Jim Davidson at ANU.

> I have found an academic and temperamental homeground here of an unusually attractive kind. There is a mountain of untouched research material in various collections in Honolulu, and much of it could be used to illuminate the social and intellectual questions I am interested in: the impact of missionary doctrine and practice on native society; the struggle for control of native government by missionary and commercial groups; the evolution of the original missionary contingent into a political and economic oligarchy in the space of a couple of generations; cultural clash and

change in the period of the great Oriental migrations; the gradual rise of Orientals to social and economic power in the twentieth century; and so on.[10]

Daws was deeply interested in and connected with the revolution in historical writing that was sprouting out from Australia National University in the early 1960s. His correspondence between 1962 and 1974, when he resigned from the University of Hawai'i to take up a position at ANU,[11] is dominated by communications with some of the most prominent members of the burgeoning Pacific Islands field: historians Davidson, Niel Gunson, Dorothy Shineberg; social anthropologist Roger Keesing; and what appears to have been a strong friendship with Harry Maude.[12] There is no question but that these luminaries considered him a colleague—though an expatriate—and that he was quite comfortable discussing the new and controversial methodologies emanating from that school.

There is also no question that while he sincerely respected the historiography of his predecessor, Kuykendall, Daws believed the new methodologies focusing on native agency, acceptance of a wider range of historical materials, and fresh examinations and interpretations of "traditional" primary sources would produce more believable and valuable histories than Kuykendall's. In a letter to Maude in 1965 he wrote:

> Kuykendall was much more happy with matters of policy than of personality, with matters institutional than with matters more broadly social. And his work shows it. He wrote the very best kind of "official" history . . . He was a smoother-over, a minimiser of strife, a constructor of consensus. For very good reasons: the generalised Calvinism which made him such a fine, honest, and industrious man also led him to believe that very little of worth could come from the examination of those who were otherwise.[13]

Gavan Daws saw no reason to avoid the memoirs and perceptions of beachcombers and ne'er-do-wells,[14] and used the reactions of native leaders and their observations to illustrate not just the course of progress but the conflicts and turmoil of the nineteenth century. The portrait he paints of many native individuals is often openly contemptuous, one reason why native readers today find *Shoal of Time* obnoxious and misleading, especially about the intentions and capacities of native Hawaiians. His flippancy here is in marked contrast to the respectful and compassionate tone of a later book on prisoners of war.[15] Daws cannot be

accurately characterized as racist—he was too much of an equal opportunity tormenter for that—but his dismissal of native actions in the
midst of terribly complex and inauspicious events clouds his analysis and
relegates many of his chapters to mere entertainment. The book, after
all, was avowedly written for a poplar audience. In reviewing *Shoal of
Time*, David Hilliard stated that the book is "marred by . . . lapses into
journalistic superficiality . . . There is a tendency to dwell on the scan-
dalous and the bizarre, as against a somewhat off-hand treatment of significant but less spectacular topics."[16]

One example is his recounting of the division and alienation of lands
known as the Mahele, a seminal event in the Kingdom's history when
thousands of years of a tradition of land tenure based on mutual obligations between chiefs and people were suddenly replaced by legislation
that allowed private land ownership and encouraged land concentra-
tions hitherto unknown in Hawaiian society. Writing in the late 1960s,
Daws would not have known that within a few years the Mahele would
come to be the strongest symbol of Hawaiian loss to several generations
of Hawaiian scholars and activists. Nevertheless, his casual dismissal of
the outcome of the Mahele as the result of the slowness of the chiefs to
divide out their interests and the *maka'ainana* being equally "dilatory"
(127) is most unfortunate and strikes contemporary Hawaiians as incred-
ibly insensitive if not downright stupid. For more than a thousand years,
after all, land tenure had been governed by a system in which chiefs and
people shared both resources and responsibilities. In the midst of one
epidemic horror after another, the Kingdom's decision to privatize land
quite understandably was greeted with uncertainty and even resistance.

Daws's analysis of the Mahele bears little cultural understanding,
but that is fairly consistent with his treatment of native society throughout. He assumes that Hawaiians would ultimately want the same things
as the Europeans and Americans and were simply fooled by unfamiliar
political and social processes. He is sympathetic with their plight but had
no conception of Hawaiian attitudes toward land and well-being, chiefly
leadership and haole intrusions and pretensions, or even toward Christianity. For Daws we were simply a befuddled and demoralized culture
in full retreat before the colonial storm.

Shoal of Time's place in Pacific historiography can be seen as a critical breaking point from imperial histories, and perhaps even one that
opened doors to native scholars who would one day provide rich and
well-researched cultural analyses of our own histories. Responding to

an interview in 1974, Daws made it clear that he saw the field of Hawaiian history being taken over by local writers doing "our history, our way," and that there was a "sizable and growing interest among locals to redefine themselves, and talk about themselves, and write about themselves."[17]

But Daws also hoped that the tone and perspective of *Shoal of Time* would encourage those kinds of histories in which writers would feel free to explore themes and perspectives of their own choosing, unintimidated by more conservative dictums of an older historiography. If he had one criticism of Kuykendall it was how closely he aligned his narratives to the preferences and pretensions of wealthy haole society in the territorial years.

> Then too, when he was active, the social and civic atmosphere of Honolulu strongly encouraged such a view of Hawaii's past and strongly discouraged alternative readings. I don't mean to suggest that muck-raking ought to be the order of the day from now on, but certainly the definition of "respectable" history might very well be broadened, so that a greater variety of source material may be utilised.[18]

The contributions of *Hawaiian Kingdom* and *Shoal of Time* to Pacific Islands historiography cannot be properly estimated without observing what the field has become, an enormously complex and contested arena for cultural and indigenous studies. It would be fair to say that this arena could never have been imagined without the painstakingly detailed archival research such as Kuykendall excelled in and the colorful, even lurid, narratives preferred by Daws.

It is too simple to say that their work prepared the way for the intellectual flowering that followed. As historians, however, they were faithful to the values of their own literary epochs and they honored their profession by the quality of their work. If Daws took greater risks with his scholarship, allowing his own judgments to stir his narrative, we should allow that he was amply repaid. *Shoal of Time* outsold *The Hawaiian Kingdom*'s collective three volumes, and his reputation as a historian, and especially his biography of Father Damien, brought him into the leadership of the ANU's Department of Pacific and Southeast Asian History. On the other hand, his passages are often cited as examples of why natives must write their own histories. Ironically, he would be among the first to concur.

Notes

1. Michiko Kodama-Nishimoto, "Ralph Simpson Kuykendall, Hawaiian Historian, 1885–1963," paper submitted to Historiography seminar (Hist. 601), 1976, University of Hawai'i-Mānoa.

2. Kuykendall passed away in May 1963 as he was completing his third volume of *The Hawaiian Kingdom*. The final chapter was finished through the assistance of American historian Charles Hunter, who had been working with the author and preparing to finish the book if needed.

3. Bob Krause, *Honolulu Advertiser*, 13 January 1963 ("About Town" column).

4. E. M. Reed to Ralph Kuykendall, 21 December 1957, Kuykendall File, Box 1, Hawaiian Pacific Collection, Hamilton Library, Honolulu.

5. Richard Van Alstyne, *American Historical Review* 45, no. 1 (1939): 190–91.

6. Davidson certainly regarded *The Hawaiian Kingdom* as "old fashioned" and unadventurous. But his respect for Kuykendall's commitment to his craft ("a humble, dedicated scholar, who found delight over many years in the study of Hawaiian history") muted his criticisms. Davidson, Reviews (of *The Hawaiian Kingdom*), *Journal of Pacific History* 3 (1968): 231–34. Davidson paid Kuykendall a further compliment in saying that *The Hawaiian Kingdom* was the only work that rivaled Richard Gilson's political history of nineteenth-century Samoa "in the exhaustiveness of the research upon which it was based." Davidson, "Introduction" to R. P. Gilson, *Samoa, 1830 to 1900: The Politics of a Multi-Cultural Community* (Melbourne, 1970), vii.

7. Throughout the volume Kuykendall revisits the theme of racial politics, regretting that they appear to dominate the political discourses of certain key elections. His notes may ultimately reveal to what extent he was affected by the discourses on civil rights in America that were taking place at the time.

8. Gavan Daws, *Holy Man: Father Damien of Molokai* (New York, 1973); George Cooper and Gavin Daws, *Land and Power in Hawaii: The Democratic Years* (Honolulu, 1990); Gavan Daws, *Prisoners of the Japanese: POWs of World War II in the Pacific* (New York, 1995).

9. See Stuart Macintyre and Peter McPhee, eds., *Max Crawford's School of History* (Melbourne, 2000).

10. J. W. Davidson to Gavan Daws, 5 April 1960, Daws File. These and other letters are original and carbon copies of letters received and sent, memos, memorabilia, outlines, and copies of speeches that were preserved by Daws and given to the Hawai'i Pacific Collection at the University of Hawai'i's Hamilton Library. The period spans over thirty years.

11. None other than the headship of Pacific History, after Davidson's untimely death in 1973. But Daws's heart was always in Hawai'i. He visited Honolulu as often as he decently could and eventually resigned his ANU position, in 1989, to return permanently.

12. Susan Woodburn, *Where Our Hearts Still Lie: A Life of Harry and Honor Maude in the Pacific Islands* (Adelaide, 2003).

13. Daws to Maude, 26 December 1965, Daws File.

14. This should be no more than a footnote. Daws may have identified strongly with the beachcomber and the trader: foreigners who came and knew a good thing when they saw it, but whose eyes were ever on the big opportunity and a chance to return home successful men. Between 1963 and 1965 he parlayed his applications to ANU into a steadily increasing salary at the University of Hawaiʻi. But from the viewpoint of this observer, he was also a remarkably good teacher and administrator.

15. Daws, *Prisoners of the Japanese*.

16. David Hilliard, *Journal of Pacific History* 5 (1970): 232.

17. David Ing, "Interview with a Hawaiian Historian," *Hawaii Observer* (October 1974): 7.

18. Daws to Maude, 26 December 1960, Daws File.

CHAPTER 16

On Hezel's *The First Taint of Civilization*

David Hanlon

The First Taint of Civilization: A History of the Caroline and Marshall Islands in Pre-Colonial Days, 1521–1885, by Francis X. Hezel, S.J. Honolulu: University of Hawai'i Press, 1983 (as vol. 1 in the Pacific Islands Monograph Series).

THE PUBLICATION of *The First Taint of Civilization* marked the debut of the Pacific Islands Monograph Series (PIMS), a joint effort of the University of Hawai'i Press and the Center for Pacific Islands Studies at the University of Hawai'i, Mānoa. It is the best-selling of the eighteen PIMS volumes published to date. Initially produced in hardcover and with two subsequent paperback editions in 1994 and 2003, total sales of the book through June 2003 stand at 3,817 copies. Half of the income from these sales is returned to PIMS, thus enabling the publication of other scholarly books on Pacific Studies. Francis X. Hezel is a Jesuit missionary from Buffalo, New York, who has lived and labored in Micronesia for nearly forty years. In addition to *The First Taint of Civilization,* he has authored or co-authored over sixty articles and four other monograph-length works, including the very fine *Strangers in Their Own Land: A Century of Colonial Rule in the Caroline and Marshall Islands,* which was published in 1994 as volume 13 in the PIMS series.

Since 1972, Hezel has headed the Micronesian Seminar, a research and educational institute sponsored by the Roman Catholic Church and currently housed on the island of Pohnpei. In its commitment to "encourage reflection on current issues in light of gospel values,"[1] the Micronesian Seminar publishes an occasional bulletin and produces videos on various social topics ranging from suicide, mental illness, and

alcohol and drug abuse to changes in family structure, juvenile delin-
quency, domestic violence, and migration. "Mic Sem," as it is often
called, also hosts conferences and workshops, maintains an active and
expanding website, and is home to a library of 130,000 titles and a growing collection of historical photographs and documentary films, all on
the area called Micronesia.

Hezel's influence on Micronesian studies is formidable. He is consulted and his work cited by almost every expatriate government official,
educator, researcher, and development specialist. *The First Taint of Civilization* is often the first book read by those new to the region; it serves
as a classroom text in institutions of postsecondary education within and
beyond the islands. It informs local historic preservation projects and the
ongoing development of social studies curriculum for secondary schools
in the Commonwealth of the Northern Marianas, the Federated States
of Micronesia, the Republic of the Marshall Islands, and the Republic of
Palau. How the book has affected the practice of history in the region
and, most especially, island peoples' own understanding of themselves
and their pasts are questions addressed at the end of this essay.

In the researching and writing of *First Taint*, Hezel considered the
approach to Pacific Islands' pasts advocated by J. W. Davidson, the foundation professor of Pacific history (1950–73) at the Australian National
University (ANU) in Canberra. Davidson sought to break from imperial histories of the region that wrote of islands' pasts in terms of European imperial interests, activities, and politics. His historical vision
focused on islands "whose coastal regions outsiders might penetrate but
whose heartlands they could never conquer."[2] Those who studied under
Davidson challenged the overly generalized, indiscriminate assumptions
of what was later known as the Fatal Impact theory. They saw Islanders
as not necessarily overwhelmed by foreign technologies, material goods,
and belief systems, but rather as active and aware peoples who engaged
these outside forces in often constructive, creative, and culturally con-
texted ways.

Scholarship tends to follow the colonial flag, a fact not fully
acknowledged or addressed by those of us who research and write from
outland rather than island locations. Davidson and his colleagues
focused much of their historical research on former British colonies and
spheres of influence where they enjoyed access and advantage because
of their citizenship in the British Commonwealth. Largely missing from
the reach of the Davidson school was "American" Micronesia.[3] Colo-

nialism had divided larger Micronesia in ways that ethnography and linguistics did not. Early Spanish colonization gave Guam and the Marianas a distinctive, pronounced, and long-standing Hispanic influence
that set them apart from the other islands of the Micronesian geographical area. Kiribati and Nauru had different, British-influenced pasts that
stood in marked contrast to the shared experiences of the Caroline and
Marshall Islands under German, Japanese, and American colonialism.

The consequence of this division often showed itself in the correla-
tion between the citizenship of historians and the colonial affiliations of
the Micronesian islands or island groups they studied. The editors of the
Journal of Pacific History, who published Hezel's first academic articles,
wondered in 1967 why American historians had neglected those Micronesian islands administered since World War II as the United States
Trust Territory of the Pacific Islands.[4] In response to this void, Hezel
undertook to write a first general history of the Caroline and Marshall
Islands in ways that evoked, though not completely or comfortably, the
Davidson school's concerns for agency, decolonization, and local
sources. In the spirit of the Davidson school, Hezel's *The First Taint of
Civilization* brings attention to an area of the Pacific deeply affected by
different colonial powers. The book concentrates on those centuries
prior to the establishment of formal colonial rule over the Caroline and
Marshall Islands, but gives prominence to the advance agents of those
later colonial regimes.

One of the strengths of *First Taint* lies in its attention to the larger
global developments that informed the outside world's first contact with
the region. The book continues to read well to a contemporary, largely
expatriate audience concerned with globalization and the transnational
movement of peoples, technologies, ideas, and material goods. Hezel's
sense of boundaries is fluid and his understanding of the effects of contact and colonization broad. He writes of European political and economic rivalries, more particularly those between Spain and Portugal,
that drove Spanish exploration of the islands in the sixteenth and early
seventeenth centuries. Spain's claim to the Philippines and its colonization of Guam provided island links for the Manila galleon trade that
connected Spanish America with East Asia. Hezel explains how the
establishment of the British penal colony in Australia and expanding
European trade with China brought increased shipping traffic that, in
turn, resulted in new sea routes through the Micronesian archipelago.

Captains Thomas Gilbert and William Marshall helped chart these sailing lanes and, in the process, left their last names on the island groups they encountered. The early nineteenth century witnessed the arrival of British and later American whaleships. Resident traders, more established commercial firms, and an American Congregationalist missionary presence contributed to the "tainting" of these islands in the latter half of the nineteenth century.

The research on which *The First Taint of Civilization* rests is quite impressive. To access the primary sources on Spain's activities, Hezel taught himself to read Spanish. He would later learn German to do the research necessary for his follow-up volume, *Strangers in Their Own Land*. Hezel traveled to Canberra, where he sought the counsel of Harry Maude, Robert Langdon, and Norah Foster, as well as the advice of Ilma O'Brien in Melbourne. His research efforts encompassed correspondence with American ethnographers of Micronesia, including Saul Riesenberg, Leonard Mason, Robert Kiste, and Mac Marshall. Hezel also received assistance with archival resources at the Micronesian Area Research Center on Guam, the Kendall Whaling Museum in Sharon, Massachusetts, and Harvard University's Houghton Library. The initiative, energy, and efficacy with which he located ships' logs in collections from Australia to New England are equally striking. Hezel's *Foreign Ships in Micronesia*, a detailed, annotated compendium of contacts between Micronesian islands and European ships to 1885, served as an advertisement for his history of the Caroline and Marshall Islands.[5]

Hindsight may very well be twenty-twenty, especially when it comes to critically revisiting books published more than two decades ago. I admit too I have found it difficult to revisit this particular history.[6] My discomfort results from the need to make some intellectual criticisms of a man who has been both friend and mentor. Along with many others I have benefited from Fran Hezel's research and his generous assistance, and am now the editor of the series that published his book. Nonetheless, *The First Taint of Civilization* invites a careful rereading in light of reigning historiographical concerns. Naming is certainly an issue. Though not in the book's title, the term *Micronesia*, coined by the French voyager Jules Dumont d'Urville and promoted by the geographer Gregoire Louis Domeny de Rienzi, is endorsed in the book's first pages. Translating from the Greek as "tiny islands," the name foreshadows the formal colonial rule to come and the ways in which that rule would be justified in part by paternalist concerns over the smallness and vulnerability of the islands. Hezel, however, chooses to avoid the history and imperial politics behind this designation.

The word *Micronesian* as a marker of common or shared identity is also questionable. Archaeological investigations suggest historical origins and cultural practices for the people of Palau, Yap proper, and the Mariana Islands that differ significantly from those who settled the Marshalls and the central and eastern Carolines. Such evidence does not deny affinity, linkage, like practices, and contact among these island groups, but rather invites an orientation to more locally based understandings that might offer very different orderings, groupings, even histories. In short, the geographical, temporal, and historical choices that inform *First Taint* reflect the ways colonialism creates its subjects, establishes alien, self-serving boundaries, and imposes its own sense of time. Terms such as *American, British, English, European, German, Portuguese,* and *Spanish* also require more nuanced, historically sensitive qualifications. While their use to distinguish among different foreign actors is convenient narrative shorthand, these designations call upon more contemporary national identities. Their usage elides the histories of nations and national identities in the often contested, violent process of becoming.

In its exclusive reliance upon written records, *The First Taint of Civilization* makes possible only a partial accounting of what actually happened in the encounters between natives and strangers in the Caroline and Marshall Islands. While conceding this point, Hezel justifies his use of sources by doubting the accessibility of alternative local histories. He writes:

> Some would say the story of civilization—in the truest sense of the word—should begin thousands of years ago with the coming of the first islanders, the real discoverers of the Caroline and Marshall Islands. Undoubtedly so, but this part of the tale is buried beneath the land and the sea—and the elements do not easily yield their secrets. Let us begin, then, with the European—that benefactor and despoiler, that cultural catalyst par excellence—who sailed halfway around the world to meet the island people in their own sheltered homelands. (xiii)

The persistence of songs, chants, genealogies, dances, and oral narratives, used or noted in other anthropological and historical works, suggests that local histories cannot be so quickly put aside. A more inclusive work might have endeavored to measure local and foreign accounts in terms of both their complementarity and difference. The use of terms like *benefactors, despoilers,* and *cultural catalysts* attributes an overly determining presence to foreigners, while the images of sheltered homelands and tales buried beneath the land and sea conjure up peoples vulnerable to the intrusion of those who write their histories and the histories of the lands they colonize.

Agency is an issue as well. The title of the first chapter, for example, is "The End of a Long Seclusion." "Seclusion," however, can be read as a culture-bound, historically blinkered term that inadvertently privileges contact with the Western world, and denies the voyaging, discovery, and settlement of the islands by those who came to be called Micronesians. Much of *First Taint* documents the disruption, depopulation, and material, technological, and religious change brought to the islands. We learn of the ravages of infectious disease on Kosrae and Pohnpei. The presence of foreign traders dealing in guns and other politically significant goods exacerbates rivalries in Palau and the Marshalls, while the introduction of Christianity challenges island belief systems, exchange practices, and chiefly privilege throughout the islands. Hezel sees "civilization," more accurately colonialism, as relentless and inevitable. The remedy for the problems brought by Western intrusion lay not among the island peoples but in the very source of the problems themselves. "If the West had inflicted these evils on the islanders, only the West could offer release from them" (298).

Despite this assertion as to the inevitability of colonialism, Hezel closes his book by acknowledging the persistence of these island peoples "with their lives, their land (regardless of whose flags flew over their islands), and their social institutions rather well intact" (318). The overall argument of this book, however, points to a fatality of impact that left island peoples ignorant of their past, uncomfortable with their present, and uncertain about their future. There is a conclusion here that is at odds with the argument that precedes it.

The analyses of cross-cultural encounters that fill the pages between the book's preface and conclusion also prove problematic in light of more recent historiographical trends. Hezel's oppositions tend to be binary as evidenced by the titles and text for chapter 4, "Two Worlds Grown Closer," and chapter 6, "The Powers of Darkness and Light." The complexities of religious encounters, for example, receive little in-depth analysis. The negative response to Father Juan Cantova's efforts at religious conversion on Ulithi in 1731 are reduced to a collective pronouncement by a group of Ulithians: "You have come to change our customs" (58). Rather than acknowledge an alternative and competing belief system on Ulithi, Hezel points to the alleged duplicity of Digal, a Woleaian catechist baptized on Guam and brought to the island by Cantova, as a possible explanation for the murder of the Jesuit priest and the Spanish soldiers who accompanied him. At a more general level, there is no sense of the fundamental challenges that Christianity in its variant forms posed to island belief systems and the social structures they sustained. Moreover, the use of the word *conversion* to measure missionary success prejudges a process that was more drawn out, incomplete, and uneven in its dimensions. To assert, for example, that the process of religious change on Pohnpei was pretty much over by 1867 is to minimize the complexity of the encounter, the missionaries' self-doubts, and their anxiety over the tentative, still contested place of Christianity on that island.

Religious change is not the only underdeveloped topic of historical inquiry in *The First Taint of Civilization*. Little substantive attention is given to the roles of women in the different island groups encompassed by this study. There is no examination of gender relations or the effects of foreign contact on those gender relations. Aside from a few chiefly wives, the only women to receive any substantial mention in this history are foreign missionary wives and those island women who had relationships with foreign men. In short, *First Taint* is very much a male-centered history. The effects of foreign trade on established exchange practices also go largely unexamined. The book presumes the preference of island peoples for foreign materials and technologies. We glimpse something of the violence these goods sometimes exacerbated or encouraged, but little of the more creative ways island peoples appropriated these foreign materials and technologies for socially or culturally enriching purposes. Of related concern is the uncritical use of European accounts on which *First Taint* relies. The limited period of contact, the linguistic and cultural barriers affecting communication, and the ethnocentric bias affecting the interpretation of meaning all necessitate a careful, more cautious use of these accounts.

While the overwhelming majority of the twenty-two reviews of *The First Taint of Civilization* were quite favorable, Hezel reacted guardedly to then emerging trends in historical practice that advanced more ethnographically sensitive readings of historical encounters, underscored the interpretive dimensions of all historical writing, urged a more critical treatment of historical texts, and called attention to the positionality of historians. In a 1988 article for *Pacific Studies,* Hezel wondered how possible an "islander-oriented" history really was.[7] While conceding the persuasiveness of the cross-cultural analysis found in Greg Dening's *Islands and Beaches* and in some of the more island-specific histories of the 1980s, Hezel wrote of Pacific historians as a nervous lot anguishing over their written works as if they were true and complete rather than provisional and partial. He saw value in recording the European side of encounters and cautioned against relying too much on oral traditions. The overcoming of ethnocentric bias in European accounts, and even in the histories produced from them, required more than one generation of scholars. Fear of being even-handed and inclusive should not cause paralysis; a good story required colorful personalities, whatever their nationality. Admitting that his stance might be considered reactionary, Hezel asserted that his intention was not to deny Islanders their place in history but rather to see that they received recognition for it. True decolonization would occur when Islanders themselves read, evaluated, and, when necessary, corrected the histories written about them.

Hezel expounded further on the practice of history in an opening address to the Pacific History Association conference on Guam in December 1990.[8] His remarks evidenced a more critical perspective on the practice of history, especially as it involved colonialism. The early Spanish presence and the later German, Japanese, and American colonial regimes over the Caroline, Mariana, and Marshall Islands afforded the opportunity for a comparative study of colonialism over time, and with particular attention to the ways in which different groups of Micronesians responded to these colonial regimes. Hezel identified these responses as ranging from outright rebellion to more subtle forms of manipulation, accommodation, everyday resistance, and even collaboration. He credited this engagement with colonialism as standing the Micronesian islands in good stead when it came time in the late 1960s to begin future political status negotiations with the United States.

Hezel went on to acknowledge the questions haunting the practice of Pacific Islands history—questions having to do with agency, representation, the place of local knowledge, the authorship of historical works, and the variety of media through which Micronesian pasts might be expressed. For Hezel, the most critical question surrounding the practice of history in the area of the Pacific called Micronesia was how far trained historians—creatures of libraries and archival collections whose canons of historical research were less than two centuries old and who perpetrated something akin to an "invention of tradition" on Micronesian pasts—were willing to go to accommodate island history. He went on:

> Authentic Pacific history means far more than a pen in a brown hand rather than a white one. In fact, it may mean taking up the nose flute or the guitar rather than the pen, in the first place. It also means different presuppositions about "truth," and the different modes of inquiry into the truth. It means a very different orientation to our work, far more different than we have acknowledged in our historical musings up to now. Perhaps far more difficult than any of us in this room are capable of making ... The genuine indigenization of Pacific history involves more complex questions than are normally dealt with (in) the prefaces of our books. Let us not be discouraged, however; we can do good history without trying to pass it off as bogus "tropicalized" history.[9]

Hezel was certainly right to see the local practice of history as markedly different from the work of academically trained historians. On many of the Caroline and Marshall Islands, the doing of history continues to be culturally formed, locally focused, vernacularly expressed, deliberately incomplete, and often contested. Within Hezel's above-cited recognition of local histories, however, there lies a defense for an established, Euro-American, documentary-based study of islands' pasts. Indeed, all of Hezel's historical writings demonstrate his continuing commitment to a chronologically ordered, empirically based narrative that tells a "good story." As attested by the steady sales of *The First Taint of Civilization* since its publication in 1983, there persists a significant audience for this kind of history. Hezel's scholarship has also aided other, more recent publications that include island histories of Guam and Pohnpei, a semiotic study of the Palauan past, an account of a Palauan traveler to England, an investigation into the relationship between history and identity around the 1837 massacre of the adult male population of Ngatik or Sapwuahfik, and a multiauthored work on Micronesians' experiences of Word War II.[10] Despite the varying methodologies and theories employed, the authors of these works list *The First Taint of Civilization* in their respective bibliographies, and most publicly acknowledge Hezel's assistance in their research.

It would be naïve in the extreme to doubt the influence of contact, Christianity, and colonialism on the local practices of history in the Caroline and Marshall Islands. How the publication of *The First Taint of*

Civilization has specifically affected these local or vernacular histories is an extremely important question that requires separate treatment. Perhaps insight into the problems and possibilities for the future study of history in the region can be gleaned from Hezel's own engagements with island peoples over a shared history. In the *Pacific Studies* article, Hezel described his attempts to do a series of historical monographs on the Catholic missions in the different islands that engaged people as not just subjects of a history but as historians. Unable to locate any local sources, Hezel relied on archival and published materials that provided details and a sequence far more specific than any oral history. By Hezel's own admission, these sources gave his monographs a decidedly Western character that highlighted European and American missionaries. Different groups of island peoples responded to Hezel's draft monographs by dancing, acting, or singing the histories of their churches. Reflecting on the experience, Hezel mused that "each of the island groups had its history, presented in an art form that best suited its genius, and I had my monographs" (103). Here is not only a difference in historical styles, but an example of how differing histories can speak to a common experience in ways that get beyond the dominance of a single, colonially privileged version. If current and future audiences respond in similarly critical ways to the writings about them, *The First Taint of Civilization* may yet become more than a first, good, and useful written history of the Caroline and Marshall Islands.

Notes

1. *Micronesian Seminar: Twenty Five years of Service, 1972–1997* (Kolonia, Pohnpei, 1997), 23. For autobiographical material, see Francis X. Hezel, "Chuuk: A Caricature of an Island," in *Pacific Places, Pacific Histories: Essays in Honor of Robert C. Kiste*, ed. Brij V. Lal (Honolulu, 2004), 102–19.

2. J. W. Davidson, "Lauaki Namulau'ulu Mamoe: A Traditionalist in Samoan Politics," in *Pacific Islands Portraits*, ed. J. W. Davidson and Deryck Scarr (Canberra, 1970), 267.

3. Two works dealing with the island of Pohnpei in the Carolines and published by American scholars with assistance from the Department of Pacific History at ANU are Luelen Bernart, *The Book of Luelen*, ed. John L. Fischer, Saul H. Riesenberg, and Marjorie J. Whiting (Canberra, 1977), and James O'Connell, *A Residence of Eleven Years in New Holland and the Caroline Islands*, ed. Saul H. Riesenberg (Canberra, 1972).

4. Editorial, *Journal of Pacific History* 2 (1967): 4. Prior to the publication of *First Taint*, anthropologists had provided what written history existed on the Caroline and Marshall Islands. See David Hanlon, "Magellan's Chroniclers? American Anthropology's History in Micronesia," in *American Anthropology in Micronesia*, ed. Robert C. Kiste and Suzanne Falgout (Honolulu, 1999), 53–79; also, the Editors' introduction, 1–9, and the chapter by Robert C. Kiste and Suzanne Falgout, "Anthropology and Micronesia: The Context," 11–51.

5. Francis X. Hezel, S.J., *Foreign Ships in Micronesia* (Saipan, 1979).

6. I reviewed *The First Taint of Civilization* in *Pacific Studies* 8, no. 1 (1984): 142–45.

7. Francis X. Hezel, S.J., "New Directions in Pacific History: A Practitioner's Practical Review," *Pacific Studies* 11, no. 3 (1988): 101–10.

8. Francis X. Hezel, S.J., "Recolonizing Islands and Decolonizing History," in *Pacific History: Papers from the 8th Pacific History Association Conference*, ed. Donald H. Rubenstein (Mangilao, Guam, 1992), 63–67.

9. Ibid., 66.

10. Robert F. Rogers, *Destiny's Landfall: A History of Guam* (Honolulu, 1995); David Hanlon, *Upon a Stone Altar: A History of the Island of Pohnpei to 1890* (Honolulu, 1988); Richard J. Parmentier, *The Sacred Remains: Myth, History, and Polity in Belau* (Chicago, 1987); Daniel Peacock, *Lee Boo of Belau: A Prince in London* (Honolulu, 1987); Lin Poyer, *The Ngatik Massacre: History and Identity on a Micronesian Atoll* (Washington, DC, 1993); and Lin Poyer, Suzanne Falgout, and Laurence Marshall Carucci, *The Typhoon of War: Micronesian Experiences of the Pacific War* (Honolulu, 2000).

CHAPTER 17

On Greg Dening's *Islands and Beaches*

Ivan Brady

*Islands and Beaches: Discourses on a Silent Land: Marquesas,
1774–1880,* by Greg Dening.

Melbourne: Melbourne University Press, 1980. Co-published, Honolulu:
University of Hawai'i Press, 1980. French translation, *Marquises 1774–1880:
Réflexion sur une terre muette*, présenté pare Hervé Le Cléach. Melbourne:
Melbourne University Press, 1999.

History is the texted past for which we have a cultural poetic.

Greg Dening, *The Death of William Gooch*

All voyages, all stories of voyages, have a beginning...
Sometimes, for dramatic effect, stories of voyages begin
at the end. Mine begins in-between. If I had a personal
global positioning system, it would always place me there.
In-between.

Greg Dening, *Beach Crossings*

REGARDING HIS inquiries into *The Great Cat Massacre* in eighteenth-century France and related difficulties of crossing cultural boundaries in anthropology and history, Robert Darnton makes a statement in passing that homes in on the heart of a postmodern problem. He writes that the "anthropological mode of history has a rigor of its own, even if it may look suspiciously like literature to a hard-boiled social scientist."[1] The rigor in this case is a code word for scientific method and interest (liberally interpreted) and the statement itself is a caution and an apology: it suggests that literature is commonly perceived to lack rigor and therefore appearing to be "literary" in certain contexts is a problem; that social science (including anthropology) both has rigor and admires it in other disciplines; and, despite appearances, that the anthropological mode of history has it, albeit in novel form, that is, with a literary spin in its frame.

This is all the more interesting given postmodern questions about ethnographic authority and the rise of various experimental writing forms as "textualism" in anthropology and related disciplines. Challenges to the authority of perfectly detached or objective ethnographic observations, especially ethnography parboiled into jargon soup by attempts to be rigorous, have made less room for overcooked declarations and more room for the softer arts of persuasion, including effective writing, in the social sciences. That's a slim cover for some old bugaboos: the tensions between art and science[2] and the subissues of who should have the authority to write anything (and be believed) and how that authority should be expressed, all of which have come to bear on anthropology and to some degree history as a kind of crisis of representation in the past twenty years or so.[3]

The anthropological mode of history sits nicely in the middle of this difficult milieu, and perhaps no work exemplifies the many facets of being there better than Greg Dening's impressive and important *Islands and Beaches: Discourse on a Silent Land: Marquesas, 1774–1880*. Readers cannot help but be struck by Dening's graceful writing and diligent pursuit of the largely tragic episodes of nineteenth-century Marquesan history. At the cusp of it, ninety thousand Marquesans were in the midst of a series of droughts, with more to come. The century's turn opened the Islanders up to an invasion of whalers, sailors, traders, missionaries, military men, beachcombers, settlers, and a hodge-podge of other adventurers who swept in with the tide of exploration and colonialism that began to swell in this part of the Pacific in the early 1800s. With them came powerful diseases and cultural collisions that reduced the indigenes to nine or ten thousand by 1863 and to about half of that by 1882. New ways of dying were added to the old in the enormous violence that was transported across the Beach—Dening's metaphor for the cultural twilight zone where it all came to pass.[4] This moving account of cultural misfires and cross-cultural casualties eventually caps itself in metonym and symbol on a rainy night that dampened the fuse of one of the last muskets aimed in a bloody war, and then slips ominously into the silence of an empty beach, even as the tropes that structure it cluster up as metaphors for us all: Natives and Strangers both joined and divided on the Beaches of life, each to the other in a pool of common humanity, diced up into sides by alien (and alienating) traditions.[5]

In its own historical moment *Islands and Beaches* was unconventional in the best sense of the term. It put new onus on ethnographic inquiry to return to the archives of its own subjects. It reasserted and redefined the inevitable entanglements and mutual dependencies of anthropology and history, and thereby raised the stakes for doing things differently in Pacific history, ethnohistory, and historical anthropology. Asking what lay behind this innovative project, what made it so different and influential, one discovers among its key elements the particular blend of anthropology and history that frames it: meticulous attention to historical and ethnographic detail that also serves as context-grounding for bright-minded (if critical) attention to what is usual in the social sciences and generally resisted by historians—the search for more comprehensive models of generalization and explanation. By fleshing out the history that is usually behind and beyond the "gaze" of social scientists without losing the larger contexts of social science questions about meaning-making, culture change, the nature of ritual and religion, and so on, *Islands and Beaches* turned out to be an inspiring and enlightening achievement on several fronts, with a twist. Covering so much ground, this work is nonetheless singularly proprietary.

The passion and power of the writing in *Islands and Beaches* is such that the reader is aware of auteur, hermeneut, ethnographic detective, human being Dening on every page as he makes sense of bits and pieces —the paper trail—in various versions of the impositions and appropriations of empire as they stacked up on both sides of this woeful Beach. One feels the presence of the interpreter in this puzzle, always triangulating and cross-referencing the circumstances and identities of the players in everything from the logbooks of ships and soldiers, to official correspondence from administrative upstarts and failures, to reality therapy crashed in on the ideals of missionaries, to snippets about Marquesan cargo (including Islanders) offloaded in some distant port—all the while sorting romanticized fictions from documented possibilities, and constantly maneuvering for a glimpse into the unwritten lives horizoned by these sources, especially those of *Te Enata*, the Marquesans. The result is a far cry from the invisible authorships and pseudo-objectivities that give us the "ethnographic present" and ethnographic or historical facts that "speak for themselves."[6] Dening himself is the beacon in this work. That makes one inquire not just about the logistics and technicalities of producing the text, but also about the attributes of Dening's own personal light: his training as a Jesuit; his deep sense of the thickness, untidiness, and drama of culture; his love of the sea and the histories touched by it;[7] his development of history's anthropology as a study domain[8] and of narrative as a theme in all such inquiries; and the sensibilities and humanity of his observations that mark him plainly as a poet in historian's clothing. All of this must be taken into account at some level in deconstructing the genius of *Islands and Beaches,* and it is not hard to argue that the bottom line in that is "literary"—influential work marked emphatically by rigor, passion, and craft.

Literature Lies in the Eyes of Its Beholders

However shallow it may seem, producing literature in the common estimation of writing for the sake of writing well provides a basis for social and moral judgments about authors. The result can be ornamental, condemning, subversive, exploitative, exasperating, and exalting—and therefore also political, a matter of social consequence, a way of deciding who is to be included and who is to be excluded from certain activities. The very idea of "literariness" evokes glamour and privilege. It acquires the subjective conviction of taste and associates it with a way of life; those who drink of it, as with French wine, drink of a totem; it is a unifying force for all who share its special meaning.[9] Authorship harvests—draws it all together, mediates the path to literariness, and confers it as a badge to be worn at the intellectual meal—in the classroom, the poetry reading, the soirée at the library. The literariness that derives from the public production and consumption of books is thus a quality to be assumed as part of the person in intellectual life. There are, after all, persons who occupy the handle of "literary giants." But grabbing at literariness as if it were whole cloth overestimates its weave: it is an "idea" anchored in the things of literature and the place of literature in society. Making sense of Darnton's suspicions about anthropological history as they might apply to Dening, the problem is getting to know the concept in a way that facilitates analysis, not just an expanded understanding of its role in public culture.

Literariness prevails as a quality of writing wherever texts are produced, in science-minded writing as well as in what is conventionally described as literature. By accentuating the form of the message rather than the contents of its speech-acts, however, the literary or poetic text takes for its primary object what science does not. Science, of course, needs language to function, but unlike literature, it neither asserts nor sees itself as situated *within* language. Such authors can also signal their separation from conventionally "objective" texts through various forms of authorial presence. The conspicuously poetic author willingly appears as a person in her text—as an artisan whose constant display is the craft of language (the language of the poem is claimed by the poet and must be read through that claim), or as a person who visibly leads the prose narrative from within. The conventionally scientific author tries to avoid both, aspiring to invisibility in every place except the opening credits of her cover page. The idea is to keep the facts in the text speaking for themselves as much as possible through the conscientious destruction of language that flags itself as partaking of the author in any personal way. Less exaggerated works find room for compromise. Given the skill and the will, such authors can saturate their works with "poeticity" through a highly original or provocative use of metaphors, without aborting their genres completely.[10] The caveat is that good writing can be both more persuasive in argument *and* resonant with deeper (richer, thicker) understanding of the subject matter, which is something we all seek to give and get as authors of any persuasion.[11]

Dening's literariness does not reach the proprietary level of display one finds in poetry per se, complete with poetic line phrasing, and so on. Nonetheless, his "poetic mentality"[12] gives him the motor power of a passionate and determined interpreter wherever we find him, without writing verse, and in various voices. In *Islands and Beaches*, he does not enter the text in first person, except (and this is important, because it frames the entire work) in his "Remarks in Preface" and his haunting epilogue, "Remarks on a Silent Land."[13] His role in the middle is exactly what historians expect: storyteller. His job is to tell the story of what happened, or what appears to have happened, given fair interpretations of the evidence, through a more detached voice (third person, past tense). But that prose is also suffused with depth of insight and emotion. Like so much of his work, *Islands and Beaches* is a telling that matters. Moreover, this particular story of islands is itself dotted and subplotted by a series of "Reflections" on larger-scale social science interests ("Models and Metaphors," "Rites of Passage," "Religious Change," etc.) following each chapter of historical particulars. Here we find the blend of the author as poet, humanist, and deep interpreter, on the one hand, and the student of Marx, Durkheim, Weber, Sahlins, social change, the sociology in anthropology, the organizing principles of society and theories about how they change, and so on, on the other. The difference between this and the usual social science is that Dening fills his structures with emotionally powerful, realistic, and motivating facts from history cut close to the ground, face to face, in the sweaty domain we call life (poets live there).[14]

The result is a balancing act that satisfies in several directions. Dening knows that a heavy analytic scalpel cuts too deep, distorts representation, and destroys particular (and therefore historical) views. The art in this is to rise in level of vision without changing too much ground, to engage the mythic qualities of being literary (and therefore the structuralist's danger of overgeneralizing form against the realities of life as lived) without losing sight of either the manifestations of those qualities in practice or the elusiveness of perfect observation. Dening understands that perfectly clinical or detached observations are impossible, that the mutual engagements of dialogic process keep the author present in one form or another in all accounts. They are all laced with selective perceptions, an ultimately arbitrary determination of beginning and ending dates for narratives, and the indelible principle that ethnographic and historical accounts are necessarily partial representations. They are also stories, by definition.

Historical Narratives (His, Ours, and Theirs)

History is for Dening a narrative act, in several ways. It is "the past transcribed into words and signs," and therefore "text-able." It is "the way we experience the present."[15] It is the past recalled to present and reenacted, remembered, revivified, storied—behaved again vicariously, with all of the distortions, imperfections, and creative appropriations that implies (36);[16] a generic form of consciousness, a "conscious relationship between past and present";[17] an "everyday thing, saturating every moment of our cultural existence. Making sense of what has happened is how we live" (xiv). And that is itself lived experience "pulled out of the stream of consciousness and given dramatic form" in a way that is "metonymic of the present, metaphoric of the past; it presents past with the double meaning of the 'presents'. Narrating both makes a now of the past and delivers the past in some dramatic display" (104).[18] We reinvent ourselves by reinventing our histories through various forms of expression: "We sing it, dance it, carve it, paint it, tell it, write it" (xiv). Through such means, history has a ritual quality.[19] It tells us who we are. Still, more than story content interpreting the past, more than "just a message," as anthropology is more than a study of "the different,"[20] histories are "the mode of the story's expression, the public occasion of its telling," and that makes them an anthropological concern (48–49). "Anthropology," he says, "has the patience that hermeneutical philosophers do not have to see and describe the everyday nature of special histories and the historical nature of everyday life as well" (49). The transforming of lived experience into narratives thus gives history "an anthropology, as it has a criticism and a history" (104).[21]

These are some of the premises for Dening's thinking on history's anthropology, part of the framework for his reading and presentation of the data on the Marquesas, believing all along "that we never know the truth by being told it," that we "have to experience it in some way." Creating the circumstances for that is part of "the abiding grace of history" (101) and the power of narrative per se (in theater as well as in historical texts).[22] It is also the art of knowing how to muster and interpret such information, and that, inevitably, is to some degree strictly personal, idiosyncratic.

The Rest of the Story

Put Greg Dening in enough libraries and he will give you history that lives and breathes its triumphs and tragedies through the eyes of individuals caught up in the cultural nets of their times and then he will tell you how that settles into the larger questions and philosophies of social science and history. He will give you history's anthropology. That is no small talent.[23] He knows that we are all Native and Stranger to each other at one level or another, and, importantly, that the Otherness of obvious strangers (including other disciplines) collapses on close inspection— given the right vehicles of communication. For Dening, as we have seen, that vehicle is carefully considered writing, and that, as any serious author must admit, comes only from deep within. Even anthropology has its muses. Dening's happen to live as poets and scholars. There is privilege in that, and Dening has had, by his own admission, "a privileged life" (4).

Seventeen years of study with few obligations beyond those of being a student preceded his academic career. His "four years of philosophy, five years of history, four years of theology and four years of anthropology" constituted for him "a magical mystery tour of life" that he "has celebrated . . . ever since" (4). But Dening did not get his poetics from Harvard's anthropology. He already possessed that quality, some of which was enhanced, along with the bear-trap mind of his scholarship, by the priesthood. He had wanted to be a Jesuit priest since he was nine or ten years old, and, as expected, there was training and regimen full of formalism in it (19).[24] He left the priesthood in 1970 and was appointed Max Crawford Professor of History at the University of Melbourne the following year. He has since retired, liberating time for additional reflections on his life and times, motivations and inspirations, and, of course, for more writing, more poetic prose, so rich in allegory and uncommon metaphor.[25] His work in that sense is conspicuously literary and emblematic of many other enviable qualities. We have come to expect from him the ease and originality through which he reveals new and enriching interpretations of old facts, new facts, and new avenues to understanding and appreciating (internalizing) the actors of history—the patterns of their lives and the consequences of their acting in one context or another, even while informing us of his own.

Conclusions: Suspicions Confirmed

From innovative forms of authorial presence to the instructive use of metaphors in unraveling the knots of Pacific history, *Islands and Beaches* has an important measure of what makes the anthropological mode of history literary in its composition while incorporating the artful interpretations and rigor of thought and method that cultural anthropology covets in the development of its own *science humaine*. The tension that emerges from this hails in its most favored form from the Enlightenment and is familiar to critics in analytic torture chambers throughout the academy: in one guise or another, it is a contest of analytic privilege and influence between art and science, and it comes to middle ground most auspiciously in anthropology and history in the hands of Greg Dening. That is ground on which he thrives. He has little use for fences, especially the disruptively artificial ones set up by academic disciplines. His genius is launched with serious craft and purpose "betwixt and between." He looks both ways, crosses intersections under several identities, instructs on all fronts, and carries the message that all knowledge is personal.[26] Determining how much practical and intellectual ground that covers depends on the space one sees between literature, anthropology, and history. Dening shows that space not only to be variable; it is in some important measure collapsible. History's anthropology is constructed—and the kind of rigor that I think Darnton had in mind for his "anthropological mode of history" is exemplified—in the process. The result is literary, to be sure. It has that wonderful veneer and spin of frame. But it is also more complicated than that. It is history, broadly conceived, powerfully stated, and rigorous in application. It is social science with its navel-gazing gates unlocked: pseudo-science jargon out, literate history in, interpreter present and accounted for, principal problems addressed.

There may also be some lessons in this for the new generation of historians and anthropologists. Dening's work can be articulated and analyzed, but it cannot be cloned. Like Lévi-Strauss, and to some degree thereby incorporating the criticism that his methods are not easily transferred because so much of what he does depends on his own individuality, Dening is one of a kind. Nevertheless, the results of his work can be *emulated*. There is hope for students who fail to keep rigor, who skim rather than shovel, who lump rather than split, who take tea on time instead of taking the extra hundred hours of back-breaking, eye-straining work that can be the bane of historical research. Like Dening, they should follow their intellectual, cultural, and historical problems wherever they lead and learn the language appropriate to each station: other cultures, other disciplines. But most of all, they should learn their craft, fear no literature, and let their muses be. Put them to work in strange places, for example, in anthropology and history.[27] There is more than one way to say (and therefore to know) things, including ourselves. Subversive of artificial polarities, fundamentalism especially, and closed worlds in general, Dening urges the point that

we history-makers must know ourselves. We must have an ethnographic sense of our cultural persons. The past is emptied of almost all its meaning by the selective texts that survive it. We realise that the meanings in the text are mere shadows the more we experience the fullness of the meanings in our ordinary living. All my academic life I taught history by first requiring my students to transcribe some event or ritual or drama in their lives into narrative. I called this ethnography. They soon discovered how difficult it was to do. They soon learned that there was nothing that they observed but was the subject of some reflective discourse by somebody else. Knowing what that discourse was, what questions shaped it and in what way their own ethnography added to it was to be the cultural persons they needed to be to write history. (30)

Or anthropology.[28]

Notes

This essay builds substantially on my review article of *Islands and Beaches*, "Les îles Marquises: Ethnography from another Beachhead," *American Ethnologist* 9 (1982): 185–90. I thank Greg Dening and Yvonna Lincoln for their generous comments on an earlier draft of this essay. They made this version better and I am grateful. Any remaining problems can be blamed on an enemy of your choice.

1. Robert Darnton, *The Great Cat Massacre and Other Episodes in French Cultural History* (New York, 1984), 6.

2. See Ivan Brady, ed., *Anthropological Poetics* (Savage, MD, 1991); Ivan Brady and Alok Kumar, "Some Thoughts on Sharing Science," *Science Education* 84 (2000): 507–23.

3. These developments are well known in most places, as are the major figures who contributed to them, including Hayden White, Clifford Geertz, James Clifford, and George Marcus. See especially the comprehensive multidisciplinary work of Norman K. Denzin and Yvonna Lincoln that not only reviews the foundations of these problems but raises the stakes on so many of them. Denzin, *Interpretive Ethnography: Ethnographic Practices for the 21st Century* (Thousand Oaks, CA, 1997); Denzin and Lincoln, eds., *Handbook of Qualitative Research* (Thousand Oaks, CA, 2000); Denzin and Lincoln, eds., *The Qualitative Inquiry Reader* (Thousand Oaks, CA, 2002); Lincoln and Denzin, eds., *Turning Points in Qualitative Research: Tying Knots in a Handkerchief* (Walnut Creek, CA, 2003).

4. Brady, "Les îles Marquises," 187.

5. See in particular Dening's widely cited "Possessing Tahiti," reprinted in Dening, *Performances* (Chicago, 1996), 126–67. Europeans not only possessed Tahiti, but it possessed them in special ways as well.

6. Cf. Alan Ward, "Comfortable Voyagers: Some Reflections on the Pacific and its Historians," *Journal of Pacific History* 31, no. 2 (1996): 236–42.

7. See Ivan Brady, "History's Poetics: An Interview with Greg Dening," in *Dangerous Liaisons: Essays in Honour of Greg Dening*, ed. Donna Merwick (Melbourne, 1994), 7–21.

8. See especially Dening, *The Death of William Gooch: History's Anthropology* (Melbourne, 1995).

9. See Roland Barthes, *Mythologies* (New York, 1972).

10. Brady, ed., *Anthropological Poetics;* idem, "Anthropological Poetics," in *Handbook of Qualitative Research*, ed. Denzin and Lincoln, 949–79; idem, *The Time at Darwin's Reef: Poetic Explorations in Anthropology and History* (Walnut Creek, CA, 2003).

11. See Clifford Geertz, *The Interpretation of Cultures* (New York, 1973); idem, *Works and Lives: The Anthropologist as Author* (Stanford, 1988).

12. A quality Hannah Arendt attributed to Walter Benjamin, and we can extend to Franz Kafka, Joseph Conrad, and others, like Dening, whose palpable poetics are contained in prose, not verse. "Poetics are not poetry," Dening writes, "but the suggestion that they might be is left with the breath of the word." Hannah Arendt, ed., *Illuminations: Walter Benjamin* (New York, 1969), 14; Dening, *Performances*, 35 (quotation), 272.

13. Much of Dening's work has the self-revealing, self-reciprocating, mutually constructing presence of first-person writing. See especially *Readings/Writings* (Melbourne, 1998); and *Beach Crossings: Voyaging across Times, Cultures and Self* (Melbourne, 2004).

14. Poetry creates and occupies sensuous space that is connected to the deepest level of existence, and it is mostly only the poets who write about experience consistently from that perspective—centering, decoding, reframing, discovering, and discoursing the world as embodied participants and observers, full of touch, smell, taste, hearing, and vision, open to the buzz, joy, sweat, and tears—the erotics—of daily life, hoping to reveal that world for what it is to them, as it is experienced self-consciously in pattern and puzzle, and can be shared with co-participants by drawing on their common humanity. It is a self-revealing, self-constructing form of discovery, like writing in general (see Laurel Richardson, "Writing: A Method of Inquiry," in *Handbook of Qualitative Research*, ed. Denzin and Lincoln, 923–48) and that most fundamental of human activities, "storying" (Brady, *The Time at Darwin's Reef*). Ethnographic poets aim at writing from one self-conscious interiority to another in a manner that stirs something up in us, finds the strange in the everyday, takes us to another circumstance, perhaps a cross-cultural one, takes us out of our inner selves for a moment to show us something about ourselves in general, what we have in common with the rest of the world. In that connection, ethnographic poems "reflect a dimension that is sadly missing from earlier forms of fieldwork"; they "help readers understand the emotional, psychic, spiritual and transcendental aspects of the . . . ethnographic experience—aspects that move us beyond the travel and the living into the experiences of the lived." Lincoln and Denzin, eds., *Turning Points in Qualitative Research*, 440. Historian/ethnographer/poet Dening is a master of these forms.

15. Dening, *Performances*, 41. Subsequent references to this work will be to the page number(s), within parentheses, in the body of the text.

16. Cf. Brady, *The Time at Darwin's Reef.*

17. Dening, *Islands and Beaches*, 3.

18. Dening says that "all the ways we transform lived experience into narratives . . . are metaphors of the past and metonymies of the present." History is not the past per se. It is "a metaphor of the past . . . the past transformed into something else, story. Metonymy: history is metonymy of the present. These stories in their telling *are* our present," and "as much about us as about something else." *Performances*, 34.

19. See Dening, *Mr. Bligh's Bad Language* (Cambridge, 1992); and *Performances;* idem, "Ritual as Cognitive Process, Performance as History," *Current Anthropology* 40, no. 2 (1999): 243–48.

20. Dening, *Islands and Beaches,* 3.

21. See also Dening, ed., *The Marquesan Journal of Edward Robarts, 1797–1824* (Canberra, 1974); and my review of this book in *American Anthropologist* 79, no. 3 (1977): 695.

22. Dening, *Mr. Bligh's Bad Language; Performances; Readings/Writings;* "Writing, Rewriting the Beach," *Rethinking History* 2, no. 2 (1998): 143–72; James A. Boon, *Verging on Extra-Vagance: Anthropology, History, Religion, Literature, Arts . . . Showbiz* (Princeton, 1999).

23. And neither is it lacking in controversy. See, e.g., Ward, "Comfortable Voyagers," 37–38.

24. See also Greg Dening and Doug Kennedy, *Xavier Portraits* (Melbourne, 1993).

25. See, for example, *Readings/Writings;* and *Beach Crossings.*

26. How could it be otherwise? See Michael Polanyi and Harry Prosch, *Meaning* (Chicago, 1975).

27. See Robert Borofsky, ed., *Remembrance of Pacific Pasts: An Invitation to Remake History* (Honolulu, 2000); and my review of this book, "Whence History?" in *Current Anthropology* 42, no. 3 (2001): 443–44.

28. There is nothing in the mix of human relations that says ethnography and history can't be reported in different forms. Poetic texts can be robust and powerful in their ability to communicate the reality of experiences at hand, achieving what Thomas Blackburn has called a kind of sensuous and intellectual complementarity, impossible through other means ("Sensuous-Intellectual Complementarity in Science," *Science* 4 [June 1971]: 1003–7). Such texts can "illuminate our experience, explore the consequences of our beliefs, challenge the ways we think, and criticize our ideologies." Poetic rendering is more than another way of telling (writing or speaking). It is another way of interpreting and therefore of knowing. See Brady, "In Defense of the Sensual: Meaning Construction in Ethnography and Poetics," *Qualitative Inquiry* 10, no. 4 (2004): 622–44. That makes the work fundamental: "To understand the nature and value of poetic creativity requires us to understand the ordinary ways we think." George Lakoff and Mark Turner, *More Than Cool Reason: A Field Guide to Metaphor* (Chicago, 1989), xi–xii.

CHAPTER 18

Disentangling Samoan History:
The Contributions of Gilson and Davidson

Doug Munro

Samoa, 1830 to 1900: The Politics of a Multi-Cultural Community,
by R. P. Gilson, with an introduction and conclusion by
J. W. Davidson.
Melbourne: Oxford University Press, 1970.

*Samoa mo Samoa: The Emergence of the Independent State of
Western Samoa,* by J. W. Davidson.
Melbourne: Oxford University Press, 1967.

11 JUNE 1950: Dick Gilson arrives in Apia and is advised to contact Jim Davidson. As it happened, Gilson was carrying a letter of introduction from Davidson's former history professor in Wellington. Gilson, an American Fulbright scholar based in New Zealand, was on his way to the Cook Islands to write a report on the dependency's administration. Davidson was on leave from St. John's College, Cambridge, as the trusteeship officer, a specially created and somewhat nebulous position with duties appertaining to the territory's advancement to self-governing status. There was immediate rapport and within a fortnight Davidson was discussing sensitive political issues with his new friend.[1] It is likely at this juncture that Davidson, who was within months of taking up his appointment as foundation professor of Pacific history at the Australian National University (ANU), earmarked Gilson as a prospective academic colleague. Gilson certainly possessed the attributes that Davidson was looking for in his choice of future staff—personal compatibility, sound scholarship, and an ability (or at least the potential) to write Pacific history in ways that took Islanders seriously and not simply as bit players in the imperial game.

In Gilson's case there was more. Davidson could see that he was an *225* alert and perceptive observer who had immediately taken to Samoa, as he himself had done. Gilson, moreover, shared his interest in contemporary affairs and, more important, his commitment to indigenous self-determination. These qualities of involvement and self-implication would, in Davidson's view, enable the writing of a history of Samoa that would transcend the purely scholarly. Gilson went on to the London School of Economics to write a thesis on the administration of the Cook Islands[2] and in 1952 was appointed research fellow in Pacific history at ANU. That is how it started. And both Gilson and Davidson, in very different circumstances, each produced a major book on Samoa—Gilson his political history of the Samoan Islands to the time of annexation by Germany (*Samoa, 1830 to 1900,* in 1970), and Davidson a bifurcated account of the historical evolution and actual creation of the Independent State of Western Samoa in 1962 (*Samoa mo Samoa,* in 1967). Their books are a remarkable duo, born of and informed by a deep affection and commitment toward Samoa and its people.

Samoa, 1830 to 1900

The affable and talented Gilson (1925–63) was a scholar's scholar. Methodical and hard-working, Gilson was described by Davidson as having "a certain thoroughness in his manner and a tendency to build an argument as an Australian bricklayer constructs a wall; the rate of work is not fast but there is no objection to overtime."[3] In addition to a four-month period of fieldwork in 1954, Gilson endeavored to locate and consult every scrap of archival evidence relevant to his theme, as evidenced by the 201 folders of carefully typed research notes on Samoa.[4] He was a perfectionist but to a self-stultifying degree. A particular difficulty was the obligation, as Gilson saw it, to reconcile the demands of compression and elaboration.[5] The sad upshot was that Gilson made insufficient progress on his book, and he found himself out of a job when the final May 1958 deadline expired. Gilson struggled on in very difficult professional and personal circumstances, to put it mildly, and the book was largely completed in 1962 when he received a teaching appointment in anthropology at the Los Angeles State College. Even then the fates were unkind with Gilson's death from a heart attack the following year, at the early age of thirty-seven. His wife Miriam completed the manuscript, which Davidson edited and saw through the press; it was eventually published in 1970. If ever a book was forged in adversity it was this one.

The critical reaction was gratifying. The reviewers warmly welcomed this "massive and indispensable book" with its rare combination of historical research and anthropological insight. Not least, Gilson's "ability to encapsulate paragraphs of meaning in a few words" would have been vindication for his concern for fidelity to every nuance of interpretation.[6] But it all came too late for Gilson to savour. Still, one can only agree with Davidson that the earlier chapters achieve a "superb" level of analysis.[7] The mastery of his source material and the correction of its European bias in the first two chapters on the Samoan way of life and its structure are exemplary. This is the more remarkable given, and contrary to received wisdom, that Gilson's formal training in the discipline of anthropology amounted to one undergraduate course and a further graduate course of instruction. Gilson was trained in political science; he was essentially self-taught in both the techniques of documentary research and anthropological method. The following pair of chapters, on Christianity and the Samoan influence on the church (not the church's influence on Samoans!), are probably the highpoints. The chapter on the American adventurer Albert B. Steinberger is a masterly unraveling of the interplay between personality and issues, intrigue and principle. While the historian Barry Rigby conclusively proved that Steinberger was an accomplished con man—which many contemporaries had suspected (and what Davidson could never bring himself to admit)—Gilson anticipated Rigby's analysis without having seen the crucial documents among the proceedings of the H.M.S. *Barracouta*.[8]

But the book rates higher in research than in readability. For all the vitality and power of its prose, *Samoa, 1830 to 1900* puts even the informed reader's powers of concentration to the test. The middle chapters especially, where complex scenarios are related in a densely constructed Germanic-style narrative, are best read in short bursts. That said, there are passages where sparkle and erudition intermingle, for example, the seven-page section on economic prospects (171–78). But a book that is finished by another hand can never be the one its author intended and the final three chapters are probably poor approximations to what Gilson would have written had he lived. To compound the problem, Gilson had consciously drafted these chapters more summarily— otherwise the book would have grown completely out of control, but the effect was to give the impression of a rush to the finish line. Imperfect it is, and heavy-going, but a masterpiece nonetheless.

Samoa, 1830 to 1900 strongly reflects its author's personality. The carefully weighed conclusions, exactness of word and phrase, and the massive research that underpins the enterprise are palpably the work of a raconteur, an enthusiast for his subject, and above all a perfectionist. His thoroughness of investigation should not be put down to an obsession with detail, as it sometimes has been. It was not detail for detail's sake, but a principled concern with accuracy and integrity of conclusions, and was reflected in his frequent agonizing over the right choice of word and phrase. This had the overtly moral dimension of George Orwell's writing, founded on a sense of obligation and duty to avoid carelessness and ambiguity, and to eschew the overworked metaphor and the hackneyed phrase.[9] At another level was a blend of the professional historian's stolidity and the storyteller's sparkle, not to mention his shrewd understanding of human motivation and a sure eye for a charlatan—as, for example, his exposé of Aaron Van Camp's shenanigans (233–39). He poured his personality into his book and the writing, indeed, proclaimeth the man.

Such is the quality of the research and perceptiveness upon which it is based, not to mention its sweep and scale, that *Samoa, 1830 to 1900* has not, and perhaps never will be, superseded as the great text on nineteenth-century Samoa. Such a commanding performance inhibits would-be imitators. Paul Kennedy's *The Samoan Tangle*[10] is also massively researched but begins in earnest in 1884, just when Gilson was tapering off. In that sense Gilson and Kennedy complement each other, but they contrast sharply in that Kennedy adopts a Great Power approach. Damon Salesa, who is working on a "people's history" of Samoa, has described *Samoa, 1830 to 1900* as a "special book." He often finds himself turning to it, "not only for its richness of sources, and the richness of sources, and the strength of its interpretation, but also as a book which has a wonderful sense of the detail of Samoan life, and perhaps most rarely, a sense of the irony of (Samoan) history . . . It has kept its feet surely for decades, and I expect that it will last in a way virtually unique amongst works of Pacific historiography."[11] *Samoa, 1830 to 1900* is a prime exemplar of the culture contact genre of Pacific Islands historiography pioneered by Davidson and the Canberra school, and a massive achievement in its own right.

Samoa mo Samoa

James Wightman Davidson's (1915–73) involvement with Samoa also began by happy accident. On study leave from Cambridge University in 1947, he was fortuitously engaged by the New Zealand prime minister to report on the political situation and prospects for Samoan self-government (6, 167). Like Gilson, his special attachment to Samoa and the Samoans transformed into a lifelong commitment, both personal and professional. He initially envisaged a 70,000-word book covering the years from 1947 through to 1962—a short and topical scholarly analysis of Western Samoa's transition from political dependency to being the first Pacific Islands territory to achieve independence. What transpired was a 165,000-word book that was "concerned with the changes of political structure, thought and activity of Samoa resulting from its contact with the Western world" (ix). More precisely, Davidson sought to show how, over the course of a century and a quarter, the Samoans lost and then regained their independence. Following a contextualizing chapter are four chapters taking the story to 1946; these are a general political history, with close attention to the nuances of Samoan culture. Davidson dealt with these years in more detail than he originally intended, partly because the Gilson manuscript was available to him and partly because of his dissatisfaction with earlier accounts, such as Felix Keesing's *Modern Samoa* (1935). He made extensive use of Gilson's unpublished work, with acknowledgment (xi, 442–43), for the period to 1900, and his lengthier than intended treatment of the pre-1946 period involved him in a good deal of extra research, especially among newspapers.

The post-1946 sections of *Samoa mo Samoa* are more detailed and thematic, including substantial chapters on the economy and on village and district government, delineating the interaction of Samoan pressures, New Zealand methods, and international requirements in the protracted exercise of reaching workable solutions for Western Samoa's independence and entry into the family of nations. Davidson was a participant to varying degrees in many of the events he describes, and these sections of the book have a heavy autobiographical overlay and are as much a primary source as a secondary account. By no means does Davidson underestimate his own role in the making of the history he chronicles. *Samoa mo Samoa* is really two distinct books—pre-1946 and 1946 onward. Perhaps the contrasting styles and purposes of the component parts could have been softened; but the eventual book was better, in terms of both content and continuity than the shorter account that was originally envisaged.

A colleague described *Samoa mo Samoa* as "lucid, graceful, unpretentious."[12] No one disputed its high literary quality. Along with professional competence, *Samoa mo Samoa* was characterized by authorial idiosyncrasy. Davidson was an indifferent archival researcher and his written sources were overwhelmingly *printed* sources—whether they be newspapers, parliamentary papers, Legislative Council debates, *fono* proceedings, reports of commissions of inquiry, United Nations reports, or the 1954 and 1960 constitution convention debates. He was also wont to get research assistants to extract relevant material from the published official documentation rather than doing it himself. Nor did he keep regular diaries while in Samoa; instead, his letters to his mother were in some respects a substitute for diaries and he used these as an *aide-mémoire* when writing *Samoa mo Samoa*. In these respects, Davidson's approach was rather different from Gilson's exhaustive researches.

Davidson's tendency to minimize his exposure to documentary sources is evident in his use of the official New Zealand files for the 1920s and 1930s. He only looked at them at all because he felt that he had to. As he explained to his publisher, "It would be unfortunate if my conclusions could either be shown to be defective because I had not seen the[se] files or even if they could be exposed to criticism, however baseless in fact, on the same ground."[13] Tapping into his old-boy network, Davidson wrote to Alister McIntosh (the permanent head of the prime minister's department), who arranged access to restricted records of New Zealand's Department of Island Territories. These files, and others in Samoa that Davidson rapidly surveyed earlier in the year, are voluminous (listed on pages 438–39) and he could not, in the time available, have closely read this material. But that was not the intention; all he wanted was to satisfy himself that his already-written chapter did not require significant modification. A greater familiarity with the documentary record would certainly have led to modifications here and there—for example, Davidson underrated the importance of the 1954 constitutional convention, which set the pace and terms of impending self-government.[14]

The singular feature of *Samoa mo Samoa* is its author's stance as a participant in many of the more recent events. While Davidson considered that his role as a participant "brought added understanding," he conceded that it "also created some danger of loss of detachment" (x). He described his position as "often that of a passionate partisan," and he certainly identified closely with the Samoans' quest for self-determination. But for all his partisanship, Davidson believed that his position as participant imposed a special obligation "not to mention by name any of those with whom I had worked when my comments on their actions were wholly critical" and to refrain from quoting, or even footnoting, official sources relating to more recent events.[15] The participant's advantage is somewhat negated if self-imposed ethical restraints prevent the disclosure of information and sources, but there was no turning back from his obligation, as Davidson saw it. A similar reticence and sense of fairness caused Davidson to write about G. R. (later Sir Guy) Powles, the New Zealand high commissioner in Western Samoa (1949–60) in ways that give the uninitiated no inkling that Davidson held him in low regard.

But Davidson had no qualms in severely criticizing the generality of expatriate (and especially seconded) New Zealand public servants in Samoa for their cultural chauvinism and general ineptitude, as well as the way in which the public service was structured, and he was ferocious in his criticism of the (unnamed) public service commissioner during the 1950s who was a law unto himself (199–201, 204–15). There was no love lost on either side, and, if anything, Davidson relished his unpopularity among the ranks of "the *papalagi* 'ascendancy'" (193), who resented his closeness with the Samoan leaders and disapproved of his identification with Samoan causes. Davidson's criticisms of the New Zealand seconded public servant, and of the public service generally, is the most commented upon aspect of *Samoa mo Samoa*. Powles was dismayed, saying that Davidson had done "grave injustice" to individuals who had tried their best. According to Powles, the "fault lay with policies and attitudes at the political and governmental level in New Zealand."[16] Powles was not being entirely frank: he might also have mentioned that he had continually beseeched New Zealand to send him people of better caliber. Those concerned took great offense at being described, even anonymously, as insensitive incompetents but Davidson had a point.[17]

There is no doubt that Davidson's involvement in Samoan affairs "was a unique vantage point for an academic study of decolonisation" and that it "impart[ed] a flavour of unusual intimacy to the book's analysis of negotiations and the motivations behind them."[18] He was aware that his version of recent events might be open to correction and he expressed the hope that other participants would set down their own version of events (x). This has not happened to any great extent. The only person, other than Davidson, to stake a claim for his part in Samoan independence was Frank Corner, the leader of the New Zealand delegation to Samoa. Via a thesis writer, Corner claimed that he was responsible at the eleventh hour for gaining the trust of Tupua Tamasese Mea'ole (one of the *Fautua*) toward New Zealand's good intentions and for persuading the Samoans to opt for full independence rather than self-government.[19]

But did Davidson's position of participant, passionate or otherwise, get in the way of Davidson the historian? He generalized the notion of the scholar as a man of practical affairs into a theory about "participant history" (and historians) and proceeded to make claims for what began simply as a happy accident of fortune—the invitation from Fraser, in his case. That is one way of looking at *Samoa mo Samoa*. But it was not a mere matter of Davidson being swept along by the current of life. He could have contracted out of his type of participant involvement in Samoa and assumed instead the posture of a detached scholar of Samoan affairs. But it was not in his nature to do this, and he actively sought continuing engagement of the participant kind. He did so partly because of his commitment to Samoan independence, partly because he considered himself indispensable, partly because he found Samoa so congenial, and partly because he was the person he was. Samoa never lost its attraction and he cherished his "entry not only into the country but into a way of life . . . [and] into a pattern of thought and behaviour that is satisfying, dignified and complete" (3). It recalls Somerset Maugham's description of Gauguin's Tahitian scenes: "They are deliberately stylised, but they have an idyllic character that does recall those lovely islands in the South Seas and for one who has lived in them they evoke memories of a kind of sensual content and a happiness of the spirit which the passing of time can never quite dim."[20]

Davidson's depiction of Samoan society was highly idealized and very kind, resulting in a reluctance to be publicly critical of Samoa and Samoans. It is not too much of an exaggeration to say that *Samoa mo Samoa* is a hymn of praise to Samoan resilience and endeavor. Stuart Inder, the editor of *Pacific Islands Monthly*, was all-too-accurate in saying that Davidson's "obvious sympathies for the Samoans perhaps carry him further than they should, and thus we are given the impression that after 1900, the Samoans were continually being sinned against by completely insensitive idiots as they struggled for recognition in a difficult world";[21] and the anthropologist Derek Freeman privately told Davidson, and none too gently, that his silences about the level of violence in Samoan society resulted in his book missing a whole dimension.[22] Davidson could not, publicly at least, admit that Samoan society had a dark side. On the other hand, Davidson secured the trust and enjoyed an extraordinarily close relationship with the Samoan leadership, and especially the two *Fautua* (royal sons). But this resulted in a high politics, or *matai* version, of Samoan society. Davidson strenuously denied that this was the case, pointing out that he consciously sought to meet people from all walks of life in Samoa. But the criticism sticks. The anthropologist Murray Groves intended to write a review along these lines for the *Journal of the Polynesian Society* but unfortunately never carried out his resolve.

So the book is open to criticism on the very grounds that Davidson claimed as its strength. But if Davidson's view of Samoa was "rather couleur de rose," he was altogether more somber on the matter of economic development.[23] He fretted about the health of the Samoan economy and its likely impact on the postindependence regime, and wondered how he should deal with it in the epilogue of *Samoa mo Samoa*. Being very much his own man, he was untroubled that what he might say would run counter to the current academic fashion to downplay, or ignore, "economic viability" (to use the terminology of the day) as a criterion for independence.[24] To Davidson, the weaknesses of the Samoan economy posed a threat to the orderly progress of the independent state, but he wondered how to frame his views in ways that would not reflect badly on postindependent Samoa. He sent a draft to a close Samoan colleague, who reassured him that "the opinions expressed needed to be made to bring the Boat of Samoa back on the course charted by the wise Tamasese," and contented himself by writing on the subject in far stronger terms in a journal article.[25]

Samoa mo Samoa can be read at many levels—as straight history; as a finely honed account of political evolution from dependency to independence; as a passionate endorsement of indigenous self-determination; as an equally passionate advocacy of participant history; as one man's assessment of his role in making history. *Samoa mo Samoa* also contains perceptive, and often comparative, theoretical statements about decolonization and constitution-making (chap. 11). Above all, he was adamant that the constitution had to reflect what Samoans wanted, and not what New Zealand deemed suitable for them. Davidson is always, if briefly, mentioned in any discussion of decolonization in the literature relating to the Pacific Islands. A reviewer rightly declared that "Professor Davidson's book deserves an honourable place among works on 'decolonisation,'" [26] but *Samoa mo Samoa* has never been integrated into the wider historiography of decolonization. One would have supposed otherwise. After all, Western Samoa was the first Pacific Island territory to decolonize, on 1 January 1962; it was a most unusual evolution toward independence; and Davidson makes so many comparative comments on the nature of decolonization as well as the specifics of the highly unusual Samoan case.

Several reasons can be suggested for this segregation. First, attention has been focused on the dissolution of particular *empires*—the British Empire, the French Empire, and so on. But the British Empire in the Pacific was tiny compared to Africa and Asia, so the Pacific territories tend to get ignored in the wider accounts of decolonization (or of colonial rule, for that matter). Discussion of the Pacific in these wider works is avoided, largely because the fiddly details do not seem to add to the story in significant ways. In any case, Western Samoa was not part of the British Empire (except, technically, from 1914 to 1919). That leads to another facet of the explanation: most colonies in the Pacific were those of Australia (Papua New Guinea) or New Zealand (Western Samoa, Cooks Islands, Tokelau, Niue). Their decolonization has been dealt with by scholars from Australia and New Zealand, creating separate literatures that seldom overlap, and neither have they been incorporated into the larger decolonization historiography that involves Africa and Asia and that emanates from Britain, Europe, and North America. For such reasons, *Samoa mo Samoa* has not made a wider impact but remains marooned within the safe confines of Pacific Islands historiography.

Even then, one suspects, both *Samoa mo Samoa* and *Samoa, 1830 to 1900* are being read less than they should be. Specialists on Samoa will always find them indispensable, but I doubt whether either book is routinely read by Pacific historians. To do so would lead to the elementary realization that the alleged new ways of a younger generation of Pacific scholars were, in fact, the norm among members of the Davidson school: as long ago as the 1950s and 1960s, many of the older scholars *were* sensitive to the ethnographic dimension of cross-cultural encounters, and consciously attempted not to interpret them in European terms. Jim Davidson was perfectly aware how difficult it was "to use documents written by Europeans as a guide to the realities of non-Western society,"[27] and Gilson no less so: "few, if any, Europeans at the time understood the intricacies of the Samoan social order or in consequence, the nature of the system of conflict and choice which defined and limited the range of action open to Samoans in the conduct of their relations with foreigners" (9).[28] Of Gilson, the social anthropologist Judith Huntsman unequivocally stated *at the time* that he "combined perceptive interpretation of diverse historical documents and sophisticated anthropological description to analyse the complex interrelationships of Samoans and Europeans and to explain what happened in Samoa between 1830 and 1900."[29] Gilson and Davidson more than satisfy the recent calls for ethnographically sensitive readings and attention to the interpretative dimensions of archival material. Moreover, the positionality of historians, which has long been recognized in the historical profession, is self-confessed in the case of Davidson and easily explained in Gilson; and Davidson's open admission that accounts by other participants might undermine his own version of events makes postmodernist notions of contingency seem positively old hat. Dick Gilson and Jim Davidson wrote marvelous books that will always be worth reading, and not least, as John Clive remarked in a different context, because they impart "the powerful impact of that encounter between personal commitment and scholarly curiosity which lies at the heart of all great history, from the Greeks to the present."[30]

Notes

I am grateful to Peter Hempenstall and Colin Newbury for helpfully commenting on an earlier version. The award of a Harold White Fellowship at the National Library of Australia has greatly facilitated my research on J. W. Davidson. The assistance of Graeme Powell and the staff of the Library's Manuscripts Reading Room is gratefully acknowledged.

1. R. P. Gilson, Fieldwork Journal, 11 June 1950 (in private possession); J. W. Davidson to his mother, 15 June 1950, Davidson Papers, National Library of Australia, MS 5105, Box 65.

2. Posthumously published as *The Cook Islands, 1820–1950*, ed. Ron Crocombe (Wellington, 1980).

3. Quoted in Nancy Phelan, *Pieces of Heaven: In the South Seas* (Brisbane, 1996), 13.

4. Gilson's papers and research notes relating to Samoa have been microfilmed by the Pacific Manuscripts Bureau in its Manuscript Series (PMB 1009).

5. W. N. Gunson, Review (of *Samoa, 1830 to 1900*), *Historical Studies* 15, no. 61 (1973): 794.

6. Angus Ross, *Journal of the Royal Australian Historical Society* 57, no. 4 (1971): 337.

7. Davidson, "Introduction" to *Samoa, 1830 to 1900*, x.

8. See Barry Rigby, "Private Interests and the Origins of American Involvement in Samoa, 1872–1877," *Journal of Pacific History* 8 (1973): 75–87.

9. Michael Shelden, *Orwell: The Authorised Biography* (London, 1991), 430–32.

10. Paul M. Kennedy, *The Samoan Tangle: A Study of Anglo-German-American Relations, 1884–1900* (Dublin/Brisbane, 1974).

11. Personal communication, 28 May 2001.

12. Deryck Scarr, "James Wightman Davidson, 1915–1973," *Historical Studies* 16, no. 62 (1974): 158.

13. Davidson to Frank Eyre, 19 October 1964, Davidson Papers, Noel Butlin Archives Centre (hereafter NBAC), Australian National University, Q25/19.

14. For an account of the period from 1945, firmly based on the files of the Department of Island Territories, see Mary Boyd, "The Record in Western Samoa from 1945," in *New Zealand's Record in the Pacific Islands in the Twentieth Century,* ed. Angus Ross (Auckland, 1969), 189–270.

15. J. W. Davidson, "Understanding Pacific History: The Participant as Historian," in *The Feel of Truth: Essays in New Zealand and Pacific History*, ed. Peter Munz (Wellington, 1969), 37–39.

16. *Pacific Islands Monthly* (November 1967): 65, 67, 69.

17. See Doug Munro, "J. W. Davidson—The Making of a Participant Historian," in *Pacific Lives, Pacific Places: Bursting Boundaries in Pacific History*, ed. Brij V. Lal and Peter Hempenstall (Canberra, 2001), 107–8.

18. R. S. Parker, *Journal of Administration Overseas* 7, no. 3 (1968): 475.

19. Justin Fepulea'i, "From Self-Government to Independence: The Development of New Zealand's Policy towards Western Samoa during the United Nations Trusteeship Period, 1946–62" (master's thesis, University of Auckland, 1994), 145–46. See also Mary Boyd, "The Decolonisation of Western Samoa," in *The Feel of Truth*, ed. Munz, 74–75.

20. W. Somerset Maugham, *A Traveller in Romance: Uncollected Writings, 1901–1964* (New York, 1984), 52.

21. *Pacific Islands Monthly* (July 1967): 26.

22. Freeman to Davidson, 27 May 1967, Davidson Papers, NBAC, Q25/19.

23. O.H.K. Spate, *Canberra Times*, 1 July 1967.

24. For example, R. S. Parker, "Politics before Economics?—A Colonial Phantasy," *Australian Journal of Politics and History* 17, no. 2 (1971): 202–14.

25. Lauofo Meti to Davidson, 9 May 1966, Davidson Papers, NBAC, Q25/19; Jim Davidson, "Samoa mo Samoa: The Troubled Present," *New Guinea* 2, no. 2

(1967): 66–71. See also Te'o Ian Fairbairn, "*Samoa mo Samoa:* A Less Troubled Present," *Journal of Pacific History* 28, no. 2 (1993): 233–55.

26. W. David McIntyre, *Historical Studies* 13, no. 50 (1968): 256.

27. Davidson, "Introduction" to *Samoa, 1830 to 1900,* x.

28. A similar awareness is evident, for example, in Harrison M. Wright, *New Zealand, 1769–1840: Early Years of Western Contact* (Cambridge, MA, 1958), 108, who emphasizes that the contemporary European observers' "unconscious habit of forcing explanations of the different Maori activities into European modes of thought pervaded every interpretation."

29. Review, *Journal of the Polynesian Society* 80, no. 3 (1971): 391.

30. John Clive, *Not By Fact Alone: Essays on the Writing and Reading of History* (Boston, 1991), 47.

CHAPTER 19

The Last Unknown: Gavin Souter and the Historiography of New Guinea

Chris Ballard

New Guinea: The Last Unknown, by Gavin Souter.
Sydney: Angus and Robertson, 1963. U.S. edition, New York:
Taplinger Publishing Company, 1966. Angus and Robertson
paperback edition, 1974.

A JOURNALIST by trade and a historian of institutions by preference, Gavin Souter is known to most Pacific historians largely on the basis of his one major work on New Guinea. Published in 1963, *New Guinea: The Last Unknown* represents an early and remarkably ambitious effort to collect or gather together the myriad documentary sources on the history of European exploration of the interior of New Guinea. It stands as the first attempt at a history of the island in all its parts, with roughly equal attention paid to the Dutch, German, and Anglo-Australian archives. Given the materials available at the time of its production, it was necessarily a history of European exploration rather than an engagement with the deeper past of the island and its inhabitants—although, as I argue, Souter opened the way for a history of encounters in which indigenous accounts might balance those of the archival sources. Grand syntheses of New Guinea are notoriously difficult, in any discipline, and historians both before and since Souter have generally refused the challenge.[1] There are grounds, then, for some biographical context, and also for consideration of Souter's research and writing methods: what inspired a feature writer at the *Sydney Morning Herald* to embark on such an ambitious undertaking, and to what extent did he succeed in this endeavor?

Gavin Souter: The Making of a Historian

Born in 1929, Souter joined the staff of the *Sydney Morning Herald* in 1949, directly after graduating from the University of Sydney. Dispatched to New York in 1950 as a Fairfax correspondent, Souter found himself working a corridor with Peter Hastings, then a journalist for Consolidated Press. Hastings was already something of a Southeast Asian expert, and would later adopt a particular focus on the fate of what was then Netherlands New Guinea. The friendship they struck up in New York was resumed on their return to Australia, and played a key role in igniting in Souter a professional interest in New Guinea. Stuart Inder, editor of *Pacific Islands Monthly*, and John Kerr, principal at the Australian School of Pacific Administration (ASOPA), were also acquaintances, and their collective knowledge of New Guinea would render them invaluable to Souter as sources of contacts and readers of chapter drafts. Having had an earlier manuscript, on a year in the life of Sydney, turned down by Angus and Robertson, Souter began casting around for a topic that might sustain a more serious attempt at establishing himself as an author. "I'd seen enough of journalism," he recalls;[2] uninspired either by the pressure of producing copy or by the lure of securing a management position, he felt that only a book-length project would allow him to pursue a line of thought or inquiry in sufficient depth.

Made aware in New York of the United Nations' interest in Australian management of its Territory of Papua and New Guinea, Souter suggested to his editor at the *Herald* that he produce a series of feature articles on the Territory. The *Herald* applied to the Department of Territories, and from a panel of some thirty imminent patrols supplied by the department, Souter elected to accompany an initial penetrative patrol in November 1958 to the Bismarck Range, as part of his tour of the Territory.[3] Led by patrol officer Barry Griffin, the patrol of twenty-one days established administrative contact for the first time with the Gants community at the settlement of Gunts. In a series of articles that ran over four days in the *Herald* in January 1959, Souter showed a keen awareness that his own brief role as an explorer was itself a harbinger of the Territory's inevitable independence.[4] His perceptive account of the lowering of the flag at Gunts is a tableau of first contact on the eve of decolonization: "the ceremony [at Mt. Hagen] was not half so impressive as the one at Gunts, when the whole unfurling reality of New Guinea had seemed to be portrayed against a backdrop of storm clouds by three lines of men: Griffin's police, confident and reasonably competent; the Jimi brassmen, learning and very anxious to please; and the Gants, wondering what it was all about."[5] A further trip of three weeks to Rabaul, Lae, and Port Moresby in 1959 enabled Souter to meet some of the more prominent administrators of the Territory, including John Gunther, Harry Plant, Horrie Niall, and Keith McCarthy; and a short visit via the Territory to Hollandia, the capital of Netherlands New Guinea, in 1960, was the basis for a series of articles comparing the Dutch and Australian colonies that won him the Walkley Award for Best Newspaper Feature Story.[6]

In preparing for his visits to the Territory, Souter had cast around for suitable reading, and the dearth of writing on New Guinea history had quickly become apparent. There were memoirs by administrators and missionaries, and a raft of early journalist narratives, most of which focused on the glamour of the goldfields—referred to collectively by Hank Nelson as "tourist histories"[7]—but few serious histories.[8] Perhaps the most thorough reviews available were the histories of individual missions such as those by Dupeyrat, Pilhofer, and Kamma,[9] the compendious chronicles of European exploration compiled by Haga and Wichmann, and the encyclopedias edited by Klein.[10] The only professional histories were those by Gordon, Reed, Legge, and Mair.[11] Murray Groves referred to Gordon, Legge, and Mair as "academic but scrappy," and Hank Nelson added that they "do not pretend to be any more than their titles suggest . . . extensions of Australian history rather than histories of Papua New Guinea."[12] Here, then, was a topic more than worthy of a book, yet little known and largely unexplored.

Writing *The Last Unknown*

The research for his New Guinea book occupied much of Souter's time during the 1959–61 period.[13] The bulk of his research was conducted in the Mitchell Library, where he had already established some familiarity with the collection of published and manuscript material relating to New Guinea. Souter's coverage of the available documentary sources is impressive: he evidently worked systematically through the Mitchell collection and then through the bibliographies of key works such as Klein's encyclopedia. In addition, Souter engaged in an extensive correspondence with many of the key actors in his narrative, including Mick

Leahy, Ivan Champion, Jean Victor de Bruijn, and Jim Taylor, to further flesh out his sense of the archive.[14]

An apparently casual system of note taking, usually on small sheets with topical headings, appears to have translated fairly swiftly and economically into the production of text. Dutch and German sources were tackled with the aid of translations of key extracts by two Sydney residents, Helga Tukk translating from the German and Dr. M. J. Loosjes, the former government secretary for Netherlands New Guinea, from the Dutch. Writing took the better part of a year during 1962, each chapter and even each sentence being produced consecutively, in the sequence of their final appearance. In privileging the flow of narrative in this way, something of Souter's emphasis on history as storytelling is revealed. Chapter drafts were then sent for comment to a series of readers, Mick Leahy, Herb Feith, Francis West, Charles Rowley, Peter Hastings, and Stuart Inder among them.

New Guinea: The Last Unknown was published in 1963 by Angus and Robertson, who were well established as publishers on New Guinea. Two further editions were published and the total print run came to over 12,000.[15] But Souter admits to disappointment with the levels of sales and royalties: "I would have made much more mowing lawns."[16] Though he would not return to New Guinea after 1960, Souter continued to write about the Territory for the *Herald* as a "temporary PNG expert" during the early 1960s. But what he now refers to as "the New Guinea book" was of more significance for his career as a writer: "[it] was a sort of first introduction to writing—an apprenticeship almost—for writing the kind of books that I ended up doing."[17] Gaining a Commonwealth Literary Fund grant on the strength of his "New Guinea book," Souter went on to write a history of Australian settlers in Paraguay, and then embarked on a second career as a political and corporate historian, all the while retaining his position as a journalist with the Fairfax press. His ability, evident in *The Last Unknown*, to fashion a flowing narrative from a complex mass of documentary and interview sources, would stand him in good stead in his subsequent histories of the Australian Parliament and of the Fairfax publishing family.[18]

The Last Unknown Considered

The subtitle, "The Last Unknown," derives from Karl Shapiro's wartime poem, "New Guinea," from which the following extract serves as the book's epigraph:

> It fell from Asia: severed from the East;
> It was the last Unknown. Only the fringe
> Was nervous to the touch of voyagers.[19]

The Last Unknown is essentially a history of these foreign voyagers and their exploration of New Guinea. In this, it should be seen as a product of its times and of the materials available—as Ken Inglis has noted,[20] there was little or nothing of any depth on the histories of indigenous Papuans and New Guineans before the publication of Charles Rowley's *New Guinea Villager* in 1965.[21]

In his opening paragraph, Souter suggests that New Guinea presented a last possibility of surprise to a European public largely sated by discoveries elsewhere:

> The terrestrial globe was by then decently, if not quite completely, covered with fine print; museums were bursting with little yellow gods, humming-birds, carved whale's teeth, kangaroos, painted skulls, and all the other spoils of exploration; and libraries were still being flooded by a stream of travellers' narratives as broad and sluggish as the Congo or the Amazon. (3)

From the first concerted attempts at exploration beyond the fringe, following the "golden decade" of the 1870s, explorers of New Guinea proved keenly aware of their place in history, writing and taking photographs of themselves and their deeds with an enthusiasm matched only by their appetites for further discovery. Any history of New Guinea composed largely from documentary sources would, inevitably, be a history of exploration—and such histories sold well. Others had already or would subsequently address many of the same events in greater depth, but Souter was perhaps the first to attempt to canvas so wide a range of sources from such a broad geographical and chronological sweep. His reviewers were swift to note the significance of his introduction of German and Dutch materials to the established Anglophone narratives of exploration history.[22]

But it is Souter's treatment of the theme of exploration that is exceptional. Where other writers evidently regarded a factual recounting of the events of exploration as sufficiently gripping in its own right, Souter grants a leading role in his narrative to a fictional character: the notorious Captain J. A. Lawson, whose 1875 *Wanderings in the Interior of New Guinea* provoked a storm of correspondence in the London press and attracted the ire of "real" explorers such as Captain John Moresby. Lawson's early near-crossing of the island at its widest point involved the ascent of the world's highest mountain (in the course of a busy day) and the discovery of an entire ark of new species, including the Moolah, a giant and ferocious striped tiger. If Lawson and other fictional explorers had been "wrong in fact," Souter contends that they were still "right in feeling" (15). At a time when "travel literature, ethnography and adventure novels were often consumed indiscriminately" by the Western reading public,[23] the contribution of such fiction to an explorer or colonial imaginary should not be underestimated. The Italian naturalist and explorer Luigi Maria D'Albertis was one of those who read Lawson, and determined to disprove the fictitious captain's claims during his first expedition up the Fly River; and even more sober authors, such as Joseph Beete Jukes, in his account of the voyages of H.M.S. *Fly* to New Guinea under Captain Blackwood between 1842 and 1846, evidently subscribed to this link between romantic fiction and the explorer imaginary:

> New Guinea! The very mention of being taken into the interior of New Guinea sounds like being allowed to visit some of the enchanted regions of the Arabian Nights, so dim an atmosphere of obscurity rests at present on the wonders it probably contains.[24]

Souter moves directly from Lawson to d'Albertis, and then through a more or less familiar litany of early explorer debacles, but throughout the book he organizes his narrative around the motivation and the action of individuals, tracing the unraveling of their dreams once confronted with the reality of the terrain and its inhabitants.

Taking as the leitmotif for the structure of his chapters a series of fragments from a poem by A. P. Allan Natachee (the nom de plume of the Mekeo poet Avaisa Pinongo), Souter divides the history of exploration into three parts: the imaginary prelude and the golden age of the 1870s ("birds that sing before dawn"), the 1880s through the 1930s ("birds that sing . . . at mid of day"), and then the 1930s until 1942 ("birds that sing before sunset"). To this is added a fourth part of two chapters that consider the impending decolonization of the Dutch and Australian halves of the island ("birds that sing after sunset")—a slightly awkward postscript that made use of his recent interviews, and may have been intended to broaden the prospective readership, but which failed to entirely convince his reviewers.[25]

Within this broadly chronological framework, the chapters are thematic, adopting the exploits of particular individuals, or the challenge of crossing the island or climbing its mountains, as the focus of the narrative. Thus the period of early exploration of the Papuan interior under the governorship of Sir William MacGregor is organized around his ascent of the Great Mountain, the highest peak in the range visible from Port Moresby, which he duly named for Queen Victoria. Other characters and other acts of exploration are then introduced but the chapter's narrative thrust leads inexorably to MacGregor's alpine success and the denouement, which finds him "among the icicles and the buttercups when no man in New Guinea sat higher than he" (69).

Souter may have been writing to the limits of his knowledge of historical events, but he did so with a well-founded confidence in his skill as a writer—a skill that he appears to have admired among his protagonists, forgiving d'Albertis his excesses in return for a lively narrative, but despairing of many of the Dutch writers: "good explorers but poor story-tellers" (132). He has a fine eye for a quotation, and the text, which at times resembles a collection of *bon mots*, is well leavened with the author's own dry humor. Describing his first successful ascent of snow-capped Mt. Wilhelmina, the Dutch explorer H. A. Lorentz wrote that "we had forgotten the many difficulties we had experienced, and were only glad that it was Dutchmen who were the first to reach that high mountain which bears the name of Her whom we all love and honour." "As they walked back down from the snow," adds Souter, "Lorentz, distracted perhaps by emotions of triumph and loyalty, lost his footing on the rock and fell, breaking two ribs and receiving concussion and abrasions" (135). And when "an English newspaper reported that 'the British Ornithologists' Union expedition to Papua was joined at Singapore by ten pickled Gurkhas,'" Souter is on hand with the comment from *Punch* "that it was 'no doubt a misprint for gherkins'" (136).

Given the broad ambit of its field and the era of its production, *The Last Unknown* inevitably betrays some substantial omissions. Nonmale and nonwhite actors are scarcely addressed, except in the moment of interaction with the white male explorers who occupy the heart of this vision of history. White women occupy a very specific niche according to the conventions of explorer literature, their carefully documented appearance as "the first white woman" in a location marking out the domestication of a previously savage and entirely male domain—a convention largely respected by Souter in a single footnote—but of indigenous women there is virtually no sign. While it is true that there are no substantial bodies of early primary source material that address indigenous history in New Guinea, it is also evident that there have been few attempts to read European sources against the grain, and to recover the traces of indigenous agency, as Bronwen Douglas has sought to do for Kanak history in New Caledonia.[26] With just a handful of mostly very recent exceptions, there have been few serious published attempts to explore indigenous oral history.[27] Where journalist writers on New Guinea commonly exoticized the "natives," and academic historians tended to treat Papuans and New Guineans as the natural objects of a history of colonial control and governance, there is a very real and unpatronizing sympathy at work in Souter's writing. Questions are posed concerning the role played by Europeans within the context of indigenous histories and systems of belief, and the vagaries of colonialism and of incorporation within a novel system of governance are exposed, as in the tableau at Gunts.

On his own terms, however, Souter's coverage of the field is excellent. One might quibble and ask why Thurnwald's remarkable exploits, including his ascent up the Upper Sepik as far as the Telefomin Valley (surely the very first European encounter with a central valley in the Highlands), are not given more prominence;[28] the break in chronological coverage between 1942 and the 1950s also serves to exclude some important patrols of exploration and early contact. But our ability to identify these lacunae rests, in no small measure, on the footing secured for the history of exploration in New Guinea by *The Last Unknown*. If there are grounds for complaint, they stem from the frustrating absence of adequate footnotes and sourcing, such that many quotations and reports of events of potential interest are untraceable.

After *The Last Unknown*

The question of *The Last Unknown*'s influence is not easy to determine. As a popular history, it was not widely reviewed in academic journals of the day, though it is unclear whether this reflected a promotional failure on the part of the publishers or a lack of interest on the part of academic reviewers. Francis West conceded that, although "Mr. Souter is not a professional historian . . . he has done a careful piece of research"; further, that he had achieved "what many professionals might envy: written a readable and enjoyable book."[29] Ron Crocombe observed that "this is not, and does not claim to be, a history of New Guinea, for no one is yet competent to undertake such a task," but added that "Souter's work gives us the best outline of [the period of European exploration] available to date."[30] In the opinion of Paula Brown, *The Last Unknown* was "likely to become the chief work of reference on New Guinea exploration."[31] But for Dutch scholars, a history of New Guinea could scarcely have chosen a less opportune date for publication than 1963, as their former New Guinea territory was transferred from the United Nations to the Republic of Indonesia, and *The Last Unknown* passed apparently without review in the Netherlands; though known of, it was seldom, if ever, drawn upon by Dutch scholars working on New Guinea.[32]

However, at the teaching coalface of the Administrative College in Port Moresby and the fledgling University of Papua New Guinea, where the first courses on New Guinea history were taught in 1967 by Hank Nelson and in 1969 by Ken Inglis, respectively, *The Last Unknown*, along with Rowley's *The New Guinea Villager* (1965) and Peter Lawrence's *Road Belong Cargo* (1964), formed a trilogy of fundamental texts.[33] Certainly the impression gained from scanning the bibliographies of subsequent works on New Guinea is that *The Last Unknown* is a book that almost every Anglophone scholar of New Guinea has read or consulted, often as the first port of literary call. Perhaps it is the sheer readability of the text, its narrative strength, which invites academic suspicion. This is evidently not a style that historians writing since on New Guinea have felt comfortable with—and that is to be regretted. If it is obviously possible to dig a little deeper into the past through the archives, or through oral history, it will always be a challenge to write as delicately and as beautifully as Souter.

Thus far, and with some honorable exceptions, historians of New Guinea have largely been content to improve on Souter through closer examination of a more extensive range of archival sources on more narrow topics.[34] If *The Last Unknown* straddles the watershed between the "tourist histories" of the 1940s and 1950s, and the professional histories that were to follow, it also represents a signpost bearing a series of largely forgotten directions that future histories of New Guinea might still elect to explore. If European perceptions of encounters in New Guinea were significantly influenced by those elements of New Guinea prefigured in a colonial imaginary, a novel and more comprehensive history of the encounter would seek to understand how Europeans were incorporated within indigenous cosmologies, and how the events of such encounters were documented under the terms of different Papuan historicities.

Notes

I would like to thank Hank Nelson for his encouragement to tackle this essay. Gavin Souter, though invariably (and sometimes frustratingly) modest about his achievements, was unfailingly generous with his time, materials, and memory. I am also grateful to the manuscripts librarians at the National Library of Australia (hereafter NLA) for their persistence in tracking down the full collection of Souter's research materials for his New Guinea book.

1. Clive Moore's *New Guinea: Crossing Boundaries and History* (Honolulu, 2003) is the most recent exception to this observation.

2. Gavin Souter, interview, 10 October 2003.

3. District Commissioner Western Highlands District R. I. Skinner to Officer-in-Charge, Jimi River Patrol Post, Tabibuga, 21 October 1958. Gavin Souter, private collection.

4. Gavin Souter, "On Patrol in New Guinea," *Sydney Morning Herald*, 1, 2, 3, 5 January 1959.

5. *Sydney Morning Herald*, 5 January 1959, 2.

6. Gavin Souter, "The Two New Guineas," *Sydney Morning Herald*, 13, 15, 17, 18, 19 August 1960.

7. H. N. Nelson, "New Guinea Nationalism and the Writing of History," *Journal of the Papua and New Guinea Society* 4 (1970): 10.

8. Frank Clune, *Prowling through Papua* (Sydney, 1943); idem, *Somewhere in New Guinea* (Sydney, 1951); Ion L. Idriess, *Gold-Dust and Ashes: The Romantic Story of the New Guinea Goldfields* (Sydney, 1944); Lewis Lett, *Papuan Gold: The Story of the Early Gold Seekers* (Sydney, 1943); idem, *The Papuan Achievement* (Melbourne, 1944); Colin Simpson, *Adam with Arrows* (Sydney, 1953); idem, *Adam in Plumes* (Sydney, 1954); idem, *Islands of Men* (Sydney, 1955). Comparable literature for the Dutch side of the island (much of which appears to have been unknown to Australian readers) includes J. van Eechoud, *Vergeten Aarde* (Amsterdam, 1952), *Met Kapmes en Kompas door Nieuw Guinea* (Amsterdam, 1953), and *Woudloper Gods* (Amsterdam, 1954).

9. André Dupeyrat, *Papouasie. Histoire de la Mission (1885–1935)* (Issoudun, 1935); Freerk C. Kamma, *Kruis en Korwar. Een honderdjarig vraagstuk op Nieuw-Guinea* ('s-Gravenhage, 1953); D. Georg Pilhofer, *Die Geschichte der Neuendettel-sauer Mission in Neuguinea*, 2 vols. (Neuendettelsau, 1961).

10. A. Haga, *Nederlandsch Nieuw-Guinea en de Papoesche eilanden: historische bijdrage, 1500–1883*, 2 vols. (Batavia, 1884); A. Wichmann, *Entdeckungsgeschichte*

von Neu-Guinea, Nova Guinea, 2 vols. (Leiden, 1909–12); Willem Carel Klein, ed., *Nieuw Guinee,* (Amsterdam, 1935–38), 2nd ed., 3 vols. (Amsterdam, 1953–54).

11. Stephen Windsor Reed, *The Making of Modern New Guinea* (Philadelphia, 1943); L. P. Mair, *Australia in New Guinea* (Melbourne, 1948, 2nd ed. 1970); Donald Craigie Gordon, *The Australian Frontier in New Guinea 1870–1885* (New York, 1951); J. D. Legge, *Australian Colonial Policy* (Sydney, 1956).

12. Murray Groves, "The History of Papua: Some Notes on Research Resources, Achievements and Problems," *Historical Studies* 5, no. 20 (1953): 386, 394; H. N. Nelson, "On Teaching History . . . or Ignoring Lines on Maps," *New Guinea* 8, no. 3 (1973): 40–41.

13. See Gavin Souter, research material for "New Guinea: The Last Unknown," 1962–63 [*sic*], NLA, MS 1209.

14. This correspondence is included in the National Library of Australia collection (MS 1209); Souter's principal correspondents are listed in the book's acknowledgments.

15. First edition, 9,578 copies; U.S. edition, 990; paperback edition, 1,650 (figures provided by Souter).

16. Personal communication, 15 October 2003.

17. Gavin Souter, interview, 10 October 2003.

18. Among his published histories are *A Peculiar People: The Australians in Paraguay* (Sydney, 1968); *Lion and Kangaroo: The Initiation of Australia, 1901–1919* (Sydney, 1976); *Company of Heralds: A Century and a Half of Australian Publishing by John Fairfax Limited and Its Predecessors, 1831–1981* (Melbourne, 1981); *Acts of Parliament: A Narrative History of the Senate and House of Representatives* (Melbourne, 1988); *Heralds and Angels: The House of Fairfax, 1841–1990* (Melbourne, 1991).

19. Karl Shapiro, *V-Letter and Other Poems* (New York, 1944), 10. Gordon had previously quoted precisely the same lines of Shapiro's poem "New Guinea" (*The Australian Frontier in New Guinea,* 20)

20. K. S. Inglis, *The Study of History in Papua and New Guinea* (Port Moresby, 1967), 14.

21. Charles Rowley, *The New Guinea Villager* (Melbourne, 1965).

22. See Robert E. Huke, *Geographical Review* 55 (1965): 447–48; Judy Tudor, *Pacific Islands Monthly* (November 1963): 85, 87–88.

23. Robert Dixon, "Cannibalising Indigenous Texts: Headhunting and Fantasy in Ion L. Idriess's Coral Sea Adventures," in *Body Trade: Captivity, Cannibalism and Colonialism in the Pacific,* ed. Barbara Creed and Jeanette Horn (Dunedin, 2000), 115.

24. Joseph Beete Jukes, *Narrative of the Surveying Voyage of H.M.S. Fly, Commanded by Captain F.P. Blackwood, R.N., in Torres Strait, New Guinea, and Other Islands of the Eastern Archipelago, During the Years 1842–1846,* 2 vols. (London, 1847), 291.

25. In defense of his decision to extend his narrative to contemporary events, Souter insists that "as a journalist I would have felt remiss not dealing with something as blatantly topical as paratroopers dropping into [Netherlands] New Guinea" (Gavin Souter, interview, 1 December 2003).

26. Bronwen Douglas, *Across the Great Divide: Journeys in History and Anthropology* (Amsterdam, 1998).

27. Donald Denoon and Roderic Lacey, eds., *Oral Tradition in Melanesia* (Port Moresby, 1981); Bob Connolly and Robin Anderson, *First Contact* (New York, 1987); Edward L. Schieffelin and Robert Crittenden, *Like People You See in a Dream: First Contact in Six Papuan Societies* (Stanford, 1991); Klaus Neumann, *Not The Way It Really Was: Constructing the Tolai Past* (Honolulu, 1994); Bill Gammage, *The Sky Travellers: Journeys in New Guinea 1938–1939* (Melbourne, 1998); August I. Kituai, *My Gun, My Brother: The World of the Papua New Guinea Colonial Police, 1920–1960* (Honolulu, 1998); Polly Wiessner and Akii Tumu, *Historical Vines: Enga Networks of Exchange, Ritual, and Warfare in Papua New Guinea* (Bathurst, 1998).

28. Marion Melk-Koch, *Auf der Suche nach der menschlichen Gesellschaft: Richard Thurnwald* (Berlin, 1989).

29. Francis West, *Australian Book Review* (February 1964): 79.

30. R. G. Crocombe, *Journal of the Polynesian Society* 74 (1965): 246–47.

31. Paula Brown, "Some Recent Books," *Australian Territories* 4 (1964): 45.

32. Jaap Timmer kindly inquired on my behalf among Dutch scholars of New Guinea active during the 1960s, confirming that few had either read or possessed a copy of *The Last Unknown*.

33. Hank Nelson, personal communication, October 2003.

34. Some of these honorable exceptions—histories that manage to integrate the archival and the oral, and the documentary and the sensory, without necessarily privileging one over the other—are listed in note 27, above. The first professional history of Papua New Guinea published after *The Last Unknown* was the school text by Peter Biskup, Brian Jinks, and Hank Nelson, *A Short History of New Guinea* (Sydney, 1968). But perhaps the most widely read general accounts of Papua New Guinea are still those written by journalists, such as Sean Dorney's *Papua New Guinea: People, Politics and History since 1975*, rev. ed. (Sydney, 2000).

CHRIS BALLARD is Fellow in the Division of Pacific and Asian History, Research School of Pacific and Asian Studies, Australian National University.

IVAN BRADY is Distinguished Teaching Professor of Anthropology, State University of New York, Oswego.

BRONWEN DOUGLAS is Senior Fellow in the Division of Pacific and Asian History, Research School of Pacific and Asian Studies, Australian National University.

MICHAEL GOLDSMITH is Senior Lecturer in Anthropology, University of Waikato.

DAVID HANLON is Professor and Director of the Center for Pacific Islands Studies, University of Hawai'i at Mānoa.

K. R. HOWE is Professor of History at Massey University's Albany Campus, Auckland.

BRIJ V. LAL is Professor and Convenor of Pacific and Asian History, Research School of Pacific and Asian Studies, Australian National University.

HUGH LARACY is an Associate Professor of History at the University of Auckland

LAMONT LINDSTROM is Professor of Anthropology at the University of Tulsa, Oklahoma.

DOUG MUNRO is an Affiliate of the Stout Research Centre, Victoria University of Wellington.

VINCENT O'MALLEY is a partner in the Wellington-based consultancy HistoryWorks, which specializes in Treaty of Waitangi claims research.

JONATHAN K. OSORIO is an Associate Professor with the Center for Hawaiian Studies, University of Hawai'i at Mānoa.

TOM RYAN is Senior Lecturer in Anthropology, University of Waikato.

JANE SAMSON is an Associate Professor of History at the University of Alberta.

FRANCIS WEST is Emeritus Professor and Overseas Fellow, Churchill College, Cambridge.

GLYNDWR WILLIAMS is Professor Emeritus of History at Queen Mary College, London.

This is a book about books (and their authors), so every attempt has been to index the monographs that are mentioned or discussed even when they are not explicitly identified in the text. An asterisk beside a page number indicates when this occurs.